Landscape & Labour

RICHARD JEFFERIES

Landscape & Labour

ESSAYS AND LETTERS NOW FIRST COLLECTED
WITH AN INTRODUCTION, NOTES AND BIBLIOGRAPHY
BY JOHN PEARSON

Drawings by Ursula Sieger

MOONRAKER PRESS

for my parents

46548346

© 1979 MOONRAKER PRESS
26 St Margaret's Street, Bradford-on-Avon, Wiltshire
SBN 239.00188.5 (paper SBN 239.00239.3)
Printed by T. H. Brickell & Son Ltd
The Blackmore Press, Shaftesbury, Dorset
and bound in England at The Pitman Press, Bath

Contents

Acknowledgement

I would like to thank Professor W. J. Keith of The University of Toronto for the assistance which he has given me in the preparation of this collection. The need for a fresh bibliography of Jefferies' works was an obvious one in view of the amount of new material now available. Professor Keith provided the basis for this bibliography, much information on newly discovered essays by Jefferies and advice on various aspects of the author's writings.

JOHN PEARSON
The University of Exeter
November 1978.

Introduction

There is a sense of uncertainty in the atmosphere of the age: no one can be sure that the acorns he plants will be permitted to reach their prime, the hoofs of the 'iron horse' may trample them down as fresh poppuations grow. [1]

This, like many of Richard Jefferies' sentiments, has a curious resonance over a century later. The late nineteenth century, and particularly the last 30 years, were, as he observes, marked by an uneasiness in several areas of English life, so much so that an 'outsider', the American economist Henry George, was forced to conclude in 1879:

What change may come, no mortal man can tell, but that some great change *must* come, thoughtful men begin to feel. The civilized world is trembling on the verge of a great movement. Either it must be a leap upward, which will open the way to advances yet undreamed of, or it must be a plunge downward, which will carry us back toward barbarism. [2]

It would be easy to see these projected alternatives as reflected in Jefferies' work in the worlds of *The Story of My Heart* and *After London*. But he does not admit such simplistic judgements. Nevertheless, his writing, especially in his early career up to 1879, radiates the doubt which affected agriculture and all other aspects of rural life. He is the recorder of the rural *zeitgeist*, the chronicler of uncertainty.

This uncertainty is the central concern in this collection of Jefferies' essays which shows his preoccupation with the difficulties surrounding farming in the Wiltshire of the 1870s, but also indicates his method of escape from the worst effects of these developments—through Nature and the spirit of Nature. This volume brings together 18 of the essays of Richard Jefferies and two of his letters, all touching upon rural matters. With the exception of a part of one sketch they have never appeared outside the pages of the newspapers and magazines for which they were writ-

[1] —*The Gamekeeper at Home,* (London, 1878), p. 58.
[2] —*Progress and Poverty,* (London, 1882), p. 488.

7

ten. It is now over 20 years since the last book of 'new' essays by Jefferies appeared and in the intervening period many fresh works have been discovered. In a relatively brief career, spanning 21 years, he contributed to more than 30 different publications, ranging from his local newspapers to *The Times*, from *Forestry* to *London Society*. My research has been conducted on the assumption that the body of writing known to be Jefferies' did not represent his total output, and so it has proved. Some 27 separate pieces, consisting of essays, short stories, letters and a full-length novel in serial form, were found among the journals of his day. It is possible, indeed probable, that other works await discovery, since many of Jefferies' early works were not signed. The essays in this collection are, however, the most recent of value to have emerged.

The obvious temptation, with so much material available, was to lump together all the short pieces in one volume. In compiling this anthology however, two aspects of Jefferies' writing have had to be taken into account. First, its diversity in both form and subject-matter, especially in his early years, and secondly the doubtful quality of some of the work. Mrs Q. D. Leavis's contention that he was '. . . a many-sided and comprehensive genius . . .'[3], is one borne out by later works, but his lack of experience in the early 1870s led him to spread his talents too thinly over subjects about which he knew too little. But variety and inexperience were not the sole factors, for Jefferies was an ambitious author with a desire to attract a mass audience; the large number of periodicals for which he wrote tells its own tale. Besetting financial problems were allied to this ambition. The author was obliged to search for the most lucrative opportunities and to write with an eye to the potential readership at this time. In short, he was frequently forced to pursue the rôle of hack writer, and to forsake the topics about which he knew most—the countryside, its workers and its wildlife. An anthology which contained such a large amount of laboured material may have told us something about Jefferies the man, but would have been of little intrinsic interest and would have done nothing for his reputation as an artist.

The essays gathered here deal mainly with Jefferies' native Wiltshire. Some of them have been known to Jefferies scholars for several years, but, because there were insufficient good essays on the same theme, they have never been collected in volume form. The majority were published between 1872 and 1879, a critical time in rural England generally and in Jefferies' own life in particular, for they straddle a time when he left Wiltshire permanently to live in the suburbs of London. The effect of this move was

[3] —'Lives and Works of Richard Jefferies' in *Scrutiny*, Vol. VI, No. 4, Mar. 1938, p. 437.

profound on a man whose imaginative sensibility was such as to make the years spent in and around Swindon difficult, uncertain ones. His dissatisfaction with life there is revealed in a letter to an aunt in Sydenham in 1870:

. . . I felt far more at home with you than ever I do at Coate—for there we are so distant and unsocial . . . I cannot say that I admire the country much after London, and the still more elegant Brussels manners. My efforts will be directed to return. . . . I shall never be happy in the country again, . . .

Remarks like these could perhaps be dismissed as youthful overstatement, were it not for the evidence of his other writing. Repeatedly, in both early and later fiction, recognizably autobiographical figures—usually dissatisfied, ambitious, oppressed, frustrated men—are created. In the newly-discovered novel, *The Rise of Maximin, Emperor of the Occident,* written in 1874, Jefferies gives us our fullest insight into the workings of his mind in his Wiltshire period. The hero of this romance, clearly an idealized self-portrait, is a man who

. . . looked back on Sandover [Swindon] with contempt—that cruel, heartless place which had treated him so roughly, and despised him a presumptuous fool.

The sense of persecution and unfulfilled ambition is strong here, for the author, like Maximin, believed that

. . . his brain was full of original conceptions. . . . He had studied the works of the ancients; he had pondered upon the stars, the hills, the waters, and the great sun, till out from the depth of his own soul there sprang forth a poem, yet not in verse, which embodied the truths he had learnt.

The clash of imaginative mind and uncongenial circumstances is thus established early. This *cri de coeur* follows in *A Sin and a Shame* (1875):

How few of us are what we should have been had circumstances given our nature scope to expand itself! But most of us have been hemmed in and pressed down, and compelled to meet daily with dull and dispiriting circumstances, till at last these react upon our nature, and warp us from our original bias.

These 'dull and dispiriting circumstances' were partly an unsatisfactory home life, where a shrewish mother and a father with a temperament similar to his son's, but without his ambition, made the atmosphere at Coate Farm an uncomfortable one. Partly too, they were the failure of those around to understand him. In a fragment entitled *Hyperion*, Jefferies presents an exaggerated picture of the situation:

There was once a youth in an obscure country village, quite lost in the rudest and most illiterate county of the West, who passed a great part of his time reading books and dreaming, so much so that he was useless upon the farm.

The contemptuous adjectives speak eloquently of the alienation felt by a sensitive, introspective youth. And all this was compounded by financial difficulties which both limited his movement and channelled his efforts into unsuitable areas of literature.

But it was the general spirit of the age, rather than home or local considerations, that most affected Jefferies the author. He was, as he intimates above, an avid reader, and was aware of national problems. These essays were written, as was most of his work, when economic depression was altering many of the features of farming and the lives of its people permanently. Wiltshire, it must be remembered, was the English county with the largest percentage of its area devoted to farming, so general agricultural difficulties tended to be felt more acutely there. The young Jefferies had been raised in the period of 'High Farming' which, even if less spectacularly successful in Wiltshire than in some other counties, generated a faith in the possibilities of unfettered 'Progress' which the events of the 1870s shook severely. What Jefferies observes and analyses in his agricultural essays is a movement away from these policies, this faith. How frequently he can be seen using the term *transition* to sum up the movement in farming. And it is more than an economic movement. Virginia Woolf's observations on a later period and in an urban context describe precisely the kinds of changes occurring in rural England at the time when Jefferies was writing:

All human relations have shifted; those between masters and servants, husbands and wives, parents and children. And when human relations change there is, at the same time, a change in religion, conduct, politics and literature. [4]

Perhaps the most obvious manifestation of these shifts was the split between masters and workmen. The formation of the National Agricultural Labourers' Union in 1872 was, in a sense, a formal recognition of a process which had been evolving throughout the century. A tetchy William Cobbett had noticed the change in this relationship in the way in which the farmer and his men no longer lived together, no longer ate at the same table:

Why do not farmers now *feed* and *lodge* their work-people, as they did formerly? Because they cannot keep them *upon so little* as they give them in wages. [5]

Yet, it is indicative of the variable rate of change that even in the late nineteenth century Hardy can show the milkmaids of Talbothays joining their employer for their meals and 'living in', and Jefferies himself can depict 'Jearge' the fogger eating at the Iden's table in *Amaryllis at the Fair*.

[4] —*Mr Bennett and Mrs Brown* in *The Hogarth Essays* Series, (London, 1924), p. 5
[5] —*Rural Rides*, (London: Everyman, 1924), Vol. I, p. 266.

On the other hand, some of the Wiltshireman's vignettes in *Hodge and His Masters*, showing the pretensions of the farmer and his family, suggest a more balanced view. The changes in the countryside from labour-intensive to more mechanized forms of agriculture, from high capital outlay to retrenchment, from a monopoly to an internationally competitive market, from partial payment in kind to payment in cash-wages for the labourer and from subsistence farming to farming as a business for his employer, were not changes effected overnight. Their full impact was longest delayed in the more rural southern counties of England, but with their advent difficulties and uncertainties were inevitable. Perched on top of events, as it were, Jefferies could not take the historical view which only time affords. But he captures, and indeed, himself epitomises, the sense of uneasiness abroad, in the probability that what has already taken place by the mid-1870s may only be the beginning. He comments in *The Future of Farming*, '. . . all the facts of the hour point irresistibly to the conclusion that the era of development has but just commenced'.

Generally the agricultural essays in this collection are confirmatory rather than revelatory—a lack of, and search for, certainty being the main concerns. They show an author who does not confine his attentions to any single class. Although the labourer's problems were, quite legitimately, occupying much of the attention of agricultural commentators in the 1870s, Jefferies ranges over the whole gamut of agricultural society from itinerant labourer to duke, in what are the most perceptive articles on the industry of the era. He is never a 'comfortable' writer, in the sense that an author like Howitt is, when describing country affairs. Rural life for its agricultural workers is hard, and Jefferies does not spare the sensitive reader. Nor can it be said that he lacks a complete understanding of agriculture. Though accused of indolence—a natural reaction in an agricultural community, where human endeavour is so conspicuous—his lack of practical attainment arose not so much from ineptitude as from disinclination. For though his health was suspect Jefferies was no 'armchair commentator', as the profound analyses of the state of farming and knowledge of various methods used reveal. Moreover, any deficiencies in practice are balanced by powers of observation which are, with the exception of Gilbert White and possibly Cobbett, unparalleled in English rural literature. These powers are seen at work in the minute fidelity of the description of the old-style sower who scatters the seed with a 'peculiar *steady* jerk', in the picture of the cows which have just been turned out into fresh grass 'lazily rioting in it', and, in this collection, in the sound of the woodpigeons in Savernake Forest which make a 'soft mellow crush.' These, and a hundred other similar examples, show Jefferies at his best.

He has, of course, like all other writers, his shortcomings. His early treatment of the 'Labour Question' is generally a somewhat blinkered one, and especially when he is dealing with the labourers *en masse* and with union activities. This can be ascribed to a basically conservative nature and to his concern for the small farmer, the man who had most to lose by the labourers' action. Though he recognizes the poverty (in this, the poorest of all the English counties) which prompted Canon Girdlestone to comment that labourers did not live in the proper sense of the word, they merely didn't die, his earliest energies focus upon blaming them for their own plight. The tone of the letters to *The Times* and of such propagandist essays as *The Power of the Farmers* are, however, increasingly replaced by a more humanitarian, understanding approach and a realization that reform of the problem is neither speedy nor satisfactory. This does not imply that Jefferies' authorial progress can be viewed, as some observers have attempted, as moving from a conservative to a proto-Marxist position. Such a perspective has become more difficult to maintain since the recent discovery that one of his more radical essays, *Thoughts on the Labour Question*, was written in the early stages of his career.[6] If any shift is discernible, it takes the form of a greater emphasis on, and sympathy for, the labourer as an individual, and away from the general agricultural articles on the classes in farming. This view is necessarily a tentative one, for the sketch on John Smith belongs to the early period and both he and Roger the Reaper *(One of the New Voters)* are, as their names clearly suggest, representative figures. Nevertheless, it is only in these more-detailed individual sketches that humanitarian considerations emerge. It is as though in examining the single example of the class or occupation the author comes to appreciate the intricacies which blanket assumptions blur or extinguish.

The 1870s saw the dispersal of the pastoral-idyllic myth as far as descriptions of the farm labourer's life were concerned. Men like Girdlestone, George Mitchell *(The Skeleton at the Plough)* and Francis Heath *(The English Peasantry)* uncovered the sordid, impoverished reality of his existence in the south-western counties. And, though Jefferies shows himself to be in harmony with this spirit of realism in several respects, he is not essentially an *exposé* journalist. His view of agriculture is different in that he treats it as an *industry*. It is as subject to industrial pressures, fluctuations and other processes as any fabrics or metallurgy concern in a town—perhaps even more so. The small operator is a casualty of such in-

[6] —*See*, G. Woolaston, 'Richard Jefferies: "Thoughts on the Labour Question".', *Notes and Queries*, March 1975, pp. 118-9.

dustrial processes. In *The Size of Farms* Jefferies states: 'The small farm appears doomed'.

This recognition that, on the whole, the small-scale farmer in competition with market forces is the latter-day equivalent of the hand-loom weaver, is a crucial one in any attempt at comprehending the changes which were occurring. Jefferies is also aware that as a result of these changes the dichotomy between town and countryside, beloved of the romantic poets, no longer has any validity. A quarter of a century before *Hodge and His Masters* appeared, C. W. Hoskyns had exhorted town and rural dwellers to remember their mutual dependence, with this assertion: '. . . you are each others Customers and Brothers'.[7]

Now, the border is even less distinct, as Jefferies acknowledges in his preface to *Hodge:*

Country towns are now so closely connected with agriculture that a description of one would be incomplete without a mention of the other.

It is, nevertheless, when he leaves the Wiltshire countryside that his most creative writing on the area commences. Then, an imagination which had dreamed up wild, impossible romances as a surrogate for artistic deficiencies in Wiltshire life was set to work on more promising material. A journalist's training, harnessed to this creative talent, was used to describe the county at a distance in newspaper serials like *The Gamekeeper at Home, The Amateur Poacher* and *Round About a Great Estate.* Some of the first fruits of this move were the vignettes of the *Hodge* series, of which *The Gentleman Farmer* (contained in this volume) is a forerunner.

It is noticeable that the disparaging remarks which Jefferies makes concerning Wiltshire centre on men and manners rather than on the larger life of the countryside. The uncertainty in his personal and professional life, the general doubt in agriculture concerning future developments, the desire for adventure and the imaginative restrictions he felt, all threw him into solitude in surroundings which satisfied him and elevated his thoughts, restored certainty and compensated for shortcomings in other areas of his life. If the past could not be restored—and he himself acknowledges this as impossible—then the more enduring features of the countryside might be proof against the spirit of the present. Thus he is attracted in solitude to apparently immutable phenomena such as the stars, the sea, the sun, the hills, the woods and forests. On the downs he muses, 'The Earth was thus, and the sun was thus and the sea was thus, one hundred generations ago'.

To these can be added certain of man's structures which blend with

[7] —*Talpa, or, Chronicles of a Clay Farm,* (London, 1852), p. 56.

Nature and her rhythms, like the White Horses carved in the side of the downs, the ancient barrows and water-mills. And even the fauna and their ways provide reassurance. In a significant observation in the preface to *Wild Life in a Southern County,* Jefferies presents the two extremes: 'Modern progress, except where it has exterminated them, has hardly touched the habits of bird or animal'.

These phenomena stand as symbols of defiance and encouragement against what Jefferies considers the base commercial haste and falsity now permeating the society he has known. In one of the early novels he refers to '. . . the thick crust of artificialism, which weighs us down more and more year by year . . .'.

His object is to escape from uncertainty, using Nature and its spirit to free him from this incrustation and to induce a Lethean relaxation. It is, of course, only a temporary release from the human world, as he makes clear in *A Summer Day in Savernake Forest,* where the place '. . . cheats us into a passing forgetfulness . . .'.

This then is the function of the landscape for Jefferies. It never fails to inspire. Its stable, non-human aspect throws into even starker relief the kind of 'controlled turmoil' of human life. Part of the attraction of the Wiltshire landscape is the sense of mystery and wonder of life which it evokes in the sensitive human frame. The fact that its innermost secrets are retained contrasts again with man's enquiring, scientific spirit, which provides and expects answers. Only receptive persons can take advantage of its influence. Jefferies is such a man: looking at the conifers in a wood this emotion is stimulated,

This, our common English pine, is indeed a tree of mystery, whose history is full of deep things, not easy to be found out.

And in Savernake he declares, 'The heart has a yearning for the unknown . . .'.

In many of these early landscape sketches we thus become aware of a man who is reaching out into unplumbed depths of the human psyche towards something he barely understands, and cannot fully communicate in satisfactory terms. This remained so to some extent, even through the ecstasies of *The Story of My Heart.* It probably accounts for his attempts to provide a simpler equivalent for the force which moves him in his communion with Nature, in magnetism or electricity. This force, he says, '. . . will not come unless to perfect peace', yet this cannot be taken as synonymous with silence—what is denoted is mental calm. So, the noise of the mill-wheel, echoing the rhythms of Nature's revolutions, lulls '. . . into daydreams and a Nirvana of forgetfulness'. The initial attraction is frequently the patent lack of hurry displayed in Nature. She does not work in terms of man-measured time, especially now that man has succumbed to the new, industrial tempo. Indeed, she appears to suspend both herself and Jefferies in a limbo outside all temporal and spatial considerations. The author ponders thus on the new industrial 'idols' of time and money in one of his favourite haunts:

To us each hour is of consequence, especially in this modern day, which has invented the detestable creed that time is money. But time is not money to Nature. She never hastens.

It would be wrong to assume that this species of natural religion experienced by Jefferies is unaffected by either a conscious desire to attain its elevating effect, or by comparison with other religions. He was an ambitious young man in the early 1870s and his writing then gives a good idea of what he felt his rôle in society was. It is a somewhat inflated view, with strong intimations of a Messianic or divine function. Jefferies, as we observe him fantasizing in *Maximin*, shows the hero as imbued with a poetic nature and, taking his religious poem 'Rah' (significantly, the name of the *eternal* Egyptian sun-god) as his inspiration, he gathers round himself a group of seven disciples. There is little doubt that Jefferies felt himself capable of leading a new cult of human spiritual advance, perhaps a substitute for organized Christianity. It is worth quoting in full what he says in *Restless Human Hearts*, written in the same year as *Maximin*:

. . . the lives of some among us do seem in some peculiar way to correspond with the singularities of nature. The coincidence may be merely accidental—but there it is: and a highly-wrought mind, dwelling upon its own aspirations and analysing its emotions, can hardly help feeling its individuality increased when it recognises these parallel circumstances. In their turn, the circumstances react upon the creature, and tend to produce a frame of mind strangely susceptible to mystic influences. It is thus that Renan, in the famous *Vie de Jesus*, accounts for what he describes as the delusions which occupied the mind of that central figure of history. The scenery of Judea—the romantic hills and plains, the seas and woods—heightened an originally poetic temperament, till a tension of the mind was produced in which it became capable of the most extraordinary effects.

The inclusive pronoun 'us' leaves little doubt that Jefferies considered that he himself was such a case. The similarities between the two experiences and the implied analogous rôles are revealing, and it may well be that Renan's celebrated work, first published in 1863, was one of the sources of his preconceptions about such elevated states of mind. Here though, the interaction of responsive mind and Nature's spirit gives something akin to the satisfaction which Christianity bestows, but without belief in an all-controlling deity.

The imagery used in some early landscape essays shows a similar religious bias. On several occasions Jefferies' excursions are clearly viewed as journeys of religious devotion and affirmation. 'The pilgrim of Nature may wander freely', on the downs, he declares, and in *The Story of My Heart* he states of a popular walk:

The idea of the pilgrimage was to get away from the endless and nameless circumstances of existence.

The sense of the fulfilment of a sacred mission, and the feeling that faith and certitude can be had or restored by such journeys, runs through many of the accounts of his wanderings in these formative Wiltshire days. In a wood he is filled with '—a sense of belief in Nature, of certainty in the life of which the cones up there are a symbol'.

Locales like this become his temples, his places of worship, at a time of personal and general decline in Christian beliefs: 'Gazing upwards—these curious trees, like green steeples, incline the eye upwards'. And even the best examples of man-made places of worship are deficient by direct comparison with those of Nature:

The silvery trunks and arching boughs more than realise all that poets and romance writers have ever said or sung of woodland naves and forest aisles, of which the noblest cathedrals offer so poor a copy.

So the mental tension produced in these surroundings is not only that of a poetic mind worked on by its milieu. There is an open comparison with less satisfactory ways of life, both physical and spiritual. It is not only a physical descent being described when the author declares, following an afternoon on the Wiltshire downs: 'it is time to leave the thyme and the sward, to descend to the cities of the plain'.

There are other aspects of these experiences in the Wiltshire landscape that are less obvious. Through the very act of writing, escape is achieved and the experience re-lived. This regeneration is evident in the method Jefferies uses in essays on places which hold pleasant memories. Thus, the couching of the essay on the Wiltshire downs in the present tense is surely no accident: 'Lying on this pillow of thyme . . . sucking the clover . . .'—and similarly in a wood—'Gazing upwards . . . a sense of exquisite langour enters in . . .'.

The author is luxuriating in the recapture of much of the emotion of the occasion and, in fact, many of these landscape essays give the impression of being almost as much for the author's benefit as for the reader's. In *The Rise of Maximin* this process of recall is taken a step further: the central figure, in walking the downs and exploring the forests, provides the author not only with a surrogate for his pilgrimages, but also a point of 'take-off' into fantasy of a more intense nature. The stimulus is the remembered experience, and both the models for the original event and for the fantastic regions are, naturally, ones which are congenial to his tastes. We are reminded of what Jefferies himself says of the forest, 'it beguiles us from the region of fact to the realms of fiction'. These surroundings, by extinguishing present problems and stimulating the imaginative element in the author's constitution to escapism, thus perform two functions.

The theme of escape is very strong in another sense in the landscape essays. In both *The Graphic* and (especially) *The Globe* newspapers Jefferies is writing for a specific audience. It is predominantly an urban and suburban one, experiencing for the first time an opportunity for leisure which was facilitated by the growing railway network. The desire to escape from often miserable surroundings to the countryside resulted in a quickening of interest in all aspects of rural life, aided by a radical if nebulous yearning for a return to supposed rural values, epitomized in the cry for 'Three Acres and a Cow' in the 1880s. Jefferies capitalizes upon this desire: thus, we see him referring to the time it takes to reach Savernake by rail and to the remoteness of some villages as an integral part of their attraction. Although his view of the more inaccessible areas as being 'as unknown as the centre of Africa' is, of course, an exaggeration, it is an understandable one, for he is indulging a repressed sense of adventure which certain features of the landscape, like forest and secluded community, free in similar ways: one can get lost in these parts, and such thoughts appeal. Part of the lure of the forest is its 'wildness and freedom', similar to that of 'an American primeval forest'. The child-like delight and wish for adventure, most strongly manifested in *Bevis* and fed by both early reading and contemporary pioneering exploits, is evident. Pointedly Jefferies remarks of the forest at Savernake that 'it reminds us of books of woodland sport read in our boyhood'. In the out-of-the-way communities it is still possible to catch a glimpse of a passing mode of living—one which equates with Nature. The absence of hurry, and the diurnal rhythms sustained by the various activities and sounds of the countryside, are faithfully caught and rendered in essays like *Village Hunting*. When incursions have been made by the modern spirit Jefferies shows that Nature has resisted and eventually reasserted herself. The symbolism of the clock that stopped 'half a generation ago', during less turbulent times, indicates both the gap between past and present and the irrepressibility of Nature in the form of the jackdaws which have built there.

In some respects the realistic attitude which Jefferies brings to his writing on agriculture carries over into his landscape essays. Nature is sturdy, resilient, sometimes harsh, rather than winning, pretty, effete, but this merely enhances her attractions. Jefferies' advice in a late essay to 'Idealize

17

to the full, but idealize the real, else the picture is a sham', is advice which he himself adheres to in the essays in this collection. A sense of the ageles. quality of much of the Wiltshire countryside is conveyed, yet any tendency towards sentimentality, or vague nostalgia, is deliberately undercut. The valley of the old mill may be suffused with the rosy glow of the setting sun, but it contains a building which '. . . stands on the edge of life, where we meet the stern facts of existence'. The downs themselves may evoke recollections of pastoral poetry, but they have also witnessed 'The shout of battle, the whistle of the arrow, the groan of the wounded . . .', and their '. . . green sward has been stained red with the blood of hapless men'. The author is purposely setting up the pastoral-idyllic convention here in order to deflate it. These essays, in the main, show Jefferies playing to early, if immature, strengths, writing from his own experiences—a far cry from the weak 'society' pieces which were appearing at this time in *The World*, and the 'silver fork' novels of the same period.

These then are the essays of landscape and labour. They emphasize the unashamed allegiance to the past of a man who felt the destruction of many aspects of traditional rural life acutely, and yet realized that change, decay and regeneration are all an integral part of the historical cycle. In his agricultural articles Jefferies saw himself as the dispassionate, factual reporter, as his numerous claims regarding the veracity of his accounts testify. But as much depends on *how* matters are seen as on *what* is viewed, and with his background objectivity in these articles remained more of an aspiration than an actuality. Only in his sketches of individuals does any fresh appraisal of the farm labourer's problems occur. For the most part, he, along with the majority of Wiltshire farmer-employers, saw the present as unstable, and the portents for the future as uncertain, unpromising. The main personal consolation resided in Nature and the example which she provided. This may seem vague and rather irrelevant to the great changes taking place in rural England. However, Jefferies takes these changes as epitomizing the shifts in society as a whole towards a new commercial attitude, which may provide many of man's material needs, but leaves him spiritually arid and is essentially opposed to Nature. She provides certitude by example and thus a basis for a new faith which is notably lacking in the aggrandized but fragile present. In a late essay Jefferies observes of the countryside, 'It is all changed and just the same'.

This, ultimately, is the most effective retort to human aspiration and a vindication of his own natural religious faith.

Every effort has been made to keep Jefferies' prose as it appeared in the periodicals of his day. However, where necessary, printers' errors have been remedied and the punctuation modified to improve the sense.

I. LANDSCAPE

The Wiltshire Downs

1877

The great sun still hangs high in the western sky, and yet, though there is no shade, it is cool lying here upon the soft turf, for the breeze blows fresh and pure at this height, and tempers his summer rays. From the south it comes, from the distant Solent where the gay yachts are dancing merrily before it—over broad Sarum Plain, till the bennets and the long grass, where the hare hides in her form, rustle as it bows them on this ancient Wiltshire hill. In that rustle as the sound now rises, now falls, is there not a faint echo of the sea, and down yonder in the valley behind there the graceful barley stoops with a passing sheen upon the stalk, like rolling waves of green. This deep fosse gives a pleasant slope to recline on, this great bunch of thyme a pillow for the head which a king might envy: soft, odorous, every motion of the arm resting upon it presses out an exquisite bouquet; and is not the delicate flower itself lovely to look upon? Let the head rest then, bury the face in this pillow of Nature, extend the limbs, and forgetting the dusty struggle of the wearied cities, breathe in as it were the very spirit, the magnetism of the grand old Earth, as Antaeus did in the fable of the Greeks. There will rise a sense of vastness, of a depth underneath, of an extension round about, and at the far away rim the ocean—beyond the ocean, space itself, and in space, *what*? It is a mystery: but it is a mystery that purifies the mind to dwell upon, and lift it above itself. The Earth was thus, and the Sun was thus, and the Sea was thus, one hundred generations ago, when in Egypt they hewed out that carved mountain the Sphinx. As in the hour-glass the sand runs, so in the hour-glass of the world the sand of the desert has risen, atom by atom, particle by particle, till now, the very lips of the statue, which once were inaccessible in their height, as it were drink the sand, drink the bitterness of Time which has reached their level. Then they prayed at the feet: now, the Arab spreads his mat by the very ear of the statue, and looking towards the east he prays on the dust of three thousand, ay, four thousand years. The mystery—but listen, the lark sings overhead, and what is our brief life besides the memory of that span of time; still less besides this dial here, this sarsen boulder dropped from the ice-rafts of a glacial sea? Shall not a little, just a breath, of this eternal youth of nature—of the earth as young now as ever, of the sun as undimmed, of the everlasting hills, of the wind that blew as freshly then, of the ocean—

> Ocean old,
> Centuries old,
> Strong as youth and as uncontrolled,

Shall not a breath of this magnetic vigour enter into us too? Shall not the soul trace back its ancestry before the very hills, and look forward to a life beyond the very sun, and outdoing Ulysses, sail farther even than

> The sunset, and the baths
> Of all the western stars.

Glance over the edge of the fosse—see hills, hills, hills, rolling in vast billows away on every side; these bright in the sunshine, those dark as the shadow of a cloud glides over them. No fence, no jealous enclosure shall stay your footstep. Whole days the pilgrim of Nature may wander freely, like the wind whither it listeth, and none shall say him nay. The track there—it is but a few waggon-ruts and the marks of horse's hoofs—passes for fully five-and-twenty miles along the ridge of these Wiltshire hills, not to mention the Berkshire, which are part of the same range, and the horseman may ride the day long from morn till eve on the finest of turf. There is a freedom in this vastness, these open downs, which far surpasses the most picturesque of landscapes where the traveller cannot quit the beaten path. It is an almost prairie-like solitude; the farmhouses are far between, and lie chiefly in the 'bottoms', as the combes are called, so that one may pass them easily unnoticed; and the hamlets farther still, placed where some never-failing spring supplies man and beast with water. Water is as precious here as in the veritable deserts of the East. The shepherds are the only human beings to be seen. As the evening grows later and work is over, perhaps a ploughboy or a shepherd lad sits him down upon the ground, hidden in the corn, and plays a plaintive tune upon his whistle, which there, with those surroundings, sounds sweet and mellow. It is curious how little the equipments of the shepherd, his 'tar-box' and so on for the aid and succour of his flock, have altered since the days, two hundred years ago, of the beautiful pastoral ballads preserved in Bishop Percy's book where the details almost exactly correspond. Something of the old poetry of outdoor life lingers yet in these far away solitudes; you may see the shepherd with his crook, a real crook, still on Salisbury Plain, of which these Downs are the northern escarpment, and it would not seem quite out of place to witness such a pastoral wooing as when—

With that she bent her snow-white knee,
Down by the shepherd kneeled she,
   And him she sweetly kissed.
Whereat the shepherd whoop'd for joy,
Quoth he, There ne'er was shepherd's boy
   That ever was so blessed!

Lying on this pillow of thyme the bees go by with 'drowsy hum' sucking the clover, and the myriads of lowly but sweet flowers which blossom on the Downs, and make the honey of the hills famous. Some farms have a hundred hives in a row, and sell immense quantities of honey; in the old times it was a regular business before sugar came so freely and so cheaply from abroad. A king may really have rested on the thyme here, for this deep trench, covered with soft turf, is the outer fosse of an ancient British fort or camp. There are two ditches, circular, one within the other, and on this steep hill in the days of bow and arrow it must have been a strong place. Down in the valley below see those half-effaced lines and trenches—they are the relics of a buried city, a British city, where the spade has turned up coin and arrow-head, and quern—the stone mortar in which they pounded and ground their corn. The shout of battle, the whistle of the arrow, the groan of the wounded has been heard upon this hill, the green sward has been stained red with the blood of hapless men. The sandalled foot of the Roman has trod the broad green track there—it was a military road then; the White Horse flag of the Saxons has floated on the breeze, when, as the Chronicler writes of this very spot, they advanced to attack the Britons in one compact body 'with such fierceness that the standards being dashed together and borne down, and the spears being broken, it became a hand-to-hand fight with the sword. The battle lasted till nightfall without either party being able to claim a victory'. There are *tumuli* close by, or rather there were within easy memory, for the plough has gone over them now; though others are within sight, low green knolls where sleep forgotten warriors. But the shadow of the hawthorn bush lengthens visibly; the disc of the sun grows red and larger as he sinks; it is time to leave the thyme and the sward, to descend to the cities of the plain. From the flint-heaps and the furze those curious birds, the 'chats', fly off with an odd cry as we pass; and in a few hours' time the hares now so cunningly hiding will be scampering over the turf under the 'glimpses of the moon'.

A Summer Day in Savernake Forest

1876

With the thermometer ranging from 130 to 135 degrees in the full blaze of the sun, few men would fail to appreciate the cool glades of Savernake Forest. Even without the tropical heat of the present summer, it is a charming spot, for it cheats us into a passing forgetfulness of the weary, horse-in-the-mill sort of life we all lead more or less in this work-a-day world; it reminds us of books of woodland sports read in our boyhood; it beguiles us from the region of fact to the realms of fiction, and brings us face to face with Nature in some of her most witching aspects. Here Summer has robed the trees in all their bravery. Vegetation has reached its prime. The leaves show no signs of the hardship to which they were exposed by the frosts and the unkind winds of May. No sickly stain hints that they must die before winter comes. They whisper and rustle in the glorious sunshine in all the pride of life. In the great beech avenues the shade dapples the walks or lays in dark masses for miles and miles. The silvery trunks and arching boughs more than realize all that poets and romance writers have ever said or sung of woodland naves and forest aisles, of which the noblest cathedrals offer so poor a copy. On either side the crisp, dry leaves lie ankle deep on the ground, and betray the light, faltering steps of the hare as she pauses to gaze a moment at the passing stranger, and then scuds away to the nearest cover. As for the squirrels, they are quite at home in these leafy strongholds. There they sit, the arch impostors, making believe that they find nuts in the empty shells of the rotting beech mast. Their bushy tails are coquettishly spread over their brown backs, and they themselves eye the invader with a mild surprise, till, startled out of their propriety, they scamper up the giant trunks and leap from branch to branch, adepts in all the mysteries of the flying trapeze.

The forest is no level plain, but, like other parts of the Wiltshire downs, its surface is broken into heights and hollows, and tiny canyons, over which the tall fern waves in unbroken patches, hundreds of acres in extent. The fallow deer muster strong in the woodlands, but show less than they will do a few weeks hence, for the does are nursing their young ones in the bracken, and have for the time given up society. Are their lords disconsolate? It is hard to say, for they seem to have formed themselves into clubs, and lead gay bachelor lives, wandering where fancy dictates, or resting under the shade, sadly oblivious of all parental duties. Yonder is a great herd of red deer. The stags are as heavy as any ever dropped by a bullet in Highland glen. The velvet has not yet fallen from their antlers, which look somewhat clumsy from the soft, thick coating, but for 'stags of ten' where may you see so fair a sight? It makes the heart beat fast, sends a wild flutter through the nerves, and is altogether suggestive of an express rifle as they glide away with a shadowy silence so peculiar to the race. What creature is that crossing a piece of close-cropped turf in so deliberate and ungainly a fashion? It is only a hedgehog, which, mistaking a friend for a foe, loses no time in assuming a defensive attitude. It is too hot for comfortable fighting, yet the silly animal is straining his muscles to a painful degree of tension in order to keep all his spears in due array. The Macedonian phalanx in battle array was nothing to him. It requires two to make a quarrel, so *requiescat in pace*. The jays in yonder oak glade chatter harshly, and flutter restlessly from tree to tree. Robin Hood and his men might have forgotten for a time merry Sherwood. The giant branches, so gaunt and bare, might each make a separate trunk that would have required at least a century for its growth. It is a sombre spot, a place where these Titans of the wood have met to lay their bones when their time comes. They stand firm in the summer air, make a brave show in their decay, and look calmly down on the bleaching limbs they have lost in some struggle with winter and rough weather. The soft mellow crush of the wood pigeon's note sounds all in keeping with this woodland mausoleum, while the flaunting, fine gentlemen woodpeckers, in scarlet and green and gold, seem a little out of harmony, not so much on account of their dress, as from their chuckling want of sympathy.

The thorns form quite a feature in the landscape, raising their twisted trunks from the green sward, or from the fern brakes. They are things to be remembered, these hoary seers. Were their memories good, and were they disposed to be communicative, what episodes in history might they not supply? Many of them must have been in their prime when bluff King Hal wended his way to the Field of the Cloth of Gold.

Savernake Forest is not a toy place. The 'rides' are endless, the roads manifold, and it may well chance that a stranger who has no compass in his pocket to point the way to Marlborough, Dudley, or Great Bedwyn, might lose his way and be compelled to make his bed among the bracken. The day seems to have less than its usual span, for the shadows point eastward, and grow longer and longer, the topmost boughs of the great clumps of beeches wearing for a moment golden tints from the level beams of the setting sun. But there is to-morrow, to-morrow, and to-morrow, in which others may dream away the summer hours in this loveliest forest in Britain. The finest pleasures are the cheapest, and few pleasures might be less costly than a day in the forest. Loitering in its solitudes, it requires some effort of thought to remember that it is scarcely three hours by rail from Paddington.

In a Pine-Wood

1877

'He who loves trees lives long', says the Eastern proverb, and the pine-wood with its intense stillness and calm, shutting out as with a thick wall the anxious cares of towns and cities, lets the mind return in upon itself, and realize its immortality. This, our common English pine, is indeed a tree of mystery, a tree of life: whose history is full of deep things not easy to be found out. For among the imagery on the walls of the palaces and temples of Nineveh, hidden away thousands of years ago, there are figures of Genii, or demi-gods, winged human-like beings, standing before the Supreme Lord of Heaven, and holding in one hand a fir-cone. Such cones we may pick up here, as we linger slowly, pondering in the warm shade of these beautiful trees; over whose tops the sky stoops lower, and becomes more richly blue; between whose branches a bright sunbeam slants, lighting up the dim crypts yonder underneath. Such cones take the swift mind back—in a second over-stepping the centuries—to the days when those creatures of the air, now to us mere ideal abstractions, whether under the name of Bel, or Apollo, hardened into human shape, and walked hand-in-hand with Earth's own fairest; when the 'Sons of God' looked with love on the daughters of men. See how this strange fruit is built up ring upon ring, scale upon scale, swelling out from the base, and then gently tapering; at its root each scale absorbed into the general mass—each distinct, and yet a part of the whole. The tree itself, too, if you will glance at the ends of the branches, grows thus: these delicate 'needles', or leaves, gradually sinking into the wood, adding to its length and size, little by little. In the palms which are common under glass in London, a similar mode of growth is so palpable that we seem almost to see the leaf become the tree, to be in the presence of life itself—symbolized by the fir-cone. The Assyrian Genii hold in their hands, in visible shape, the mysterious force, which, neither heat, nor light, nor electricity, nor magnetism, we vaguely call life: the stirring of which all nature feels about the time of the rising of the Pleiades. In our own limbs and bodies, the 'cells' of the physiologist, in

like manner to the pine needles and the palm leaves, live a short life and build up the larger organism—as a great poet says:

And the individual withers, but the world grows more and more.

The fir-tree is above all trees the friend of man. Some even find that its appearance upon the earth in geological time corresponds with that of the human race. In the strata preceding man remains of other trees are found; lastly comes the pine, and with it the rude implements of primitive life. This may not be wholly correct, yet it is certain that the part played by the pine in human history is very striking. The vast population of our own times could scarcely have existed had it not been for the discovery of the almost inexhaustible pine woods of America. Our English woods and forests, quite seventy years ago, showed signs of quick extinction, so immense was the demand for shipbuilding. American deal, imported in timber ships in quantities so great as to baffle calculation, alone rendered possible the marvellous development of towns and cities, by providing the materials of building. Let anyone just glance over a house, and note the extent to which pinewood (deal) is used: floors, beams, rafters, staircase, banisters, doors, ceilings (laths), window-frames, cupboards, furniture—the list is too long for recapitulation. Without the fir-tree much, if not most, of our civilization would be impossible—the very locomotives, typical of the age, roar on over a framework of pine. Concerning that period when first the demand for wood became so great there is a sad anecdote; sad because showing how liable the keenest human foresight is to fail, as Xenophon put it—it is as if we guided our steps by the chance casting of the die. A great landowner, to whom an heir was born, set to work and planted one million fir-trees on his estate: 'For', said he, 'when the child is twenty-one, each of those trees will be worth £1., and he will come into a fortune of £1,000,000'. The trees grew, but meantime the American lumber trade sprang up, splendid balks of timber came over in enormous quantities, and the puny English firs of such short growth fell in value to a few shillings. The 'oaken walls of England' are a national tradition; yet pine was used long before oak for ship-building, the latter not coming into use till a comparatively late period, and still the masts and spars are chiefly pine. When Ulysses in Calypso's Isle wished to build a ship, the goddess led him where—

> On the lone island's utmost verge there stood
> Of poplars, pines, and firs a lofty wood,

and these formed his materials. In the extreme north, where vegetation is stunted, the bow of the Lapland hunter is formed from the root of the fir, and its slim poles support the tents of the nomadic races over vast regions.

The transition from the pine to the cedar is to ordinary eyes easy; time fails to even mention the historic sweep of the cedar tree, now rising in majestic grandeur on Lebanon, now in the creeping variety, trailing along the ground. The Norfolk Island pine, the stone-pine, endless varieties, and reminiscences of southern climes crowd the memory, dreaming in this English wood. Grim is the story of the ancient tyrant who threatened to cut off a whole people *as a pine tree*. They could not understand this till at last it was remembered that the pine alone, when cut down, sends forth no shoot or bud. The stump and roots decay till they totally disappear. This may be seen in any fir-plantation where the axe has been at work. He meant utter destruction.

It is the most artistic of trees, beautifully balanced, with drooping branches, and delicate 'lines'—a noble sight in winter, when the snow clings thick, and contrasts with the dark green of the boughs. Something weird, mystic, hovers over it; thus Retzsch, picturing Walpurgis Night, places the Demon-band up in a pine, squatting on the branches, with horn and cymbals, playing to the rout of witches dancing. Though so still now, yet at times when the wind rises there is a sound among them as of the distant sea. Here is the squirrel's home, here the pigeons love to rest, and the noisy jays chatter and scold, and the shy grossbeak hides. Pheasants delight in the thick covert.

Under the warm sun these trees give forth a sweet odour—an odour for which invalids seek the pine forests of Arcachon and Hyères; but which may be inhaled in any English coppice. We have many flowers, some flowering shrubs; but alone of our trees the pine scents the air with a delicate perfume. It is not permanent; now it comes and now it goes, you must sit down and linger, you must begin to dream, and then it will seek you. The spirit of Nature will not come unless to perfect peace. Gazing upwards—these curious trees, like green steeples, incline the eye upwards—a sense of exquisite langour enters in with the bouquet of the pines, a sense of *belief* in Nature, of certainty in the life of which the cones up there are the symbol.

The Commonest Thing in the World

1877

Nothing affords so comfortable a seat when tired of walking down a country lane as a log of timber lying on the sward under the shadow of tall elms, lit up with the red glow of the sinking sun whose beams shine level over the fields,

> Where the poppy plants his banner
> Scarlet bright amid the corn.

The wayside weeds are trying to hide the flint-heap near by, the tiny wild pink geraniums, and the larger blue crane's bill, and the creeping tendrils of the convolvulus have lovingly nestled up against the hard stones, fringing them with beauty. The flowers do not disdain the flints even, so in the idleness of the moment let us pick one up; a rough, sharp-edged flint, common, despicable, yet the whole history of the human race lies now in the hollow of the hand.

When the noble sun yonder was—ah, how many thousands of years younger, there stole stealthily through the primaeval forests an all-but nude animal, fighting, struggling daily for bare existence with the huge beasts of the earth, hiding in caves fearfully, wondering at the darkness and the dawn, hailing the sun there as a god, yet walking upright, and already pondering deeply in a dim way—in brief, a man with the divine spark of intellect in his brain. His naked foot stepped on a flint whose sharp edge cut it; a beast of the forest would have simply rushed from the spot in anger and pain, but the man stooped down and picked it up, just as we have done, looked at it, turned it over in the hollow of his hand, till an idea occurred to him. What had cut him would cut anything else—he tried it on a branch, and marked and gashed the bark. It would cut deeper if it was thinner; he dashed it against a larger stone, and it split up into flakes. There was the first knife, there was the germ of progress, the tool which gave him dominion over the beasts of the field, and even the elements themselves. With the flint-flake the rude club torn from a tree could be fashioned into shape; such a flake attached to the end of a long stick formed a javelin with which game could be dexterously transfixed at some little distance. A larger and heavier piece made a spear for close attack; a smaller, an arrowhead, when the bow at once became a powerful weapon. Knives of the same material cut up the animal the hunter had killed, and with flint scrapers the skin was cleaned and prepared for use as dress, or the sinews for string and thread. The peculiarity of flint is that if tapped in a particular manner it chips off, or splits almost to a nicety in proportion to the strength and direction of the blow. Thus primitive man was able to make spear-heads and arrowheads, knives, and so on of really exquisite workmanship and artistic shape. It answered admirably for cutting or stabbing; but would not stand the jar of chopping; hence axes were generally ground of stone with a grain that did not readily split into laminae. But when the tree had been laboriously felled with such dull tools, the sharp flint knives or chisels hollowed it out into the canoe, and shaped the paddles. Here already was dominion over the beasts, and over the element of water. With these knives wood could be fashioned into the fire-drill for the obtaining of heat by friction, and so fire.

Still higher yet. The keen edge of the flint-flake carved out lines and designs upon the paddles and sides of the canoes, on the posts which supported the hut, and on the handles of the weapons and tools themselves. Such horn handles cunningly cut out into the likeness of couchant animals still exist; and yet more. On a famous piece of ivory there may be seen the outline sketch, if one may so call it, of the mammoth—that prehistoric monster—graven probably with a flint-tool, and not without spirit. Here was Art. Then came rude images of the gods—idols sculptured with the flint, and certain ceremonies of a religious character performed by such an instrument. Some have thought that even the advanced Egyptians chiselled out their statues with flint, since copper tools could not touch such hard material; and did not Zipporah circumcize her son with a 'sharp stone', i.e., a flint? It is known that sacrifices were cut up with flint knives. The spear, the javelin, and the arrowhead of flint made something like an organized army possible, and hence war and conquest, and the migrations of tribes and races of men ages and ages since. Thus, the chase, war, art, and religion itself owed almost everything to the discovery of the flint. From it sprang civilization. He was a genius indeed who first used the flint-flake; and note this, no monkey—though the monkey tribe has existed for ages and ages and ages—has ever advanced to such intelligence. The line is distinctly marked between the first man, however rude, of whom caves bear record, and the cleverest ape or monkey. The most primitive of men used *a tool*: there it is.

From the distant East—India—to the distant West—America, all along the vast caravan route, so to say, of the human race, from the sunrise to sunset, in cave, and mound, and river, the chipped flint is found, the hieroglyphic of man; the stamp, as it were, of his presence. Ay, and even at the bottom of the sea. Off the eastern coast of England the trawl and dredger now and then at intervals brings up to the surface from the silence of the deep—miles and miles out at sea—just such tools and weapons, adding to the accumulated evidence of the enormous changes which have taken place since the Stone peoples hunted over what is now the home of the mackerel, since this island was part of a continent. What a history has yet to be written of those strange times! The chapters are being slowly spelt out word by word, in caves, in *tumuli*, by stones and flints, and shell mounds, and carved horn and ivory; just as the cuneiform inscriptions were deciphered by patient ingenuity.

Later down, the flint won the battle of Waterloo in the flintlock guns of our gallant soldiers; and to this day glass of the finest quality is manufactured by its aid, and with glass lenses and prisms the mystery of the stars was solved. Give this round flint a smart tap; see: as it cracks open, the centre is hollow—there is a little dusty substance in the concavity: men of science say it is the remains of a sponge (sponge-spiculae) which once flourished in the ocean till the liquid silex poured round and enveloped it, destroying yet preserving. This large and shapeless block is full of crystals, which glitter in the sun at first, but soon grow dull after exposure to the atmosphere. Here, on another, see what exactly resembles the outline tracing of a delicate fern, as if a fern had been stamped into the stone; some consider it an effect of what for convenience sake we may call crystallization, any way it is beautiful. Our forefathers, in their powdered wigs and gaiters; and silver knee-buckles, and rapiers, lit their candles by the aid of flint and steel for long, long generations.

But pause—a solitary star, it is Arcturus, which Job the great poet watched and wrote of in the old-world days, shines down through the elm branches, and the bats are wheeling in mazy circles round the trees. It is time to go. The flint, dropped from the hand on the sward, rolls out into the road, to be crushed with all its marvellous history under the careless wheel of the thoughtless carter, ground into powder, to the last serving man by mending his highway.

The Old Mill

1878

There flashes back from the topmost window, under the grey slates, a fiery gleam, like the red blood-shot eye in the brow of the Cyclops: it is the light of the sinking sun, whose level rays fill the valley with a rosy glow. The wheat, slowly crushed under the ponderous stones there, was ripened by the same sun which, in the old, old days, lovingly shone down upon the yellow grain in the year when it was said, 'Two shall be grinding at the mill, and one shall be taken and the other left'. How many weary centuries have the mills of the world ground on? For, in one shape or another, this is the oldest machine on earth, rivalled only by the potter's wheel. This great weather-beaten building stands at the mouth of one of those curious, winding, narrow 'bottoms', or deep valleys—across which one could almost throw a stone—so characteristic of the chalk formation. The walls are of flint, set in cement, hard as adamant, and thick enough to stand the fiercest tempest, or even a shot from a 'culverin' in the times when every Englishman's house was literally, and of necessity, his castle.

Once, while dragging his heavy shoes over the fallow, and guiding the slow team in the cornfield yonder on the slope, the ploughman saw the share turn up a strange-looking hollow stone, which he placed on one side till work was done, and then carried home to his master. It was a quern, a rude utensil, not unlike a coarsely made mortar, in which the women of the primitive peoples painfully laboured to grind or pound their corn—Saxon, and Dane, and hardy Norseman—chaunting of the famous sword:

> Quern-biter of Hakon the Good,
> Wherewith at a stroke he hewed
> The millstone through and through.

The bones of the warriors have long since mouldered into dust—dust dried by the sun, and blown hither and thither over the field, dust moistened by the dew of Heaven, and finally working its part in the germination of the seed-corn—the wondrous marvel of life coming out of death. So there was a mill, a rude hand-mill, at work here 1,200 years ago. Then follows a brief,

U. L. Sieger '79

curt entry in the Book of Doomsday, as the Saxons, with a certain poetry, called the Norman's register of their plundered lands; all the entries in which book are short and curt, as if written by hand to which mace and sword were fitter than the pen. It records that here was a mill which paid 5s. taxes, a large sum in the days of William the Conqueror, to be raised from grinding in so small and outlying a place. Not very long after a Norman 'Comes', or Count—Earl as we should say now—held a mill here. This was one of the most valuable of the manorial rights, and jealously guarded, so that no poor serf dared to take his corn elsewhere than to his lord's mill to be turned into flour. A crushing despotism it must have been when these little kings on their separate estates had 'right of gallows', and could hang the wretch who offended them; when everything a man could do—to buy or sell, or travel, every detail of life—rendered some tribute, or in some way came under the dominion of the 'lord', and nothing could be done without his license. Yet later, and it passed into the hands of a neighbouring Abbot and his cowled company, who stinted not the wheaten bread, and

bade the goblet pass,
In their beards the red wine glistened
Like dew-drops in the grass.

It was reckoned in with their *columbarium*, or dovecote, their stews or fishponds, coney or rabbit warren, and other appliances for ease of good living. That was the day when Chaucer's miller flourished, a stout knave who could burst a door in running with his head, like a battering-ram, who grew so fat and 'podgy', with constantly dipping his hands in the sacks of meal to take toll of the poor folk's corn, that the 'Miller's Thumb' became a byeword, and is still the local name of a fish which lurks at the bottom of brooks, and is notable for the hugeness of its head in proportion to its body. It was an Abbot who built the major portion of the present walls, within which the grain was ground to feed the Crusaders, for the men who fought in the bitter wars of the Roses, for Cavalier and Roundhead, and so down to our own time. Still the wheel goes round, and still the ceaseless current of human life flows on. The oldest buildings in every parish are the church, the manor-house, and the mill, and very often (as in this case) the mill can be traced back—though not, of course, the actual walls that now stand—far deeper into the mists of hoar antiquity than either.

The still pool there which drives the wheel may be but a common pond in the eyes of the waggoner who comes for the sacks of flour, and yet in that pool there is a mystery which has baffled all the efforts of our philosophers and men of science, and that is—the storage of force. In every drop of water force is stored up waiting till man comes to use it; now no mechanic has yet succeeded in constructing a strong room in which to lock up the energy of the sun, and tides, and the rolling world like this. If they could, all the steam-engines and inventions of the age would fall into insignificance beside it. The dew and the rain on the downs up yonder sink into the chalk, and presently ooze out—filtered to crystal clearness—at the head of the narrow valley, where the grass is a vivid green and the water-cress flourishes. These dew and rain drops drive the mill, and they have been first lifted up to the hill-top by the sun, and so it is really a sun-mill, and the same planet which ripens the grain grinds it for man's use. Perhaps it is the direct incidence of Nature which has ever surrounded the mill with a certain mysticism, so that the Greeks used it to illustrate Fate, and the inevitable Nemesis which overtakes every deed. 'The mill of the gods grinds late, but it grinds small', was their proverb. Unto the third and fourth generations minute retribution was ground out. Proverbs and sayings cluster about the mill, for it stands on the edge of life, where we meet the stern facts of existence, and it has furnished endless illustrations—'hard of heart as the nether millstone', 'better that a millstone had been hung about his neck, and cast into the sea', 'our teeth were broken with gravel'—i.e., because the corn was ground badly, and full of grit. Mills are the pioneers of civilization as opposed to nomadic life; so in the American backwoods a grist mill is the first building erected after the log shanties of the settlers.

In the osiers yonder by the side of the pool the swallows gather of the early autumn evenings in Parliament assembled, when, after 'motion made and question put', and much reporting of progress in the debate, and tremendous twittering, away at last they go to warmer skies. There are pike, and roach, and perch in the depths, and ducks and drakes with glossy necks merrily quacking as they swim between the broad water-lily leaves; and hark! there goes the kingfisher with his melancholy long-drawn whistle. Clack-clack-clack-at-a-clack! the wheel swings ponderously round and round on its axle of a solid oak—green with dripping moss, making the earth close by tremble as if afraid. The wheelwright who made it was a proud man, when after months of labour it was completed, to last a generation itself, though the hard apple-tree cogs of the lesser wheels within the mill have been renewed time after time. Alas! he will tell you since ironwork became so cheap his vocation is almost gone, and, he might add, since men gathered so thickly in cities, and had their corn ground by steam.

Still there the miller, with his white apron, stands at the door, podgy and thickset as in Chaucer's day, with 'slow, wise smile', till we think of the miller's daughter, and remember how once, mayhap—but no matter:

> And she is grown so dear, so dear,
>> That I would be the jewel
>>> That trembles at her ear.
>> For hid in ringlets, day and night,
>>> I'd touch her neck so warm and white.

Or the grimly grotesque scene when the farmer's daughter was pushed in the pool, and:

>> The miller he 'fot' his pole and hook
>> And fished the fair maid out of the brook,

only to steal her guineas ten, and thrust her 'back agen'.

>> But the Crowner he cum, and the Justice too,
>> With a hue and a cry, and a hullaballoo!

For poet, and humourist, the wise men of Greece, and even the inspired writer have all had something to say of the mill.

Village Hunting

1877

Every year a larger number of pleasure seekers, who have grown tired of the bustling cities by the sea, who have exhausted Brighton and Scarborough, and a host of similar places, endeavour to get out of the beaten track of holiday making, and to discover some quiet spot where they may really rest awhile. But the difficulty is that there is no guide, no carefully got up volume, 'with map', to show them where to go, and the choice of a village in which to spend a few weeks' retirement is pretty much a matter of chance. Nor can we altogether wish it otherwise, for the moment a thing is 'organized' it loses half its freshness and charm. The fun of 'prospecting', as the gold diggers say—only for health instead of wealth—of exploring districts which, to a resident in the suburbs of London, are as unknown as the centre of Africa, would be lost if all the routes were mapped out, and people told exactly what they were expected to admire. It is much better to arrive totally unprepared and ignorant of what is to be seen and enjoyed—to find it all out for oneself. Then every ramble affords something new.

Villages lie in such unexpected places. Mounting a long, dusty hill, not a house or cottage in sight, suddenly on the other side, down in a deep hollow, you see just the tops of the chimneys, and could pitch a stone into them easily. All the rest of the place is hidden by tall elms, and even the church tower is so green with ivy that were it not for the weathercock on the top it would hardly be distinguished among the foliage. Or, passing on the plain between the thickest of hedges, with the white convolvulus trailing over them, behold at a turn of the road an inn, whose sign hangs from a tree, and without knowing it you have actually gone half through the place. The cottages and houses stand far back from the highway, fenced in with hawthorn and orchard and yew; till you are tempted to change the nomenclature, and call it Hedge-town. Others there are set in the midst of rolling prairies of meadows and green pastures, studded with oaks, till at a little distance a stranger might imagine he was approaching a great wood.

Here, again, a brook seems to run before every door; to get to the cottage or the farm you must cross a broad, flat stone, laid over a clear stream bordered with flags and rushes. Had the original choosers of these sites any 'Fung-shuy', any health necromancy, or art of divination like the Chinese, by which to pick out the places best fitted for human habitation? 'Fungshuy' has often beaten our engineers in China in the knack of selecting sites for barracks and residences free from fever; and so 'the rude forefathers of the hamlet', without any knowledge of geology or sanitary science, nevertheless generally settled just where the trees, or the water, or the hills gave them the largest supply of ozone.

How few ever seek the precincts of the beautiful forest of Marlborough, so easily accessible, and so completely open and free to all comers to roam whithersoever they will. There the red deer move grandly among the huge oaks and natural avenues of beech in great herds, or start up suddenly out of the endless bracken, tall as a man's shoulder. It has all the wildness and freedom of an American primeval forest. If 'mamma' and 'papa' only understood the strengthening, invigorating quality of the breeze on the downs of Berks and Wilts, and over the vast Sarum Plain, how eagerly they would take their delicate children thither, to run at will over the elastic sward searching for mushrooms, to slide gleefully down the steeper inclines, and inhale the peculiarly dry air so valuable to weak chests. But even village hunters run very much in grooves, and go where somebody else has been, instead of striking out a bold, original course for themselves. Take up a railway map; see, here and there are wide spaces between the lines of rail. There you may be nearly sure to find quiet and health combined, for such spans have been avoided by the engineers because of the hills, which have saved for us just a little of the old-world life in England.

You may find traces of that life in the strange indifference to time which seems to brood over the village. Even at their work in the fields the men and women do not hasten; their arms move slowly, and ever and anon they pause and talk. There is no noise of whirling wheels, no bustle and puff and hurry. The very sun appears to hang in the sky. The days are longer here; very likely you will hardly be able to discover what o'clock it really is in any of the houses. They will always say 'It is about six' or 'nearly seven'; never the precise time to a minute as a man would answer in London. The clock in the church stopped half a generation ago, and has never been started since—the jackdaws have built in the works. In this drowsiness there is a moral change for the mind as well as a change for the physical man. The doctors say when one has heart disease that it is not the actual exertion of running to catch a train which causes sudden death, but the anxiety, the eagerness, the strain upon the exquisite fibres of the brain. 'Time is money', often, it is to be feared, 'time' in this sense 'is death'. Therefore, when the village hunter has chosen his land of the lotos, let him or her lay aside that carefully wound-up watch, lock it up out of sight. Measure time as the villagers do, by the increase of heat in the middle of the day, which demands a pause of work; by the contented lowing of the cows as they, towards half-past three or four, of their own accord, come up to the pens for milking; by the sinking of the sun and the lengthening of the shadows. Go and sit by the mill sluice, where the ferns grow among the damp stones in tropical luxuriance, and listen to that great clyssydra, that vast water-clock, the mill-wheel, with its monotonous yet pleasing sound, till it lulls you into daydreams and a Nirvana of forgetfulness. Then the mesmeric influence of nature will enter into and strengthen the whole frame.

If sometimes it is felt necessary 'to do something', then put into practice your favourite study, that hitherto you have only read of in books or followed indoors. Is it history? There is the entrenchment on the hill, the old church tower once used as a fortress in a skirmish in the civil war, the manor-house. Visit these, and, avoiding books, try to get at their origin and story. Is it geology or botany?—the earth and stones and plants are all around you. Is it only light literature?—well, there are the legends, the odd tales, the ghost stories of the people to collect, for never yet have they been collected fully. Or art?—then there are faces of children, dark-eyed girls of ten and twelve, with curling locks and shy black eyes, a handful of wheat ears in one little hand, a scarlet poppy in the other; old men sitting in the porch, or a village bridal perhaps; and if your genius be realistic, local industries to limn with the stern fidelity of Holman Hunt, such as the stripping of the osiers or the making of gloves, which still lingers in unsuspected places. Never plan anything out to be done on the morrow—go where the fancy leads you on the spur of the moment, or leave it alone; if it is arranged beforehand it will be a failure. That very method which succeeds in business spoils pleasure; enjoyment must be impromptu.

The area is very wide. Till lately people have for years gone in crowds to about a score of places, mostly by the sea, and have left, therefore, broad districts untouched by the tourist. Were not some statistics published lately to the effect that there were something like 12,000 parochial clergymen, say 8,000, in charge of rural parishes as a rough guess? There are, then, as many villages to explore; enough and to spare for many years to come.

The Contents of Ten Acres—May

1883

The ten acres are grass, and are divided into three fields: one on somewhat elevated ground, the second sloping down to a brook, and the third, much smaller, in the corner. A private path goes up the higher field, and on entering this path the first plants that are seen are the plantains. These grow thickly: the larger variety under a wall, by the fence, and everywhere where shelter is afforded them; the lesser variety grow among the grass of the meadow, mingling with it. The veins of the plantain leaf run parallel, and not branched like those of the Oak. The larger kind, with broad leaves, is not at all welcome in meadows: it is too coarse to make hay. The leaves of the other are narrow and lance-shaped, and if not too numerous, are good in the swathe; but if a little over-dried by the sun when mown, these leaves, like those of most other herbs, crumble to dust. For grazing, herbs and plants seem valuable; for making hay, nothing but grass appears of much use. In the new method of preserving fodder for cattle in silos—that is, putting it in the green state in caves and covering it up till wanted—probably herbs and plants will do quite as well as grass. If it proves so after sufficient trial, and if silos, or artificial caves, become general, it is likely that a change may slowly take place in our meadows.

Various plants which have long been recommended for forage may be sown, and a meadow will wear a different appearance. Ever since meadow lands became so valuable, care has been taken to root out herbs and plants, till by degrees grass practically occupies whole fields. Some indeed cannot be destroyed, and some are not injurious enough to pay for eradication: these remain, and the rest have been driven to corners. All creatures that graze are fond of herbs, from cattle to hares. The reason hares occasionally enter gardens, even close to houses, is for the various herbs which shelter in the odd places, as well as for those that are cultivated. As the arable farmers at one time sacrificed everything to wheat, and drove everything else from their domains, so the grass farmers for generations now have striven to root out all but the finest and most profitable grasses. It is not at all improbable that both will be found by the change of the times to partially retrace their steps, and pay attention to more diverse and special cultures. Not only do the leaves crumble to dust if the least over-dried, but in other plants (not the plantains) the stalks become as hard as wood, sapless, and useless for nourishment. They may be picked out from a truss of hay like little brown twigs. Green, these stalks are edible by cattle; dry, they are useless: perhaps the silos will render the stalks profitable too. The lesser plantains being among the grass are mown off; but the larger sorts, hiding in corners behind the defence of stones and sticks which, like a breast-work, protect them from the scythe, remain, send up a tall stalk, and ripen their seeds on it. These stalks, with the seeds attached, are known to all who have kept caged birds. The finches, and indeed half the lesser birds, eat them, often bearing the stalk to the ground in their claws by the force of their weight. By the roadside, when the footpath is elevated a few inches, you may see the green-finches get on the edge of the path, as on a step, and so reach the seeds.

Carried away by the birds the plantain seeds reach every place, and the plant springs up the moment a piece of ground is let run to waste. Though so common and so well known, the plantain should not be overlooked by those who feel an interest in natural history; because, if they will note where it grows freely, and will watch the spot, they will have the pleasure of seeing these birds feeding. Near the path also the dandelions grow—another bird-favourite when it seeds; though the seeds seem too minute to be of much consequence to them. But they are fond of variety, as much so as we are, and next to us they enjoy the most, being in this particular more fortunate than the animals. The earliest dandelion—as early as January sometimes, and as late as December—is usually to be found on a sheltered bank rather than in the open field. This I mention for the children's sake: they are always so delighted to find the bright dandelion when few or no other flowers are out. Except the children have them, the flowers are of no use. Let them look too for the lesser celandine, which they will call buttercups, where the ground is moist, at the verge of plantations. They are the earliest flowers of the buttercup shape and colour. Some I once found growing at the foot of an oak: there was a ledge of soil over a large root; and the tree, leaning forward, formed a lichen-hung cave over the yellow celandine petals. The earliest true 'craisie', ranunculus, or buttercup will probably be found on a mound—often under brushwood. It is not so brightly tinted as the meadow one, nor does it stand on a tall stalk. Of the thousand thousand grasses that grow in the ten acres, it is not possible to say much, because so few of them are familiar either by name or shape to general readers. Unless one has some previous idea of a plant, or grass, or tree, it is not much pleasure to read of it; there is no sympathy, and the most brilliant colours fail to awaken interest. It is like looking at an inscription in an unknown alphabet—curious, but a blank to the mind. The grasses are an unknown alphabet, unlike the ferns which have attracted more attention. This alphabet of grasses is one well worth studying. Not only are the grasses beautiful in themselves, but they are constantly associated with the lives of wild creatures and birds.

Some birds eat grass, plucking it and eating it; numbers feed on its seeds; numbers find shelter in it; and some have their nests among it. Wherever you go, there some species of grass is to be found: a place without grass is synonymous with utter desolation, hard rock, and desert sand. Wherever you can find a single blade of grass, however small, there you stand face to face with the mystery of life, and all the possibilities of existence. It is of more interest than many of the stars; for if astronomy is right, some stars are ceaselessly burning, and therefore, beautiful as they are from a distance, life upon them (in the sense we understand life) is impossible. The roots of the humblest blade of grass go down to the beginning of life on the world, and its tip points to the sky. If you should chance to find a blade of grass withering in a rocky place, carry it a little water for the sake of the thoughts that spring from it.

Fibres of dry grass are used by several birds in constructing their nests; the summer mice use them also. The moment the grass is mown, the finches, and indeed almost all the birds, flock to the exposed ground. The mower first examines the field to see which way the grass lies, for it has usually a list to one direction or another. Wind causes it to lean, rain beats it down, and where very strong and thick it falls of its own weight and becomes a tangle. Stepping round the field, the mower selects the best place to begin, and soon opens a drift like a roadway into it. To this drift the birds flock for the seeds of the fallen grass, the insects in the swathe, and those that move in hundreds over the turf, and are now easily got at. Standing grass does not give the birds much opportunity, as, on descending into it, they find themselves enclosed on all sides as in a forest. The ants' nests are cut off and the eggs exposed; they do their best to remove them inside, but when it is quiet a partridge is sure to visit the spot, and the green woodpecker will swoop down in his rapid flight and prey on them. Some fields are almost denuded of flowers, so careful has been the cultivation of grasses, properly so called, to the exclusion of plants. Here there are scabious, knapweed, germander speedwell, and the large daisy, sometimes called moon-daisy, besides sorrel and buttercups. On the swathe of mown grass the moon-daisies make the most show; the sorrel when it is standing. The under soil of these fields is clay, a deep strong clay, well covered at the surface with mould—originally formed of felled forest. Perhaps this is the cause that butterflies are not so forward as in warmer districts. Besides the yellow and white it is not often that any are seen till the end of May. Ragged-robins are plentiful, but the woodruff is not out. The difficulty in constructing a floral calendar is, that in one place it is noon while at another by the same calendar it would be, say, ten o'clock. Oaks are not yet in full leaf: when they are still ruddy, while the Elms are tenderly green, and the hedges have filled, as it were, with leaf, is the finest time of spring. When the Oaks are in full leaf, it is summer, no matter what the day of the month may be.

The Ash is an interesting tree to watch as the spring advances. Stubborn and unimpressionable, its storm-beaten bark yields so grudgingly to the increasing warmth. On the lower branches of the Sycamore, where sheltered by banks, leaves came forth towards the end of March. The Ash gave no sign. By degrees the hardy Hawthorn became green under it, and scattered blue-bells appeared. There were eggs in the thrushes' nest, and the nightingale came, though silent for awhile. The black ends of the Ash boughs began at last to swell; but slowly, and not till the cuckoo called did they begin to open; some not even then. Let no one think these little things to note, unworthy of attention. It is the reverse. Unless you do observe these apparent trifles and dwell on every bud and leaf, you will wake up presently and find the summer gone. In order to enjoy the summer you must take it before it comes. When it comes it is gone like a dream. It is like Time's forelock, to indicate that to grasp time you must be prepared beforehand, and seize the lock of hair in front. Once present he is bald. By holding back and keeping its green sprays for King Charles' day, the Ash marks the advance of all other trees and bushes. The Ash hangs back in the ranks, and does not come in till they are nearly full. Sternest of winter's warriors—like Constantine hoary-headed, in the Saxon war song—he is loth to put off his armour which took the frost, and snow, and rime so blithely. A true and loyal tree is the Ash, symbol of firmness of character, straightforwardness of heart. Did not the rooks caw so continually, their nests would not be noticed towards the end of May for the foliage. Though some have been shot, many broods remain to be fed. The larches have concealed the wood-pigeons' nests with their green needles.

Far back in the northerly winds the brambles sent out shoots along their curving stems, buds starting from the upper side of the arch, and they are now a two-fold green, the dull green of the old leaf that has remained on, and the fresh colour of the new. Brambles are nearly evergreens. I observed a plantation the other day in which men were busily engaged rooting up the brambles, and substituting the common laurel for 'ornament'. Could anything be in worse taste? The yellowish, sickly green of these laurels will

M. L. Sieger '79

Brambles.

Wood Anemones

stay of much the same hue the year through. Nothing will find refuge in, or under them, unless it be snails, and even snails do not care for such shelter. Snails have better taste. There are plenty in every trailing piece of ivy; scarcely any in laurels, unless indeed they have no other resort. Lizards, snakes, frogs, toads, all these avoid laurels if they can, because no insects frequent them. Something in the laurel is poisonous and hateful; birds will have nothing to do with it. The appearance of the plantation is entirely spoiled, and half its attractiveness to birds gone with the brambles. There is a thicket of bramble in the ten acres which is a place of call with the birds of the hedges round the three fields. The stems of bramble are nearly as thick as those of the great briars which grow in old hedges. Brake fern is pushing up under it at the outskirts, and some anemones flowered at one side. A pair of thrushes have already had their nest in it, and gone: the fledglings are hiding about the hedge and calling for food. There will be other nests in it before the summer is over. Sometimes a rabbit starts out if the bush is kicked; but he will not start if he believes he is not observed, and there is no dog to alarm him. A man might hide in it unseen. The parsley, tall grasses, climbing 'cleavers', and brake fern would conceal him below, and the bramble sprays above. In this great thicket the birds roost at night: it is a favourite roosting place. Bramble is a true old English bush. What thickets of it there must have been in the olden time—when the country was unenclosed, and also in the deer parks! The flowers are not out yet, but there will be flowers and fruit in season, so that all the year through the bramble is interesting.

In spring, nests are built in it; in summer, it is covered with white and pink-tinted bloom; in autumn, it is red and black with berries; in winter, the birds roost in it, and the leaves stay green till the bluebells appear again. If this paper should chance to be read by any one about to lay out a plantation, let me beg them to think of the bramble, to have at least one good thicket in some corner, if merely for the sake of old England—the old England that these times have done so much to destroy. The finches already find a plentiful supply of seeds in the grasses. The red dock seeds of last year have but just failed them. As early as March, groundsel seeds, if the weather be favourable; and the goldfinches seek waste places by towns for it. Soon after come the dandelion seeds, and now the grasses in the meadows. Seeds scarcely fail them all the year round, though, of course, small in quantity, and restricted in variety as the year draws to an end. There are three polled Elms at one side of the larger field, close to the hedge but not in it, which are noisy now with the chirk of young starlings. What a business nesting is to the starlings! They came to these polled Elms, and rushed to and fro the feeding grounds a month before the cuckoo's first note was heard. A polled Elm becomes hollow at the top, like a wooden basin—sometimes two or three basins, or bowl-like cavities—and in one of these the starling's nest is made. It is merely a little dry grass, straw, and fibres; a lining on which to rest the eggs. These number four or five, a pale blue-green, often quite white. But the excitement of the starlings precedes the first egg, or even the putting in of the mattress of fibres on which it is to lie. Perching on the bare branches they talk to each other and to their neighbours at the top of their voices; in a moment or two off they go to the field they fancy—very often to the same field ten times in a morning, back again with a fluttering of wings, chattering and whistling. There is nothing whatever to do at the tree, no reason whatever for so much discussion and agitation, but the starlings are so full of life and spirits that they must talk; their discourse bubbles from them as a spring of water from the ground. When the young fledglings are being fed, the 'charm' is constant. Though May is often so cold, it is a month crowded with incidents in hedge and tree; and unless these are observed at the moment, when the sun shines and the soft south air comes, they are past, and half the nests empty.

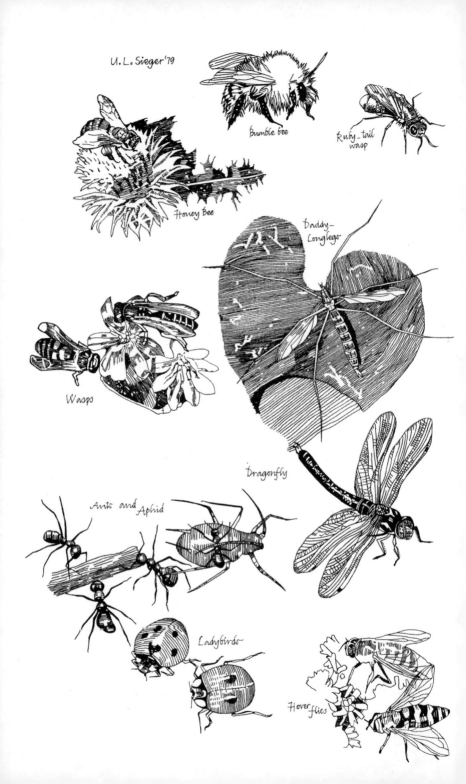

U. L. Sieger '79

Bumble bee

Ruby-tail wasp

Honey Bee

Daddy-Longlegs

Wasps

Dragonfly

Ants and Aphid

Ladybirds

Hoverflies

Butterfly Corner

1887

Three oak logs happened to lie athwart each other in a corner, hazel bushes and brake fern behind them, oak boughs and brake fern on one side, and in front a great stack of hop poles. From the right hand the sun shines into this green angle, and the south wind comes up over the beeches. The surface of the split log grows warm in the rays, and attracts the insects that pass upon the wing. Packs of flies settle and walk interminably round each other; a great chequered fly, a little chequered fly, black flies, and flies green as glass beads, all too occupied with the heated surface of the wood to annoy anyone. A sand wasp, much smaller than the common species, comes, but only stays a moment; a great common wasp passes low down the grass looking for a hole. He alights on a little branch, and walks right over a fly, which shows no alarm. If it were October the wasp would have eaten the fly then and there, for the first frosts turn him into a furious cannibal. The plums are ripe, but the wasps seem scarcely to have begun their nests, so that next year one would think they would be very few in number. Next a drone fly came to a pink bramble bloom, then another large drone fly to a yellow hawkweed and a wild bee to some heathbells. The logs lie among heath and heather, and I have seen a hive bee visit the tiny flowers of the ling first, and then the purple bells of heath. It is true these flowers belong to the same class, and are something the same in appearance, but hive bees are supposed to be very rigid in visiting only one kind of flower during each journey. I have also seen a hive bee go from ling to blue scabious. There must be a scarcity of honey in the community, which may account for the bees being less particular. I think that bees, birds, and animals would change their apparently immutable habits without hesitation if they found an advantage in doing so. Humble bees will go from yellow hawkweed or yellow tormentil to purple heathbell, but not always. Sometimes they seem as particular as the hive bees, and at others less choice. The humble bees come along one after the other, now a monster with broad orange golden band, now a smaller one like beautiful black

53

velvet, now a grey kind. They are very assiduous at the small yellowish green florets of the wood sage, never leaving a bunch of these inconspicuous flowers till they have sucked at every bloom. I have often seen humble bees lying half stupified in places where there was much wood sage—can it be that the honey of this plant has some deleterious action on them? It is one of the bitterest plants that grow. A single leaf placed between the lips will dry up the mouth. If you only bruise the leaf and smell it, it gives a sense of dryness like hops. Perhaps the bitterness may imbue the honey of its flowers. One sunny morning, when the surface of the log was unusually heated and the packs of flies most numerous, a large insect came with a feeble flight and settled by them, only half folding its wings, so that its whole back was exposed. Three-quarters of an inch long, the upper half of the insect was a bright emerald green; the green of a glazed surface; the lower half of an equally bright ruby, shining as if the sunlight penetrated the surface as it sinks into glass. Like a gaudy fly from Brazil, the green and red insect shone on the dull surface of the oak. In another minute it folded its wings completely, which were laid parallel along the back, but the colours still appeared through their texture. This was a rubytail, well-known in museums and books, but not always to be seen in the open. It might very well pass among a collection of tropical insects. I could easily have captured it, but refrained. After a while the rubytail flew off with the same feeble flight, as if its wings were hardly powerful enough for its weight. With a low hum a great fly settled on my knee—a large bulky body, generally yellow, with narrow black bands, and a great head and yellow back—something like a drone-fly made yellow. There is a great fly here of similar shape and similar beak, but with a window in its body, just as an old writer suggested that man would be improved by a small pane of glass in his waistcoat over his heart, so that his true character might be seen. The upper part of this fly is black, and the lower part is also black, but across the middle is a broad whitish band, which, when looked at nearer, is found to be translucent. Insects are slow in motion at night, and if you put him in a tumbler and hold it towards a candle, the light passes right through; so does the shadow when he crawls over it. It almost looks as if you could read through him, but he is not really transparent. To my sorrow he has no English name, so I must give him his Latin label—*Volucella pellucens*. Through the heath and over the long grass the daddy-longlegs climb and fly and drift very much like thistle-down before the wind, crowds of them, thick as locusts. A boy saw a small heath lizard with a daddy-longlegs in its mouth. He clapped his cap on the lizard, which struggled so hard that it pulled itself into two just in front of its hind legs, leaving that part behind while the front part crawled under the heath.

The tail part still moved, though separated. Motion, indeed, seems often to continue when, according to our ideas of its depending upon consciousness, life should stop. A hive bee caught in a handkerchief left its sting behind with part of its abdomen, and flew away self-mutilated. Carefully picking up the fragment of abdomen, we saw the sting dart in and out several times; finally a drop of poison exuded from its tip.

I have been down to the three logs every day, waiting for the patrician butterflies. Last year they came to this corner like an army on the march, resting for breath whenever a cloud came over, rising again directly the sun shone, company after company, endlessly drifting. A great army sometimes takes days to pass a given spot, being encumbered with artillery and baggage and camp followers. With the swiftness of their wings to help them the butterflies took all the summer of 1885 to pass the three oak logs, and their number I cannot tell. Hour after hour they came and went till the spot seemed to name itself Butterfly Corner. This Summer they have been slow to come; still I have been to watch, and while waiting for them these other insects appeared.

A ploughboy brought word that the wasps were coming—there was such a lot of very little ones just come out of a nest—evidently another species. The spot was on the purple bank leading to the logs, purple with heath, where the sandy bank was bare. Ranks of trumpet-shaped lichen turned their grey-green tubes upwards. There was a hollow, and heat radiated from the sandy sides of the concavity, so that to put the hand anywhere near was like putting it in an oven. Slender wasps, much smaller than the common species, were dotted about on the sand and flying over the green larch tree above. These slender creatures, brightly banded with yellow and black, moved on the sand with the peculiar quick walk of the wasp tribe, almost running, and as they turned the hinder part of the body formed a curve something like a rudder. One of them seized a small insect banded with red and immediately carried it into a little hole in the sand. Before this hole there was a little mound of more finely divided sand, like the earth a rabbit throws from his burrow. Putting a stalk of grass in the hole to try its depth, some fragments of sand were detached and blocked the mouth. By-and-bye the head of the wasp appeared returning, all dusty, and, finding the way obstructed, he set to work with his fore feet, exactly like a terrier in a rabbit hole, and dug a passage out. Another wasp pounced on a great bluish green fly, far more ponderous than himself; this was among some grass, entangled in which he could not for a while get out with his prey. He stopped and seemed to sting the fly repeatedly. After a rest, he struggled out of the grass and made a large circle in the air, carrying the fly, which bore about the same proportion as a dog to a kestrel hawk, and returning to the sand bank dragged the fly deep into a hole. After a time larvae will doubtless be hatched in the nest, and the carcase of the fly will supply them with food till developed into wasps. So it went on hour after hour in the hot sunshine, these cruel Malay pirates seizing the miserable flies in their brief hour of sun-warmed life and devoting them to this wretched end. I had long wished for an opportunity to see the fossores at work—here it was found by chance, as usual; but the process seemed so demonlike in its cruelty that I took no pleasure in watching it, and left the spot. Never was there such a spot for "ammuts' " nests (ants), emmets in other districts. The whole bank, from end to end, beneath the heath is undermined with them, under the trumpets of the lichen, under the moss, everywhere. It is a common trick to take a handful of yellow ants and drop them among a colony of red ones. A savage battle instantly ensues and they tear each other to pieces with fury. A small species of ant seems to be fond of the dark pine trees, and has regular tracks up and down under the scaly bark.

There are hop gardens near, and the aphis is a great enemy to the crop. Ants keep these green flies, and even take care of their eggs, so that some think the ants injurious to hops; on the other hand, the 'ammuts' devour myriads of insects. The lady-bird—friend to the hop grower—is often eaten by spiders, in whose webs the spotted wing cases hang empty, sucked dry, like the shield of a slain knight. The ploughboy next knocked down what he called a 'gurt adder-spear', that is, a dragon fly, which he brought me dripping from the pond into which it had fallen. The dragon fly's eyes seem all his head, two half-spheres that meet and see in every direction; the quickest fly cannot escape their fatal glance. They are somewhat iridescent and pearl-like, and through their translucent glass some spots at the bottom of the eye are refracted into the middle of the bead. Suppose a man with eyes on his shoulders, each as big as his head; even then they would not be so large in proportion as these green and greedy lanterns. His four wings seem clear and colourless, except a black mark near each tip. If you place a piece of paper under them they are seen not to be colourless, but an exceedingly pale brown, and you can read anything through them like glass. With these wings he has more power than any bird of the sky. His jaws open the same as other creatures; within these his mandibles work at right angles to his jaws like a pair of sharp reaping hooks, meeting each other at the tip. His thirst for insect blood is insatiable. Between the bare trunks of the fir trees, where the flies play, he rushes at full speed in and out, his wings clattering together at his frequent jerks, and pauses to take an insect snip. You can hear the collision between the fly and the dragon.

Back again down the ditch just above he rushes, suddenly up into the air straight like a rocket, twice as high as the fir trees, down again as if shot from the sky, stopping dead short under the shadow of a great hawthorn. He can stop dead in full career, back water, or proceed sideways without turning—the proud eagle cannot do it. Once within the grasp of his not-ched limbs the fly is held to that terrible mouth, the keen blades of the reaphooks meet, the head is off, the wings sheared, the trunk devoured, while still the dragon's eager eyes are watching, and his four wings careering for fresh prey. In the Tower of London, among the mediaeval in-struments of torture and death, there is a figure called the Maiden; the vic-tim was told to embrace her, and as he did so the arms clasped him and pressed him with irresistible force against sharp knives placed in the hollow bust. It was a clumsy and merciful device compared to the dragon fly's mouth. All the torments invented by man in centuries of cruelty are as nothing to the tortures hourly endured and inflicted in the insect world. The vitality of the dragon fly was remarkable. Though struck down and run through with a pin the creature breathed for some time, the long tubular body expanding as regular as clockwork every four seconds. This aerial beast of prey when at last weary seeks the hawthorn boughs that overhang a ditch, and, after hovering a little while, clings to a spray and hangs tail downwards with wings expanded. If disturbed it will make a few circles and come back and suspend itself again.

There is an old quarry in the heath close by, and in the dry sand at the top a whole colony of wild bees have their nests in holes. The beautiful heather hangs over, sweet as honey, and bright in the sun. There they glan-ce to and fro, and play in circles round each other, and take the honey of the heather to their homes. It is a pleasure to watch them at their task, which harms no creature small or great, and gives them so much delight in the happy sun. They seem, as it were, several thousand years morally in advance of the sand-wasps; a contrast between the barbarous Chinese choppings and sawings and torture, and our modern ideas of the heroism of saving life. The bees seem happily born to the light, the wasps to the darkness. How fond all the bees are, hive bees, humble bees, and lesser bees, of the flowers of the bramble! I think they are more unanimous about the bramble flower than any other. The hum is incessant over a bramble bush all day long. They all come, the hover flies and drone flies as well, each so intent on its own purpose it cannot see another; a hive bee almost alighting on and thrusting a fly aside; two bees to one bloom, at once all oblivious of each other till they nearly touch. The instant they are con-scious of each other's presence one invariably gives way, and two are never seen at the same time sucking at the same flower. I have seen a large humble bee on a head of white clover suddenly knocked right over on to the grass by a hover fly alighting on its back as if it had mistaken it for part of the flower. The humble bee rose and flew off, taking no revenge. I have seen them do this to humble bees several times. A white butterfly settled on a white flower of wild camomile, and after leaving it, alighted on the ground about six inches away. Immediately afterwards one of these hover flies came to the same flower, and on quitting it flew to the butterfly, examined it carefully, and was on the point of settling on its wing as if it had been a petal when the butterfly moved. Another tried to alight on the wings of a gatekeeper butterfly. Could these have been attempts at parasitism? One little bee that comes to the bramble flowers is so small it can but just struggle with the stiffness of the anthers, pushing them laboriously aside as if it were a work for Ajax Telamon, and at last when it reaches the honey is half hidden beneath them.

Flowers and Fruit

1877

When an artist desires to charm the eye with a glowing picture of luscious fruits and gorgeous flowers, he groups them together—intermingles them—carefully studying the harmonies of colour and tone. He does not draw an arbitrary line down the centre of his canvas and say, 'All the flowers shall be on this side and all the fruit on that'. If he were to commit such a glaring departure from good taste, and the picture were hung in the public galleries, not a passer-by but would exclaim upon the formality and the artificiality of the design. Yet at home in their flower gardens and pleasure grounds nine out of every ten of these very critics would be found to have put into practice—to have realized in actual fact—this precise separation of fruit and flowers which they condemned in the picture. They have placed all the fruit-bearing trees out of sight in what is called the vegetable garden, divorcing them from their natural companions the flowers, and practically banishing them completely from the house. For who cares to gather a peach when to get it one must encounter the spectacle of half an acre of decaying cabbage stumps, not to speak of the odour of manure, and all the unpleasant refuse which gravitates towards the outskirts of the vegetable garden. How is a lady to trail her dress over the earth, perhaps damp, to reach fruit from the wall in such a locality? The whole pleasure, the whole poetry of the thing is lost.

The residents in a house or villa, whose grounds have been laid out in the modern manner, scarcely so much as get a glimpse of the exquisite beauty of ripening fruit. To watch the peach, nestling in the warm nook, day by day deepening its delicate hues under the loving touches of the greatest of all artists, the sun; to note how the dark green of early summer gradually melts into the rich blue and luscious bloom of the plum; or how the pear grows heavier, dragging down the over-weighted bough; these pleasures are totally lost. What blossom is so marvellously white and pure as that of the cherry? Where are the white rose and the red so delicately intermingled as in the apple-bloom? An apple tree in bloom is one vast bouquet. Yet even the beauty of the flower must yield to the colours of the apples themselves as they gradually assume the golden tint of maturity. Strawberries upon a plate—no matter how fresh, no matter how valuable the china itself upon which they lie—are not so sweet as those we gather with our own fingers in the open garden. Not even the black hothouse grapes or the pineapple can compare with the fruits we gather in freedom and profusion; shaking the damsons from the bough, or the ripe cherries from the topmost branches, or stealing the largest plum with a merry laugh in some hidden nook. The grand beds of rhododendrons which are now so much in fashion have a stately beauty, it is true, yet it is a fleeting one indeed, and one sense alone is gratified, that of sight. Why not recall the fruit tree in some degree at least to its ancient and natural companionship with the flower? Why not let a few apple and pear trees, a few peaches, plums, and cherries, lurk as it were in corners with the pleasant surprise of their burden, if we are ashamed to grow them openly? For remember that while the flower pleases the eye only, or at most sight and smell (and a great many now fashionable flowers have no perfume), fruit has colour, scent, and taste, a threefold recommendation.

Our forefathers did not deny themselves these delights; nor did they disdain the orchard, as is easy to be seen from Shakespeare alone—see 'King John', and many other plays. A memory of an ancient manor-house (now a farm) in the west rises up, thinking on this topic, where you may stand literally ankle deep in flowers, and choose your cherry from the bough. From your chamber window, when you rise in the morning, you may put out your hand, and take more bunches of the same fruit—that is, from the left side of the window: if you come in the autumn, and look out on the right side, there will hang great ripe pears for your breakfast. From the lawn there trends away a low, arched avenue—a shady, sheltered passage under green boughs; it is a filbert-walk. Of all the ideas that ever entered into the mind of man to render his dwelling-place pleasant nothing can exceed the filbert-walk. It is shade; it is colour—a grateful green early, a brown later; it is fruit, and fruit of the finest kind. Yet where, in all the villas which modern wealth has built, in all the grounds which gold has laid out to order, will you find such a window as in that farmhouse, such a filbert-walk as that? Walnuts and wine have been the theme of many a writer; but those who crack the walnut by the side of a roaring sea-coal fire, boxed-up indoors away from the wind and rain, know really nothing at all about that fruit. The time to eat and enjoy the walnut is long before then. It is while the autumn sun yet lingers and is warm. Then take a long, slender pole, and, selecting those branches where the dark green of the rind is cracked, or partially blackened, strike them gently, and down will shower

the nuts. The fall on the ground will loosen the rind, or peel; the nut will crack with ease when just fresh from the tree, and then you taste the walnut in its true perfection—ripe and firm, and yet juicy, white, delicious. But to do this you must have the walnut trees, and how few—may we not say that no one—thinks of planting these when they lay out a garden? The fruit of the Spanish chestnut is, perhaps, hardly so delicate in flavour, yet the tree is one of the finest and most stately, and ought never to be omitted from a plantation. As for the poor currant trees, white and red and black, are they not utterly despised and cast aside? Yet some sorts are beautiful with the large clusters of grape-like berries, and the slightly acid flavour is welcome in the heat, while the leaves of the black variety yield a fragrance if crushed in the hand.

If fashion is imperative, and the decree has gone forth, like that of Darius the King, that fruit shall no more be seen side by side with flowers, then, at all events, give the apples and cherries, and plums and peaches a place to themselves. Let them, with their beauties, their colour, scent, and taste, be no longer thrust out into the outer wilderness of the vegetable garden; but give them a province of their own, distinct and separate. Let there be no cabbage-stumps, no stable refuse, no heap of rotting weeds to offend the eye or nose; nothing, in a word, that savours of utility alone. Make paths winding in and out, so that ladies may gather what tempts their fancy without spoiling a sweeping dress or soiling a shoe. Place therein seats with easy curved backs, well sheltered from the sun, and also well sheltered from the east, whose wind even in summer is dangerous for tender throats. Nor forget a sun-dial, with brazen face and quaint motto; and if it be possible, have a level space of grass hard by for lawn-tennis, so that, while reposing under the shadow of the trees with cherries and strawberries before us, we may watch the fortunes of the game.

Birds of Swindon

1871

To The Editor of *The Swindon Advertiser*

Sir,—Passing leisurely down the High-street, Marlborough, one lovely day last summer, on my way to enjoy the shade of that beautiful forest which M. Lesseps declared to be the finest in Europe, I paused in front of a window, attracted by some chromo-lithographs, when I caught sight of a little green book with the title in gold letters of *Birds of Marlborough*. Now, for years past, I have been in the habit of wandering about the meadows, and round the copses, and sitting on the banks of the hedges with my gun, ostensibly pigeon or rabbit shooting, but in reality watching the habits of the fauna. Hour after hour have I sat under a grey ash tree on a certain sunny bank drilled with rabbit holes, dreamily reclining with my feet in a dry ditch, and between my knees a wasp's nest—a veritable wasp's nest —swarming with the yellow venomous insects. It was built in a rabbit hole, and my seat was just over it, my knees, one each side, and every wasp that came pitched first on my knee and then flew into the nest, just as bees alight on the projection in front of their dwelling. I sat perfectly still, and they took not the slightest notice. Hundreds of them came, and this day after day, yet I was never stung, nor did they ever buzz round me angrily. The very novelty of the idea made me frequent the spot more than perhaps I should have otherwise done, and this amusement continued for months of the warm season. There I sat, gun at hand, leaning against the grey lichen-covered ash, with my yellow friends peacefully coming and going. Snakes rolled along the bank and out in the narrow grass, doves came and perched overhead, cooing softly, black-eyed rabbits peeped cautiously out, and, gaining confidence, proceeded to browse at my very elbow. Two woodpeckers had made their nest in a hollow willow tree, not ten yards distant, and their green and gold plumage—imperial livery—was constantly flashing in the sun. The corncrake sometimes came stealing along with his harsh note. Ants came and crawled over my legs, but I sat still and they crawled off peacefully. This was my pastime—to watch all nature enjoying itself. Once only did I fire from my covert. A partridge suddenly flew over, uttering loud cries, pursued by a hawk, who made the pounce just after passing the hedge. I snatched up my gun and shot. The hawk fell dead, but the partridge escaped unhurt. Many, many similar nooks have I discovered for myself in rambling about—winter nooks as well as summer ones. With these tastes it may be understood it was with pleasure I caught sight of the little green book in the window at Marlborough. I had long desired to meet with such a work. I desired to find a book which divested of scientific technicalities, would give me an account, not only of the birds, but the whole flora and fauna, and geology and natural productions of this beautiful part of England, in simple terms, so that I might easily identify the living creatures which, in the course of time, had come to be almost acquaintances to me. Here was one step in this direction. *Birds of Marlborough* would probably include the birds of the Swindon district also. Nor was I disappointed. In plain simple language the author gives a description of the birds which his own experience and that of his friends establish as residents or visitors in the neighbourhood. Without any desire to act the part of a critic, my wish is to be permitted to make a few remarks, and perhaps add a few facts upon the ornithology of a place lying at the extremity of the radius—8 miles—adopted by the author. I will go through the book. About hawks, which come first, I can endorse the statement as to the wanton destruction of these birds. Here it is a common thing for parties of four or five 'sportsmen' to go out in the evening in the spring with the avowed object of killing them. In the evening one of the pair is sure to be on the nest and the other probably pretty close by. The plan is to steal up cautiously and shoot the hen bird through the nest, sitting, thus destroying the bird and smashing the eggs; the report startles the cock, who flies out of the tree and is shot by the others. Missel thrush: A pair of these birds have built in an orchard to my knowledge for full fifteen years, usually choosing an apple tree, but sometimes a yew. There is never more than one nest, so that it is natural to suppose they have made it a kind of ancestral home. The hen will sit till almost caught, and the cock will fly round an intruder's head threatening assault with loud cries. Blackbirds: White variety. Can this be ever inherited? I knew a farm on which there was a race of white moles, which existed till they were all caught as curiosities. White sparrows are occasionally seen. While on the subject of hybrids, I may mention that a friend has a bird which he shot and stuffed, much resembling a starling in general contour, and with the iridescent feathers distinguishing that bird, but marked like a snipe, or between a snipe and a sparrow. Rooks with white feathers are occasionally seen. One haunted the fields here for a long time, and was daily observed. Tomtit: One of the birds commonly going under this name makes a noise almost exactly resembling the sound of a file used in sharpening a saw. The labouring people implicitly believe that when the tomtit sharpens his saw there will shortly be rain. Goldfinch: The author says these birds are uncommon at Marlborough. Here they seem common and plentiful enough. There are invariably two or three nests every spring in the orchard mentioned above. They frequent it in small flocks of eight or ten all summer long, and their song greets my ear every morning on awaking at that time of year. Birdcatchers with nets and decoy birds make this a favourite station for capturing goldfinches for sale. These birds seem particularly fond of hedges where thistles grow, and frequent them in flocks when the thistle down is ripe. Starling: I have observed these birds on sultry days flying in a most peculiar manner as if they were catching flies in the air like swallows; rising and falling, and flying round and round in direct contradistinction to their usual straight arrow-like flight. It is amusing to watch these birds riding about on the backs of sheep with the utmost gravity. What orators they are from the chimney tops! There one will perch himself, and use all the arts of oratory to his fellows in an adjacent tree, now almost screaming, and flapping his wings to give emphasis, now sinking his voice to the softest and most winning accents, till presently having succeeded off he flies, and the rest follow. Those who still believe in a blind instinct, and reject intelligence from the possession of birds, need only watch the starling carefully. Woodpecker: the gamekeepers say this bird is scarce, but it is not. Any attentive observer will frequently hear its wild eldritch chuckle, like sardonic laughter. The old Wiltshire name was yuckle, a word which represents the sound made by the bird.

'Just then a yuckle passing by
Was asked by them the cause to try.'

OLD BALLAD

There are two other species of woodpecker besides the common green one—the greater spotted woodpecker, and the lesser spotted woodpecker. Both are rare. I have, however, seen both in the neighbourhood of Burderop. The lesser spotted woodpecker is easily recognized by its harsh note which is like the turning of a crank. It is called the crank bird in some districts. Wren: During the late severe weather it was observed that as many as six wrens regularly passed the night together in one hole in the thatch of a cowshed. Woodpigeon: I remember shooting a woodpigeon which was found to have no less than twenty-four acorns in its crop, hard and brown. Pheasant: The cock birds invariably crow at every flash of lightning during a thunderstorm—day or night. It is curious to listen to

Goldfinch

Blue
Tit

Nightingale.

U.L.Sieber '79

not to scale

them in a large wood in a storm. The poachers make use of this fact to discover the birds at roost. Heron: They are very common and numerous at the reservoir at Coate, Swindon. As many as nine have been seen all standing in a row close together. Butcher birds: *Query.*—I have occasionally during summer observed large humble bees spitted or impaled upon long thorns on the hedges. Is this the work of the shrike? Yellow wagtail: Is a common summer visitant in this neighbourhood, but seems to confine itself to certain spots. Cuckoo: To the list of birds in whose nest the cuckoo has been know to lay eggs, I may add the robin redbreast and the common wagtail. The last instance was in a garden, within ten yards of a bow window. The cuckoo was seen sitting on the nest and the egg found upon its flight. Redwing: Last summer the redwings, usually winter visitors only, remained the whole year; which had not occurred in the memory of the oldest living inhabitant. The fact was first made apparent by the song of a bird being heard which was not recognized. People watched it and found it came from the redwing. The notes were very beautiful—loud and yet mellow. The bird usually sat in a tree and sang. I was so incredulous that I spent a whole day following the note with a gun, till at length I shot the bird in the very act of uttering its ringing song, and found it to be precisely similar to those I had so often shot in the winter. Subsequently the note became so common as not to excite the least attention, but I kept my eye upon the birds and succeeded in finding a nest, and first seeing the eggs and afterwards the young birds. It was built at the side of an ash pollard at some considerable height, and much resembled a blackbird's nest. I was much interested in these birds never having heard of their remaining during the summer; and endeavoured to account for it by some peculiarity in the weather. A careful watch will be kept this year. I should mention that the fieldfares last year also remained till very late, and one or two even into the summer. Snipes: Are common here of all descriptions. Wild duck: I have seen Coate reservoir absolutely black with waterfowl, and on one occasion, drawing an imaginery line, I counted two hundred that swam across it in a few minutes, and was then obliged to desist by the great numbers making it impossible to keep a correct reckoning. Merlin: A fine specimen of this hawk was shot about a year ago at Wanborough Nythe, near Swindon, and stuffed. Nightingale: Common in this neighbourhood. In the season four or five may be heard in the evening answering each other. They frequent particular spots. For instance, the nightingale is never heard in Burderop wood, except in a particular place. They sing as much in the morning as at night, and it is then more pleasant to hear them. They are not at all shy, if approached without making a disturbance, and will sit and sing within two or three yards. Raven: I never saw a raven in this neighbourhood, but while upon the genus Corvus, I would call attention to some, to me, strange birds visiting the reservoir here this winter. In build they resemble a rook and in flight, and appear to go in pairs; but the back is of a shining glossy white, or grey. They frequent the edge of the water, and seem intent upon finding muscles like the crows. I saw one with a small fish. Is this the hooded crow (page 86) which is commonly called the grey crow? Goatsucker: Is occasionally seen. I shot one myself some years ago, sitting on a rail asleep in the day time, and preserve it stuffed. Bittern: A fine specimen was shot a few years ago in a brook here, and is still preserved. It is the only one I have heard of. Waterrail: Formerly common in certain spots, now rarely seen. Usually one or two specimens are shot in a season. Teal: Common, same with widgeon. Gull: Often seen after storms. A bird locally called a sea-swallow often comes to the reservoir, after storms three or four at a time. It resembles a swallow in its habit and flight, rarely pitching, but is much larger and grey, somewhat like a diminutive gull. Two birds said to be the Great Northern Diver were shot at the reservoir last year. I understood they were stuffed. A friend preserves a bird also killed at the reservoir, said to be 'Columbus Crestatus', and evidently some aquatic bird.

It is much to be desired that some gentleman, or gentlemen, would compile a work containing an account of the whole flora and fauna, and geology of this very interesting district. I would most willingly contribute my mite of local knowledge. In the absence of such a book, the work called *Birds of Marlborough*, is very welcome, supplying as it does one great gap.

I am, &c.,

R. J.

II. LABOUR

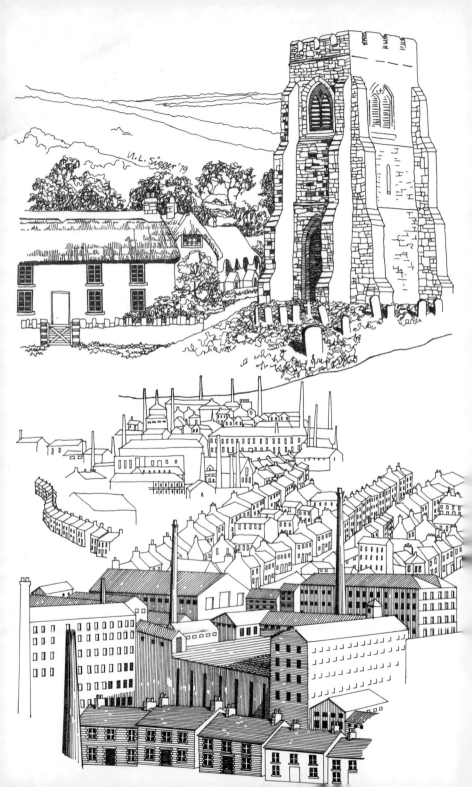

The Future of Country Society

1877

The relations between the various ranks of men, and the customs of social life, have sometimes, in the course of history, seemed so fixed as to appear immovable. The castes of ancient Egypt and India, during an existence not measured by centuries but by thousands of years, maintained their hereditary positions, and transmitted their habits and traditions unimpaired. So in the physical world, the sun rises and sets day by day, the stars proceed in regular procession, the green corn bronzes unfailingly summer after summer, in short, the whole secular system seems to exhibit an eternal stability. But the gentle rain removes atom upon atom from the plains, the tides and the frost sap the cliffs, the silent coral grows: presently the island becomes a continent, the continent disappears, and the astronomer finds that the zodiac has moved a whole sign. Kings live and reign; war follows peace; the historian chronicles their marches and decrees; the crown and the sceptre, the mitre and the sword, remain still nominally as of old, but, meantime, the faith and thought of the living mass of men dies out and is born again, till at last the realities correspond no longer to the names. The very language, like a snake, casts aside its slough, and assumes new colour and force. Fresh gods, in the form of nobler ideas and philosophies, are introduced. The ranks change their places, power slips from the patrician to the trader, and thence to the plebeian. While outwardly the authorities are the same, and the names remain unchanged from the monarch to the lowest magistrate, the real distribution of power is completely altered. Such changes alter the destiny of a race.

What is here expressed in generalities has literally occurred in detail during the last fifty years in the rural districts of the kingdom. These local changes, in fact, reflect the great moral and social revolution which has noiselessly passed over the entire country, and which may, perhaps, be better illustrated by instances drawn from a familiar source, and on a smaller scale, than in the more ambitious pages of the historian. Briefly defined, may we not say that the spirit of the past was deference to authority, and that the apparent spirit of the future is to supplant, by education and development of the individual, the gradually lessening hold of tradition and dogma?

A rural parish, if a well-selected specimen, forms of itself a miniature state, and contains representatives of the chief varieties of human life. It has its political boundaries, within which it enjoys considerable self-government. These have been carefully surveyed and mapped, and the map is preserved in the local archives. It has its constitution, and its geography—brooks in the place of rivers, coppices for forests—and one or more special products for export. The vestry forms an independent local council. Not many years since the resemblance was still more complete, when unpaid labour was expended upon the internal roads; each farmer taking his turn with waggons, horses, and men, to repair them. The poor of the place were relieved upon the spot, and the administration of that relief gave to the overseers an indirect power. At the same time there existed a local *esprit de corps*. The village had its hero, rudely resembling the warrior of the Homeric age. He was the strongest, or the swiftest, or the most dexterous player with the ashen backsword. To the annual feasts and revels came sturdy competitors in bands, striving to carry away the prizes for wrestling, running, fencing, leaping; men who 'refused not the hand-play', in the stirring words of the Saxon battle-song. These made their homes famous by victory; the nut-brown ale flowed freely on return, and a certain rough prestige was theirs. If not 'for a hundred year', at least a generation remembered, and talked by the hearth, over their deeds. For these 'sports' were those of men who fought fairly, but spared not; and it was well-known that he who won must not only possess strength and skill, but the stern courage of endurance. If Waterloo was gained on the playgrounds at Eton, so far as the rank and file of that day are concerned it was as much won on the village greens. Such a Berseker education of knocks and blows, coarse fare and exposure, could not but turn out a race who stood like a stone wall.

The counties were composed of a collection of such parishes, and each county also, in a still more distinct way, resembled a separate kingdom. They formed a Heptarchy, not of seven, but forty states. Each had, and in a lesser degree yet retains, its particular language, difficult to understand by those who dwelt on the borders, incomprehensible at a day's journey, and to the modern a dead speech, curiously compared now and then through fragmentary vocabularies, as one might a provincial dialect of Greece with the classic authors. The pride of one was sheep and wool, of another cheese, a third bacon: men really felt a patriotic pride of their county, an idea now so extinct as to be with difficulty conveyed. The ancient county towns were but greater villages, and the same spirit imbued them throughout; a firm belief in home, in the superiority of the place, a local faith, in short, and no man looked beyond the spot where he was born for applause. The council of aldermen, with their little monarch, the mayor, were great men. Now the cosmopolitan spirit is abroad, and even the labourer laughs at the local 'bauble', the mace of office.

England herself in this agricultural age, which came up till within fifty years, was a collection of such counties, and, as a whole, full of similar insular traditions, thoughts, hopes, and social faith. Everything foreign was detested; everything outside her own fields and hedges was despised. Then the nation might have been compared to a circle gradually narrowing inwardly; now, to a circle rapidly expanding outwardly. Yet to this day, so strong is ancient custom, men from the rural districts fill almost all the offices of the State, and, till recently, monopolized the services. Who form the Cabinet, whichever party is in power? Is it not men of large landed property, with ancient titles and old descent, the very impersonation of The Country? These are the body, if the leader himself be from a different and more modern class. Their sons, and those of families of a similar character if lower degree, crowd the bar, the pulpit, the army, and the navy. From their upper ranks are drawn the members of the diplomatic service. In short, the manufacturing masses may vote, but their will is still executed; the very ministries of their own choice are formed of men whose traditions are agricultural. In this sense the country-seat continues to rule England.

To appreciate the changes progressing in rural society, it is necessary to revert to the smallest division—the parish—of which, in the past, the church was the centre. Without staying to plunge into archaeology, it might almost be conjectured that the church and the parish, which was the temporal dominion of the church, were the very first agents in the organization of society. The age demands that the ecclesiastical powers should renounce temporal authority; and a reflection of this wide-spread spirit may be found in the country parish, where the position of the State clergy becomes more and more divorced from the local administration. But the church still remains the nominal legal centre of the parish, though not the exclusive centre that it used to be. The church-door is the local Gazette. There the proclamations of the monarch are posted, notices are affixed of rates and assessments, lists of voters, those liable to serve on the juries, licensed carriers of fire-arms, etc. Latterly, some of these have been also placed at the entrances of chapels; but still the church-door is the royal advertisement. Could we suppose a Commission of Array issuing in our time, as in the early years of the civil war, where would it be made known but here? The church was, and still remains, the visible representative of the State, and more especially of the Crown, in the parish. Perhaps its character of perpetual duration contributed to this selection. While houses decayed, and even whole villages disappeared, the church still stood. Instances are not uncommon where the pew accommodation in the building is many times larger than the present population could require, showing clearly that the homes of the ancient inhabitants are buried. Mansions were burnt, castles battered to pieces, often changing hands, but the church was there still. The very ground it occupies is held 'for ever'. Without the insertion of that word—satire as it is upon human affairs—in the deed of gift, or transfer of land, no bishop will consecrate a new church. Within, over the Decalogue, observe the Royal Arms, and motto; significant in itself. You will not find this ancient heraldry elsewhere in the parish. By the brass upon the floor, or the marble monument, the local is again connected with the national history through the name of some knight who played his part in the State.

Here is the Register, musty and fusty, but nevertheless a thing of great meaning. In these brief sentences, curiously written in the old flourishing hand, is contained the sum of the human life of two centuries and a half. Births, marriages, and burials were not recorded in the muniment chest at the mansion, the castle, or the farm; but in the church, making it still more the centre of the little state. There is now a centralized system of registration; but the old plan is not yet abolished, and consequently a dual record is kept of those who belong to the Established Church, or who are buried within the precincts of her consecrated ground. Does not the parish church then supply the place of the *hotel de ville* of continental towns? Here are the Royal Arms, here are displayed the governmental proclamations, here is the register; here, in brief, is the history of the past, and many of the potentialities of the future. Though now schoolboards, voluntary or compulsory in character, sanitary boards, and so forth, have been created; still the vestry is the local parliament, the legal assembly from which these others spring. Other forms of religion may have their lands for burial; to the churchyard alone belongs the sacred and exclusive character which is conferred by State consecration. Let it be always remembered that we are analysing, not arguing; we are describing, not contending. These churchyards too are fast filling, new ground is not always forthcoming, and village cemeteries are rapidly becoming necessaries of the present as well as of the future. Who is to provide them? The questions arising out of the parish church are great indeed. Round the old grey tower there cluster things that may shake a nation.

The parish church is not society: no, but from the building to the man who officiates is an easy transition, and the position of the one throws a light upon that of the other. The custodian of these records, of this virtual *hotel de ville,* as the personal representative of the State, must naturally occupy the front place in local society; especially in rural districts, where the only two houses above that of the farmstead in condition are the rectory and the squire's mansion. Here are no villas and no villa people as in great cities and their suburbs to balance the central figures with the power of wealth and education. The vicar is higher than the magistrate: nearer to the throne. This is from an earthly point of view: spiritually, his elevation is so much greater that no comparison exists. The Sovereign is the supreme head of the Church, the vicar is the vicegerent of the Sovereign in this particular. True, much of his temporal power is gone, unless, as often happens, he is also a magistrate. He can no longer fine those who do not attend church; he cannot levy a church-rate; nor compel the profligate to do penance. Ecclesiastical law, so far as the people are concerned, is dead. The rotting remnant of the village stocks usually lies near the churchyard gate, telling of a time when the terror of local punishment was within the power of the parish authorities—the vicar at their head always. Is it the Sovereign's birthday? The church bells ring. If a great victory comes, the church gives expression to the general gladness. The State you see in all this. The vicar has the charge of these things. He baptizes: he marries: he buries: he keeps the archives. Should a bountiful harvest fill the wains, behold a thanksgiving service; should the heir to the Throne recover from serious illness, special praise led by him announces the national gratitude. The great events of history come as it were to the parish church. The vicar is nearest of all in the village to the Crown; naturally then he is the foremost in the local society. The Ten Commandments suspended for centuries in the chancel lie at the root of all the law and order in the place.

He can point backwards to a long line of ancestors, so to say, in his office: an unbroken succession lost at last in the dim mists of antiquity, far exceeding the genealogy of squire or farmer. The shadowy influence of Time dwells near him.

Smollett and kindred writers have satirized the fox-hunting parson, the sottish parson, and the sycophant chaplain of 'my lord'; but these have long been extinct, and were never true types of their class, merely exaggerated cartoons of single instances. Taken as a whole, no men have had such moral influence in their hands as the rural clergymen. Much is with them still: but the mere echo of the past.

For generations the vicar was the only educated man in the parish: in one sense, he not unfrequently remains so still. He has been to college, in itself a prestige morally speaking. He reads the dead languages, Latin and

Greek, the unknown tongues, for which even yet reverence exists in the dwellers without the cities. The belief that the clergyman can lay the unquiet spirits from the grave lingers still. The rude labourers, bold with the strength of the Union, saucy with more money, defy the farmer: but never insult the clergyman. He is tacitly granted a special protection: an impunity from annoyance. The noisy brawl is hushed for the moment as he passes. They see him intimate in the highest circles, penetrating easily where the farmer never goes, and even the squire but rarely. If a girl wishes a situation, much importance is attached to the clerical certificate of good character; not only by the servant herself, but by the worthy wealthy people at a distance who engage her. Those who live in an atmosphere of literature will hardly comprehend the way in which the ignorant look up to the man who can compose a sermon. Nor is the pulpit powerless upon passing questions of the day, allusions to them from that hoary rostrum still carry a semi-superstitious weight in places where current literature does not enter in any sense into the life of the people.

Lastly, from the vicar's hands proceed the endowed charities of the village. The income from the lands left to the poor by benevolent persons, is distributed by him and the churchwardens, and practically by him. Luxuries and necessities given away by the Hall at Christmas, or in time of sickness, usually reach those whose cases the parson or the parson's wife recommend. In some parishes where the vicar chances to be a man of strong personality, he often acts as a species of private arbitrator, deciding disputes between members of his flock.

Here are immense opportunities, such as fall to the lot of no other class in these days. Then why are the parish churches so often half empty? Why these dreary echoing unfilled aisles? Why do chapels rise up in the smallest hamlets where it does not seem possible that two congregations could be found? The clergy are making enormous efforts. The churches themselves have been repaired almost everywhere regardless of expense; free and more comfortable sittings have been provided; all attractions are held out. In the charities distributed, the greatest care is taken that no jealousy shall be caused between chapel and church. Local benefit clubs are encouraged. The Hall and the farmers are persuaded to enlarge the allotment grounds. Glebe lands are turned into gardens. The new schools are vigorously carried on. Rectors, vicars, curates, rural deans—all the parish and county clergy, meet frequently to discuss plans for the improvement of their charge. Certainly money is not spared, nor time, nor personal labour—most self-sacrificing labour too in many instances. This work is not thrown away. Without a doubt the general tone of the rural population is rising in consequence. But 'Zion' chapel, brick-built, lowly situated in a back lane, flourishes and draws the poorer class yet more and more, than the great grey building on the hill. The sum and substance of it all is this: the recent work of the parish clergy does great good, but it is outside the church. It is difficult to express this fact. They sow the seed, but when reaped the grain is not carried into their granaries. They enlist and drill soldiers, who range themselves, when taught, under other banners. The truth is, and it stands out so clearly that it is strange any one can close his eyes to it, that the personal hold, and the hold through a popular faith of the clergy, is either gone, or waning fast. A new leaven, not by any means wholly religious, but principally secular, has been at work. Disregarded for years, it is now so strong that it cannot be conquered, and barely even guided. This leaven, or rather these leavens, will be touched on when we come to the labourer. Having sketched the rectory, let us now pass on to the mansion.

It stands so near to the church that those who run may read the general community of interest and influence between the two. The right of presentation often belongs to the family at the mansion: naturally a son, or nephew, is educated for the living. The history of the great mass of rural gentry is inextricably bound up with the church. That history has yet to be written, and an instructive one it would be in reference to the leading political questions which have agitated the kingdom. In this light, even the study of dry genealogies is not despicable. The intermarriage of families has exercised an extraordinary effect upon the course of events. If any one will examine the pedigrees of the rural gentry, speaking, of course, in general terms, he will find that they date as a class from Queen Elizabeth, or at earliest from Henry VIII. A very large number go no farther back than the eighteenth century, in which the influence of the wealth made in India about that time may be traced. The period which immediately followed the dissolution of the monasteries, saw the foundation of a class of independent lesser gentry. Independent advisedly, because though there had been gentry previously, they were either within the direct influence of noblemen, or of the religious establishments. But at this date an enormous area of land was, practically speaking, re-distributed, and out of that great change there arose a new class of freeholders, owning more than yeomen, and less than peers. They dwelt in the moated granges, not long before the property of monks and nuns, or erected mansions on the site and with the ruins of ancient abbeys. Some of these men were scions of noble houses, who took this opportunity to become possessed of estates at a low price and with comparative ease. But truth also compels the admission that large numbers of them had obtained the wealth, now expended on the purchase of land, in the cities in trades and professions. The ancestors of county families were often merchants, and, doubtless, once apprentices. Taking a few cases which happen to be easy for illustration, the founder of one family, which began its career at this time, was a goldsmith, a second was a member of the Merchant Taylors, a third was an Alderman of London, a fourth was a wool merchant, a fifth a physician of repute, a sixth a lawyer. Up till this date, such men, however wealthy, had but little chance of becoming landed proprietors. The monasteries never sold their lands: their possessions always grew, and were never dispersed. The estates of attainted noblemen were transferred *en bloc*, to favourites of the Crown. The break-up of the religious foundations threw vast tracts of land into the market, and the city men of those days eagerly snapped it up, and as a rule got it remarkably cheap. Their descendants became a new power in the State, and remain a power to this day. The value of their estates has gone on progressively rising ever since. Their names are not often seen in the pages of the historian, but they were the silent agents in most of the great events of history since Henry VIII. The monarch who forced them to accept of knighthood, who invented a new order (of baronetage) specially for them, was not so foolish in this respect as he has been represented; judged from the facts of that time. Here was a new class of untitled noblemen, owning large properties, manors, villages, mills, daily gaining more power in the state, and practically independent of the Crown. They could not be easily brought under its influence, and, further, they paid nothing for the honour of their position, no fines for succession to a title. He forced them, in part, to acknowledge their position. Their estates being entailed, were not dispersed on the death of the first owner; they were not a shifting population. Each mansion was a fixed centre, round which local influence accumulated, and a policy upheld for generations of necessity made itself felt. The power that had anciently been exercised by the castle was gradually transferred to the manor-house.

The glory and stability of Queen Elizabeth's government was in great measure owing to these families, and they contributed in no slight degree to the ultimate triumph of the Protestant faith. There was a good and sufficient reason for their marked fidelity, and even abounding loyalty to the Crown at the time of the Armada. For though it may now be almost forgotten, the country gentry were extremely active in concerting measures to repel the threatened invasion. Not only by assembling armed men, not only by furnishing forth ships, but by heavy monetary subscriptions they did their utmost to strengthen her hands. Some put down fifty pounds, some twenty—not despicable amounts in those days, according to their estates. Why this eagerness? Why this general uprising? We know that a very considerable section of the population was still Catholic; yet reading the inner history of those stirring times by the light of family papers and records, it is pretty certain that the landed proprietary, as a whole, dreaded the return of the Catholics. The reason is clear. Half their estates would have been forfeited to the Roman Church if the Spaniards had succeeded in re-establishing her authority. To the terror of rack and bonfire there was added the very real and substantial fear of loss of property. For their lands had been taken from monasteries, from abbeys and convents. Was it probable, or even possible, for those institutions to be restored without claiming their own again?

Such a thing, of course, sounds absurd now. We cannot imagine the broad acres, grouped around the manor-house, well-wooded and watered, lying in a ring-fence, torn from the owner, and converted to the use of cowled friars and veiled nuns. But it was a very real matter in those days, hardly fifty years after the dissolution of the monasteries. No wonder the new men were determined to fight for their hearths and homes, and social rank. Conversing only recently with an otherwise intelligent Roman Catholic on this topic, he took out a pocket-book, in which he had taken the trouble to make a list of the lands in one small locality which had once belonged to the Church, and were now in the possession of two worthy justices of the peace. Though acknowledging with a sigh the improbability of such an event, he did not conceal his conviction that these acres still morally belonged to the Church, and should, if rights were observed, be returned. His argument was that if, as the agitation for tenant-right and for the disestablishment of the Protestant religion seemed to point, the time would one day come when the land would be redistributed, then the Catholic claims ought to be recognized, being the oldest of all.

Long before the great Civil War this class had become the representatives of the country in Parliament. Sir Walter Scott, and other popular writers, have created a belief in the honest old Sir Geoffrey, the country squire, who loved
> 'brandy and mum well,
> And to see a beer-cup, turned over the thumb well,'

who fought for the King. This type is usually accepted as the representative of the country gentry in the days of Charles I. It is an utterly mistaken one. These men sat in the very Parliament which declared war against the King; though doubtless carried on by circumstances far beyond their original intentions. They resented the attempt to impose arbitrary taxes, because they would be the chief sufferers. If the records of those times be examined, and even far later—as the parochial assessments at the end of the seventeenth century—it will be found that, taking a small country town or village, the resident squire, and, perhaps, one or two members of his family, paid more than half the whole rates and taxes of the place. Of course, there were other causes. But these two things are plain: first, the Parliament that opposed Charles I was chiefly composed of country gentlemen, returned for boroughs and counties; secondly, that they had a preeminent interest in repelling arbitrary taxation. The lists of the Parliamentary Committees in the various counties may still be obtained, almost perfect, and a very large proportion of these Committees were county gentlemen of good families, and by no means the ignorant, rude fanatics it has suited the purposes of fiction writers to represent them. Parliamentary independence, and the freedom of the country at large, is under great obligations to these men. There were exceptions, of course; and it is also pretty certain that towards the close of the interregnum the once Parliamentary-disposed gentry were strongly in favour of the Restoration. They saw the power, in fact, for which they had risked so much, taken out of their hands, and vested in the towns and cities. Naturally they disliked this. But, before the cities formed their trained bands in the early days of the Rebellion, how could the Parliament have raised an army at all without the assistance of the country gentry?

From that date, down to the passing of the Reform Act, the country gentry composed the majority of the Members of Parliament. Even great towns usually returned landowners, as, indeed, they very often do now. The history of Parliament for the last three hundred years is the history of the rural gentry. England, indeed, was ruled by families with almost innumerable branches and members. Instances are common where as many as twelve or fifteen large estates in one county were held by relatives, all of the same name, in the early part of the present century. When voters were few in number, such families as this, of course, possessed an almost absolute power. The subject is capable of much development, and would yield interesting results if closely examined; but here it can only be briefly added that these were the men who made war against Napoleon. They dreaded all French ideas and sentiments, imbued as they were, even under the modern Caesar, with what, to the English mind, were the dangerous principles of revolution and infidelity.

The Reform Act and the repeal of the Corn Laws were stoutly resisted: but they have affected the manor-house very little, nothing to what was expected. Nor have the recent lowerings of the franchise much reduced its power. To this day, the majority of the members of Parliament are country gentlemen. You may find men now in the House of Commons, untitled, and anything but notorious—just the very reverse of the notoriety-hunter, whose father and grandfathers have sat there before them, and whose family name has never been absent at important divisions for a hundred years. Counties, boroughs, rural or urban, still as a rule choose their representative from among the country gentry.

The truth appears to be that there is something in the very nature of Englishmen—an intense hereditary attachment to The Land. Nothing has such a fascination for the tradesman and the middle class as the possession of a farm. And it is remarkable how soon a cotton-prince, or millionaire who has purchased an estate, assimilates his ideas and habits to those whose associations go back several centuries.

From this brief history of the class may be gathered the main views of the men whose houses stand so near to the parish church, and who walk arm-in-arm with the clergy. Those views are plain and simple enough. He likes local administration: but to attribute any deep designs upon the government of the kingdom to the country gentleman would be to wrong him extremely. He has no objection to popular representation.

Looking backwards, his position would seem as fixed and permanent as that of the clergyman. Looking forward there are many signs that the social future of both orders is likely to be somewhat different to their present. These indications come from within and without.

It appears an ungrateful task to accuse the hard-working rural clergy of failing to appreciate the times: and yet it is true. The monks and friars of Catholic days certainly did not greatly encourage learning: but they entered intensely into the life of the people. A picture of Chaucer's times would be recognized as incomplete without the monk. A picture of the nineteenth century which omitted the clergy would not be accused of untruthfulness. Art, and all things beautiful, both physical and spiritual, were then engaged in the service of religion, and the parish church really was the pivot round which life revolved. It certainly is not so now. The ideas of the people are utterly changed, yet they run more now than ever parallel to the *spirit*, if sometimes opposed to the dogmas of Christianity.

There was a monk, founder of the abbey of Malmesbury, known afterwards as Saint Aldhelm. He taught Christianity to the rude Saxon pagans: but he did more, he taught them civilization. Standing on the bridge over the river there, where the traffic was, he addressed them upon art, science, and history, even upon music. He was in short, not only a priest, but what we should call in our time, a lecturer. His success was enormous.

There was a monk whose deeds are not so highly prized now, St Dunstan. He worked in iron and brass as a blacksmith. This is all of his history that we need trouble about. Note: the monks were blacksmiths, carpenters, musicians, lecturers; all trades and all learning was theirs. They were not monks only.

Have we now any Aldhelms or Dunstans? Any clergyman teaching to the labourers the ennobling, the fascinating story of science?—lecturing, experimenting, announcing discoveries among the stars, in electricity, in history, towards the North Pole, each in their separate village? Any curates toiling in the hay-field, reaping among the reapers, or hammering on the anvil? The legend of the magician tells how he drew an invisible circle round his body, and lo, none could touch, or approach. The black coat forms such a circle round our clergy. They are not of the people; a distinct line marks the separation. No more need be said upon the *within* of the rural clergy. Of the *without* presently.

The sons of country gentlemen once thought it no disgrace to enter into farms, as the tenants under lease of their parents, or of elder branches of the family. Old muniment chests in many a country mansion still contain dozens of such antique leases to younger sons, nephews, cousins, and so on. Here was a great source of family power—extinct now. The same young men till very recently went into the army, into the navy, the church, or the bar. Military position can no longer be obtained by purchase: nor are Indian appointments so open to influence. The bar is not so easy to enter as it used to be: witness the strict examinations of a barrister. The Church is open yet: but suppose it disestablished? Moreover, none of these professions offer the same pecuniary, or social advantages they used to do. All arcana are abolished. The church and the bar have no longer the monopoly of knowledge. A man may attain to a European reputation in science or literature, and yet never have been to college. The social position, the receipts, and the chance of a share in the government of the country, are less and less. It is even becoming a little commonplace, below good society, to belong to a profession. The competition of intellect produces some of the effects—vulgarizing, depreciating the tone—as the competition of trade. What then are these young men to do? What is the most powerful factor in achieving social or political rank in these days? Money. Title, descent, influence, intellect itself in most superior degree, barely ever rise to high position now without some share of wealth. Lord Beaconsfield was long a favourite instance with some writers to the contrary. We all know now (as of course certain circles always did) that the young author started with a pretty large income, and by a wealthy marriage secured himself the sinews of war. It comes to this: the rising generation, take more and more to trade, manufacture, commerce—for money, not from genuine liking.

How many country families are there at the present day who rely for their income upon the rentals of their agricultural lands alone? If they did, they could not make the annual visit in the height of the season to town.

The ponderous wealth of the manufacturer would put them utterly in the shade. Brief analysis will demonstrate this. An average area of 3,500 acres may be taken as the estate of the ordinary country gentleman. Small portions may let at high rates: the average rental would not exceed 30 shillings per acre, if as much. This gives £5,250 per annum; which, however, taking a term of years, must be reduced by nearly a thousand to account for repairs, salaries, and losses from farms out of occupation. Four thousand a year is a small income for a man with, say, two sons and two daughters, claiming and justly, social rank. There may be also encumbrances left from former holders; debts of predecessors, or incurred in improvements not yet giving much return.

Hundreds of city men who go to their offices at nine in the morning, and return to their suburban villas at five in the afternoon, boasting no descent, could show an income double this. And they have no hereditary position to maintain, they get more out of their money. Country houses have, therefore, no other resource left if they would keep up the traditions of the family. They must trade, or bank, or speculate: and they do it to an unsuspected extent. The head of the house may conceal his connection with the coal-mine, the railway, the share-market, the bank, or the counting-house; but, depend upon it, his money is there. Note also the marked anxiety of the country gentry to get the railway system extended to their estates. What a number of short links have been constructed lately for the convenience of little outlying villages—they can hardly be called towns. The money for these lines has been chiefly found by the landed proprietors. Not to import navvies to steal the game, not for personal convenience, not to bring tradesmen down to join the hunt, not from a disinterested desire to further the advancement of the sparse population, but from an honest and declared desire to raise the value of their estates.

If the head of the house conceals his connection with trade out of deference to certain traditions, which had a social force in his early days but are now extinct, the sons, who have no such scruples, enter openly into business. They can find illustrious examples enough set before them.

The position of the country gentry is, then, at the present moment, undergoing change from within, owing to these causes. First, the closing of former avenues of employment for the young, as the army (abolition of purchase), the bar, Indian appointments, and so on. Then the terrible pressure of the riches obtained in trade and speculation, and the increased disposition in consequence to seek fresh openings in commerce, engineering, and even emigration, as sheep farming in Australia.

From without, powerful agents are at work; some of the strongest of which arise out of the very land which seems at first sight so completely beneath their feet.

The tenant-farmer, not the small freeholder well-known in some counties, but the occupier under lease or agreement, came into existence with the country gentry: and his history forms a corollary to theirs. They were found at the back of the squire, following with unhesitating step up till a very recent period, gathering round him in war time, answering his call at the poll, supporting him through thick and thin. The last vestige of the ancient feudal system of making war survives in some sort in the yeomanry cavalry. Not that it is a direct descendant, but the principle is similar. The largest landowner usually commands the local troops, who are one and all farmers, or sons of farmers: in point of fact, the yeomanry are a body of armed retainers, drilled once a year at the public expense. It is symbolic of the former relations between landlord and tenant. One led, the other followed. The inventor of the steam plough changed all this. The moment farming ceased to be a rude traditionary occupation carried on by rule of thumb, the moment science and skill and personal intelligence were required, the tenant began to grow independent. There is no difficulty in finding men who can follow a well-known routine, simple and plain; but there is very considerable difficulty in finding men who can adapt themselves to continually changing conditions. In a word, once the tenant followed and depended upon the landlord, now in the mass, if not in the individual, the landlord depends upon the tenant. First, farms have grown larger, and as a result more capital is wanted to work them. Secondly, the expenditure upon stock, implements, and machinery, labour, etc., has risen sixty per cent., in some cases perhaps absolutely doubled. This again means more capital. Thirdly, science enters into the calculation, and requires a man of education and mental ability. Fourthly, competition upon a most extended scale has set in, to meet which, singular energy is necessary. Now tenants who combine practical knowledge, education, and business capacity, with scientific information, and large capital, are not to be picked up at a moment's notice. The sequence supplies itself. A tenant of this kind cannot be treated as an inferior, or in an offhand manner. His views upon even such very sore points as game are not to be overlooked entirely. Suppose, for instance, a great landed proprietor receives notice one quarter day that six of his largest tenants will quit unless some grievance is redressed. To lose them means the sudden reduction of his income by several thousand pounds, and it may be years before he finds good responsible men to take their places. There was once a popular impression abroad, that farmers went about on their knees begging for farms. It certainly is not so now. A man of experience and skill, with capital, can always get a farm. A landlord cannot always get a tenant. This, of course, is putting the case in an extremely plain way. It comes to this. If the country gentleman goes to London in the season, he finds men there of no descent or name spending three and four times his income. If he returns home, he finds his largest tenants holding their heads almost if not quite as high as his. They can dine at seven as well as he, and actually do it. So much for what may be called personal pressure: then there is the pressure of abstract principles, and public opinion.

Abstract principle number one has been extensively discussed under the name of unexhausted improvements, and was at last formulated into the Agricultural Holdings Act. Abstract principle two, rising out of this and looming in the distance, is Tenant Right, which certainly means restriction of the landlord's powers, whatever else it may mean. Public opinion says very strongly that the tenant shall have his political, moral, and social views in the most independent manner, and shall express them freely, without let or hindrance; for which, in one way, the Ballot Act provides, and Chambers of Agriculture and the newspaper press in another. No such thing as moral or social pressure can be put upon the tenant, supposing, of course, he resists. The shadow of tenant-right is but a shadow yet, but a terribly dark and ominous, and, to all appearance, we must add, an unjust and tyrannical shadow. Better give way now, and yield up precedence and quasi-feudal privileges, than provoke that question. Briefly, the agriculturist has acquired social rank in the county. He is a separate, and distinct, and well-defined power—an independent power. He goes also direct to the Government without the intervention of the landlord. His local Chambers send representatives—tenant farmers—to the Central Chamber, and the Central Chamber waits at once upon the Ministry. This is a very striking fact, and in itself points to a remarkable social change. There is a talk too of a Minister of Agriculture: if so, he will represent the farmers, the tenants, and not the country gentry. A tenant-farmer, who as the bearer of his chamber's vote, can walk with an official deputation, straight into the presence of a minister and demand measures on their merits alone, is not very far behind in influence the landlord who sits in the House of Commons, and obeys the dictates of his party. Such men may claim a higher social place than the old humble farmer, who held his peace at home and accepted what was given to him. Sooner or later, it is clear that a class who thus seek in the most determined manner to obtain direct influence at the seat of Government, will not rest content unless they are granted a share in county administration. The agriculturist may yet sit as a magistrate, or at least vote at quarter sessions upon finance questions. Political advancement invariably means social advancement. In personal manners, habit, thought, and general intelligence, these men are not greatly, often not at all, behind their landlords. The sum of it all is, the social barrier is breaking down. The classes may not mingle any more, but the inequality is gone, or going fast. The one cannot claim, and the other would not admit, any superiority.

Social and even political changes arise from below quite as much as descend from above. If increased intelligence and a spirit of independence in the class immediately above them, the farmers, have insensibly acted upon the labourers, so the very decided step forward taken by the agricultural working population has re-acted upon the tenants, and indirectly upon the landlords. To put it shortly, the cottage is as much a castle now as the farmstead, or the mansion. The labourer no longer works *for* others as well as under others; like Harry o' the Wynd, 'he fights for his own hand'. It is hardly likely that the employer will consent to be less independent than the employed. The mistake is often made of attributing the altered position of the rural working-man, the agricultural artisan (for he will soon disdain the very name labourer) entirely to the rise of wages. That rise was rather the result of several causes which had been silently working under the surface for years. Those causes were mainly three, each more or less connected: first, the spread of dissent, secondly, the promulgation of those ideas, which for convenience we may call 'international'; thirdly, to great public works as railways, and factories. The leaven worked its way very slowly among a stolid and unsentimental people, such as the dwellers in village and hamlet; but by now it has effectually leavened the whole mass. The history is curious and instructive, please accept it as passionless history with no leanings either way.

Firstly, Dissent. We have seen how the parish church was by all laws, human and divine, made the centre of the parish. Dissent dissolved the connection between the lower ranks and the church, introducing a new centre especially their own. For in its commencement, the revival among the rural population was almost entirely confined to the poor. Those who were in authority, those who formed the ruling class at that period, were bitterly opposed to it. The preachers were stoned in some country villages and towns, buffeted in others, pelted with mud and filth, by command. The meetings for years, were liable at any moment to be broken up by a violent mob. At that date, the right of public meeting, in fact, was not recognized. This sounds incredible in our age and quite opposed to tradition, but any one may easily find proofs enough. The first chapels were simply thatched cottages in outlying hamlets. To this day such cottages are pointed out with something approaching to veneration by members of the rich and powerful Nonconformist bodies. The 'Ranters', as they are still called, met with closed doors and shutters in fear and trembling, like the political clubs in the latter days of Cromwell. Remember this was in the present century. Stones came against the door, or smashed the windows. Bladders full of gunpowder were let down the cottage chimney and exploded on the hearth, some of the simple-minded frightened people thinking it was an evil spirit who interrupted them. The old chimneys were very wide, built to smoke bacon, and once a young calf was dropped down, emerging as black as soot with terrified bleatings into the room beneath. After awhile, the Nonconformist places of worship were protected by special act of Parliament. At once the annoyance ceased and the new religion rapidly spread. Today what do we see? More than half the rural population frequenting their own chapels, listening to their own ministers. In summer, great meetings are held in the open air. A farmer lends his field, a waggon under a tree is used as a temporary platform. Crowds come for miles, praying and singing with intense fervour. Though both sexes are present in great numbers, and remain on the ground almost the whole day, no complaints arise, their behaviour is orderly, their faith evidently genuine. Now this is a striking fact, and it is not the ephemeral phenomenon of one season, it has gone on for years, and it occurs all over the country. In the days of the monks, travelling friars wandered from one end of the country to the other, finding good cheer, welcome, and reverence, wherever they came. Now, today, in each village and hamlet, nay, in every rural place of habitation, whatsoever, be it but half-a-dozen lowly cottages, you shall find one in which dwells a labourer, who himself once a week assembles his friends and addresses them in his humble way. If an itinerant preacher comes past, here he can obtain food and shelter, and thus, like the friars of yore, a preacher of this persuasion might travel east and west, and never want a rest for his foot, a roof for his head, or a crust for his mouth. This is another striking fact. Many farmers now belong to the Dissenting communities, and of course, form the strong props of the local congregation. Here and there, a retired manufacturer or mill-owner has purchased an estate, and quickly becomes the rallying point and leader of half a rural county, as the layer of foundation stones, the chairman of meetings, and so on. If the labourers had the franchise these men would go into Parliament. Add to these the support of the tradesmen and congregations in the towns. Reflecting upon these facts, which all who choose may verify for themselves, must not we admit, that the introduction of Dissent has been a powerful factor in the past, and will be in the future. You may divorce the Church from the State, you cannot divorce religion from politics. A man's religious faith will have its own particular political expression. These rural congregations when they vote will have theirs. Dissent divorced the poor from the church, looked at as the centre of the parish. It was the first step towards independence.

Secondly, the 'International'; using the term as a convenient equivalent for the Rights of Labour, etc. How did these views get disseminated among the rural poor, so many of whom can neither read nor write? Their own special preachers rarely, if ever, allude to such topics from the platform, except perhaps in the way of abstract principles. Whether they do in private we have no means of knowing: probably not. From whence then come these ideas? The railways and the factories were the prime source. Half the navvies were drawn, and are so still, from the rural districts. Among the hundreds employed in a cutting, or in a factory, some from the great cities could read, write, and speak: and speak they did with effect, for the seed thus sown was carried back by the navvy or factory labourer to his native village. Latterly the newspapers, the local Radical press, has been the chief agent in this dissemination. The fact of so many being unable to read has actually assisted rather than retarded these results: for the more ignorant men are, the more importance they attach to anything written, or printed, besides the incapacity of criticism. Daily papers the labourer rarely sees. The paper he does see, or learns the contents of at the ale-houses or elsewhere, is one printed in an adjoining town, and he prefers it to be composed of three things. First, the most sensational topics of the week, as murders, fires, startling discoveries in California. Secondly, local intelligence, village gossip from places he knows. Thirdly, leaders, or articles of a somewhat violent character attacking the powers that be. All this would afford much matter for thought, if we had space. The *Illustrated Police News* with its cuts of savage murder, or awful explosion, finds its way largely even into the most outlying hamlets. But such papers of themselves would effect little without the local prophet to expound them. Just as the cottage of the local preacher may be found everywhere, so in every village there is at least one man, the wheelwright, the blacksmith, or hedge-carpenter, who can read and think for himself. He dilates upon the paper which supplies him with secular texts the whole week long. If the union comes that way, he becomes the local secretary. If any agitation arises he becomes a leader. Such men in the aggregate exercise immense influence. Unsuccessful emigrants often return from America, and bring with them the story of a land where no master is known, only a 'boss'. This was the leaven that prepared the rural world for the peaceful revolution of the last ten years. It still works, and grows stronger. We cannot predict what course it will take: its most ardent champions are divided and uncertain. But may we not be certain of this: that the labourer must sooner or later be enfranchised. Schools are educating the rising generation with tenfold speed: when these become men and see their brethren in towns voting, will they remain content alone unrepresented? Most certainly not. And what a power they will have! Already the remark has been made that the enfranchised rural population would be too strong for the mechanics and the working men of towns, their numbers are so large. But collision between the two classes would hardly take place. Of this we may feel sure: when the labourer votes, the last blow will be given to the influence so long enjoyed by the middle classes: nor does any idea of 'order' in the French sense, suggest iself.

Unless in the meantime men of intellect, calm thought, and noble views can somehow obtain a hold upon the people: such a hold as Saint Aldhelm had. No one could find better material to work upon than is afforded by the rural population.

Glance for a moment at their history, and see what manhood they have furnished forth, remembering that our cities are but things of yesterday. The labourer has fought the battles of England. He comes of a fighting stock. Fragments of the tongue of the hardy Saxons linger yet, and are used in his daily life. Against William the Conqueror how they whirled their heavy axes on the field of Hastings! These thanes and their men were farmers and labourers, nothing more. Under the Edwards and Henries they filled the ranks in the gallant if needless struggle with France. The Armada saw them once more ready for the field. Not a war but has called its thousands from the plough-share and the threshing-floor, from Hastings to Waterloo. Their blood has been freely shed the whole world over.

To this hour the romance of war is believed in among the cottagers of the vale and the shepherds of the hill. The bugle sounds, the flag is unfurled, and the hearts of the young men are stirred. It is not the recruiting ribbons with which Johnny comes marching home from the fair that have taken his fancy, it is the deep-seated love of adventure. If they are called upon, they are the first to volunteer; it was so with the militia regiments when the garrisons were sent to Corfu only a few years since. The village recruit does not join the army from drink, from desperation, from utter loss of character; he joins it from sheer hope of fighting, from pure desire of adventure, much as he becomes a poacher. Splendid men they are, the pride of the recruiting sergeant. Tall and sturdy, with chests far exceeding the regulation girth; accustomed, too, all their days, from childhood upward, to exposure and hard fare, the very men to form the backbone of an army. It is strange that no attempt has been made to organize this natural enthusiasm. If England should ever have to maintain forces in some degree equal to the huge armies of the Continent, the men for the purpose will have to be sought in the rural districts. Here there is a vast magazine of sturdy manhood willing to be drilled. Drilled they will have to be too, mentally as well as physically, as the years go on.

The origin of most of our regiments was distinctly agricultural and local; they were raised by commission. The meaning of that term is quite forgotten now. An officer who receives a commission receives with it his men already raised, drilled, and armed. In the origin and beginning, the nobleman or gentleman to whom the King gave his commission actually had to enlist his men as best he could, to drill them and get them into shape, and give them cohesive power. Naturally such a gentleman went down to his own native village, his document in his hand, and there set up his head-quarters. Round him gathered the youthful of his father's tenants and their friends, and with these came the labourers out of the cottages on the estate and thereabouts, and these became a company and the nucleus of a regiment. These men had known their officers from childhood, a local *esprit de corps* bound them firmly together; they went out as the retainers of old behind their knight. Of late the war authorities have discovered that the system of centralization, under which no man knew his officer's name even till the day he was appointed, man and officer being total strangers, is not one calculated to give a vigorous life to an army, and have appointed each regiment a local habitation, forming military centres in the counties. This step will have an indirect effect upon rural society, but it does not go far enough.

Probably, the day is gone by when the old system of raising companies could be practised with success. Neither can we go to the severe length of the continental conscriptions, which, however, in a certain sense, is not so un-English a procedure as has been argued. Under the feudal system, there was a universal conscription in England. Have we not all laughed at Falstaff and his pack of rascals, not worth powder and shot, with but one shirt between them? How did he raise these? As he marched across the country, he stayed at each village, and called for the list of the men who were capable of arms. What was this but conscription? The inimitable scene is in Shakespeare: no need therefore to describe it. Later, in Armada times, each county was ordered to find so many men—the papers are still extant—and they were found by the aid of the local lists of capable persons, furnished often by the tithing-man, an officer still appointed in many villages, but who would not believe that this was once his duty if you were to tell him so. The orders of monarchs of England, commanding all those who could shoot to assemble so many times a year, and practise at the butts with bow and arrow, are well known, so are the weapon shows—annual exhibitions of skill for prizes and honour. We cannot expect ever to see her armies like those of Russia or France, formed of men taken from their homes for months or years. We can hardly expect to get to the length of an universal militia; but could not the lads of the village be organized in some degree, as they were in the olden times by these lists of capable warriors, by these shootings at the butts and annual showings of weapons?

Something to plant the germ of organization, without the stern restraint of conscription, might be done on the former model. The lads would be willing enough, and the young farmers also. Why should not a list be kept in every rural parish, revised once a year, of all males between certain ages, and not suffering from organic disease; and a rifle and accoutrements be provided ready for each of them? Why should there not be a local rank, so to say—rank only acknowledged in the parish—just sufficient for the officer to give the word of command in peace time? If butts were made for shooting and rifles found, the lads would subscribe for ammunition, and speedily become adepts at the targets; and glad indeed they would be of so congenial an amusement as shooting. Let certain days, once or twice a year, be appointed for the local weapon show or assembly, and some old non-commissioned officer sent round as judge or instructor. There would not be a man missing if it was held in the parish. No uniform would be needed—the world has several times been conquered by armies who had no idea of uniform—for, of course, no one would dream of marching such soldiers straight to the battlefield; but in case of war threatening the vital interests of the country, they would form splendid reserves, who could be drafted to camps of instruction, and quickly made into good soldiers. The idea is of course crude, but might it not be worked out practically?

The volunteer system does this admirably for the towns, but it does not do it for the rural places. Country volunteer corps are chiefly composed of men who either live actually in the market town where the head-quarters are, or close by in the outskirts. It is too far for the villagers and dwellers in the hamlets to come to drill after a hard day's work in the field. The volunteer system hardly touches the labourers. Something ought to be done to organize these, if in ever so loose a manner. As remarked before, here is splendid material in abounding quantity wasted. These men have not only fought the battles of England, they have planted her colonies; at this day, the Governments of New Zealand, Australia, and Canada, are doing all they can to induce this very class to come, above all other classes, as the best emigrants, and of most value to those states. Their qualities are understood abroad, if not at home. Oh, for a hundred Saint Aldhelms!

We have now gone through in a rugged way the four classes of country society—the clergy, the gentry, the farmers, and the labourers—and noted their history, their characters, and tendencies. Now do the existing nominal authorities correspond to the present attitude of the agricultural people, and are they likely to continue? Or will the former shortly become obsolete, and will new ones be needed? Certainly, we can say that the leaven has been at work, and if the ferment has been slow it has been penetrating. Slowly also the outward forms of government have altered, in each case assuming more of a representative and broader character.

The first step was taken in this direction, when the Union system of poor relief came into operation. At a blow it knocked away half the local power of the vicar and churchwardens. The church-rate abolition was another step towards change. The institution of county police, as vice the antique and impotent parish constable, was still more important. Pages might be written on the influence of the new police, who have insensibly smoothed away, and polished the old rudeness and boisterous brutality of the hamlets. The parish constable lingers yet, a name only. Now sanitary boards are opening up their work, though it must be said in a sadly slow and incomplete way. Most important of all, the school is re-organized. If the school board is not recognized much in rural districts in *name*, it is there nevertheless to a great extent in reality, in this way. Those who support the school by voluntary subscriptions form among themselves a board, and thus a new element is introduced into village government. Will official and outward evidence of change stay here, or will it proceed farther? Schemes of county re-organization have already been started and openly discussed. Excluding details, they present a general similarity, and are all based upon the principle of representation. The present boards of guardians, for instance, are composed of farmers elected, or rather nominated and returned without the trouble of a contest, by their parishes, and of magistrates, who are members of the boards by virtue of their office as justices. This system it has been proposed to extend to the county administration, to add to the present committees upon finance, etc., at Quarter Sessions, which are formed exclusively of magistrates, a certain number of what we may call laymen, agriculturists not in the commission of the peace, from each petty sessional district. The plan is simple enough and has much to recommend it, but there are two things to be considered before it is adopted. First, what view will the rising generation of labourers, well educated, and enfranchised as they undoubtedly will be, take of local, or county administration? Suppose they insist upon working-men representing them at such county boards as they may reasonably claim to do, if the principle of representation be once admitted. At present the magistracy exhibits a mild form of oligarchical government. Secondly, if such county boards or provincial parliaments are to come into existence, ought not their powers to be very much extended, so as to embrace and cover the lesser local authorities?

There are now so many kinds of authority in county government, that no one seems to know exactly where their power begins or ends. The Lord-Lieutenant takes the lead with the nominal command of the county forces; under him the sheriff. Then the magistrates in Quarter Sessions, and in petty sessions. Next the poor-law divisions, the rural sanitary authorities, the local vestries and school boards, voluntary or governmental. One parish follows one course, another adopts almost the very opposite. Cavillers have declared that the law itself is not the same in each division, but varies with the locality. No such thing exists as a general object throughout the county, no such thing as organization. It is a muddle. If these county boards, or provincial parliaments ever do come into existence, will it not be a capital opportunity for reforming the whole administration? These local vestries, and school boards, these sanitary boards, and boards of guardians—would it not be desirable to bring them under something like a superior county council, or authority, instead of leaving them to commit their present vagaries? Nothing like general progress can be expected till the whole population is guided in the same direction. The falling in of the turnpike trusts may very likely bring the subject before the world shortly. If anything of the kind were done it would probably lead to that most desirable of all things, a complete revision of the rating system, which again would also result in a great relief from overwhelming burdens. The fact is clear that a rate spread over a large area does not press so heavily as one upon a section of the same area. The police rate, for example, in some counties, is barely a penny in the pound. Suppose each parish paid its particular constable, or constables, does any one imagine the same degree of efficiency could be attained for the money? If the police, the most useful of all modern institutions, can be maintained by a rate levied over the whole county, why not other necessary establishments? Why should not all rates, except those peculiarly incidental to towns, as paving and sewage, be equally widely distributed? The cry that to revise the rate-book is a task so gigantic as to be impossible, is simply absurd. It should be done by a commission composed of members of the judicial bench. The impartiality and high sense of honour of our judges are matters of world-wide fame. They could do it, and do it quickly and well. There are plenty of surveyors and valuers to furnish them with the facts to decide upon. Such values would not be questioned in a court of law, or in selling an estate; why then should not they be equally trustworthy in this case? What is there so mysterious and unapproachable in a rate-book?

Certainly the present county boards, or committees, with the limited power and means at their disposal, have done their work cheaply and well, on the whole. Gaols have been removed, or rebuilt, and reformed internally; lunatic asylums put upon an entirely new and satisfactory basis:

and the general finance business of the county carried on efficiently. All the more reason for extending their authority, and, while admitting representation in accord with the spirit of the age, for retaining the unpaid class who have done their work so well. They would act like the House of Lords upon the House of Commons: no real impediment, but as moderators.

Nowhere are the classes so distinctly defined as in the country. Though day by day the lower classes become more independent, the line of separation is never overstepped. The agricultural labourer is farther removed from the farmer today than he was a generation ago. Then, he often ate and drank at the same table, slept in the same house, and his rude *patois* was used by his employer and his family. Some few indeed do still sleep in the farmhouse, but never sit at the same table: excepting at harvest home supper, which institution itself is disappearing, many giving the men money in lieu of beer and victuals. The carter, fogger and shepherd take their meals outside, or in their own cottages—they do not enter into the farmer's sitting-room and help themselves from his dish. He does not use their *patois* more than he can avoid: he educates his children to disuse it entirely. So that the links between them, the social bonds, apart from political and religious ties, are completely gone. The country grows more republican year by year, and yet at the same time more exclusive.

Very rarely do the gentry invite their tenants to dinner, or a party: so rarely, that never might almost be written. The great noblemen do still in a sense, once a year, but their position is different, and the entertainment is not supposed to possess much of a personal character. Even the old rent-suppers are becoming extinct. A few bottles of wine may perhaps be produced at the rent-audit, but the genial dinner afterwards is usually omitted. The farmer scarcely ever visits the squire, or the squire him: excepting of course those very large tenants who must be made much of. There is no place where they mingle with freedom; not even the hunting field. The freedom is more with the upper ranks, with the peer and the viscount, than with the neighbouring landowner. The ranks are quite distinct. Here and there a popular landlord has aroused something like the old enthusiasm: such cases may still be found, where real geniality and mutual confidence does exist, but they are the exceptions which prove the rule.

Signs there are, too, that the old county cliques, or parties are weakening and breaking-up. The Whig and Tory coteries grow less and less cohesive. Families do not intermarry so much, or form connections at home like they used to do. There was a time when county politics afforded room for much clever manoeuvring and intriguing, when the county was divided around two hostile camps, or rather courts, each striving year by year to increase its influence. This imparted a reality and life into politics now quite extinct, and perhaps happily extinct. Every nerve was then strained to add new estates and villages to the family influence by the marriages of heiresses and heirs, so as to combine properties, property carrying with it votes and power. Family genealogy was really of importance. All this has gradually died out. The Reform Act and its extensions of recent years, the ballot box, and above all the transfer of power to the thickly-populated manufacturing districts, were the chief causes of the decadence of family influence, and party jealousies. They linger in a measure it is true, but the virulence is gone. Scandal used to whisper that the lord-lieutenants of counties only nominated for commissions of the peace men whom they knew to belong to their own party. It is a good thing that this is gone, or going. The network of railways spread over the country giving such easy access to London and the sea-coast has also had its effect upon the upper ranks of county society. Less and less time is spent by gentry and landlords at home: more and more in London, or on the Continent. County balls are notorious now for their exceeding dulness. To put it vividly, a Duchess of Devonshire, the pride of a county and part afterwards of the social history of the nation, is now almost an impossibility. Ladies whose beauty and social rank, and wealth, would in the olden times have made them the toast of the country are now unknown off their immediate estates. Such a phrase as the toast of the country is meaningless. Absenteeism is a very real fact. The romance of country society fades away rapidly.

No village revels, no Maypole or feast, now brings together representatives of all the classes. Such fêtes as there are, are either wholly given over to the lower classes, who find much the same amusements provided for them as they would at Greenwich—shows and conjuring, tight-rope and acrobat, a brass band, and so on, or they are formal and stiff. The lord and the lout, the lass and the lady, never dance a jig or country dance together. The farmer's daughter would scorn to mingle with the agricultural labourers; the labourers would feel constrained in their presence. The old social links are gone, and no new ones have yet sprung up. The very mummers are extinct, or nearly so; as for the morris-dancers, old men just remember them; there is no colour or vitality in village life. The labourers and lower orders do not intermarry either so much as they used to do. Emigration, great public works, etc., entice many away, and they form connections far from home. The rural population insensibly acquiring a roving spirit, assumes more of a floating character. New blood in this way is infused into the villages. Some hamlets, and even small towns, seem once to have been almost all related. The same clan name was met with at every step. Even now this may be found among the farmers; in some districts, seven or eight farms are held by men of the same name and descent. But this, too, is fast passing away, as the young men grow dissatisfied with work like that of the labourer, and seek their fortune in towns or abroad. The feudal and local spirit is all but dead.

The market towns are fast losing their former distinctive characteristics, and assuming a dead level. That the old system of business was dull enough and slow enough, it may be added vexatious and disobliging enough, is true; but still there was an individuality about it. You could not get your watch mended quickly without a good deal of coaxing, and even study of character. You had to begin about the weather and the crops, and gradually arrive at a complete understanding upon almost every subject under the sun before the watch could be taken in hand; and then, if you happened to hit the old watchmaker's ideas on the head, it might be ready in a 'matter o' three weeks'. Now, instead, observe a brand new shop-front, full of flash jewellery and American clocks, bravely lit up with gas at night, where your wishes are almost anticipated, and your wants supplied at a moment's notice. Plate-glass windows, mahogany counters, show-rooms upstairs—every London plan may be found copied as far as circumstances will permit in a small county town. The individuality of each place is wearing away, and a sameness succeeding. Nothing can be more utterly different than the modern commercial hotels in such towns, to the ancient hostelries. Some of these still survive far away from civilization, on old post-roads now nearly deserted. There the traveller, after an appetizing drive across down or heath, may call in vain for food. He can have small beer and bread and cheese, but nothing else for love or money. In the market-town he will find a glittering bar, a smoking-room, and parlour—every possible convenience down to 'Bradshaw's Guide', and a local omnibus to take him to the station. No one will 'pester him' with the ancient curiosity. Even yet, if he be foolish enough to enter into conversation with a 'chip off the old block' out in the hamlets, he may be asked questions as to business and family matters, that in town would seem the height of impertinence; but in the commercial hotel no one notices him. These towns literally compete to obtain railway communication. If the capital available is not sufficient to lay down a line for heavy traffic, they move heaven and earth for a small gauge, light railway, or at least a tramway. They are overdone with crowds of commercial travellers, who beat each other down. Out into mere villages they go, taking up their quarters at the town, and driving out daily in every direction, calling upon the petty retail traders in the veriest hamlets.

There is a complaint that society in and around county towns is far less genial and pleasant than in former times. Though business seems to increase, and consequently, money must circulate, yet a certain constraint appears to pervade all classes. Without any desire to criticize ill-naturedly, it does seem as if there was a general desire on the part of everybody to be above their business or occupation, as if they were afraid the fact of being a tradesman or a farmer, if it became known, would be disgraceful. On the other hand, there is a very marked increase of independence. The social tyranny which ruled little places of this sort not very many years ago is impossible now and sounds ridiculous even to talk of. No man now would dream of asking the permission, or at least of humbly requesting the opinion of some local magnate, before he repainted the sign over his door, or added a wing to his house. Such a petty spirit of interference undoubtedly once reigned in county society of this kind. A labourer takes a ticket and visits a mining or manufacturing district, without first saying 'May I do this?'—he comes back and obtains work at once without having to give a full account of himself. Certainly this is a far preferable state of things.

The study of country society, its changes and future, may perhaps appear a trifling matter to some who think only of the present. But in the past, the country made and ruled England. The town and the manufacturing district rule us now. When the agricultural labourer obtains the franchise, there will be a re-distribution of power. In the preceding remarks, some of the most important elements now at work preparing for that great alteration have been pointed out, and their apparent direction indicated. That there is a movement every one must admit, though its precise future cannot be foreseen.

The Future of Farming

1873

The changes which have been crowded into the last half-century have been so numerous and so important that it would almost seem reasonable to suppose the limit had been reached for the present, and that the next few generations would be sufficiently occupied in assimilating themselves to the new condition of existence.

But so far from this being the case, all the facts of the hour point irresistibly to the conclusion that the era of development has but just commenced.

The only result of this vigorous exercise of the intellectual faculties is an ever increasing interest and even anxiety in the possible combinations of the future. No one is satisfied with things as they are: neither the one nor the other party contentedly accepts the existing order, or wishes that the world should relapse into quiescence. In hard practical money-matters even, the modern habit of speculation induces an extending reliance on the times to come. Whether that reliance will be justified or not remains to be seen, for progress is not necessarily improvement.

Still there is the fact—Churchman, secularist, politician, capitalist, communist, all invest their capital in the future, and eagerly scan the slightest sign of fluctuations in the value of their funds. In this struggle, not so much for existence as for pre-eminence, old methods of practice handed down are found incapable of meeting the strain put upon them, and have to be relinquished for machinery and procedures founded upon theories rather than tradition. There was a time, and not so long since, when a farm was an epitome of human economy. The relation of a farmer to his landlord was that of a retainer to his baron, whom he followed to the hustings as his progenitor did the knight to the battle. The farmhouse contained in itself the appliances of half a dozen trades. The bread was baked in the oven from wheat grown in the tenant's fields; the beer was brewed in the brewhouse, often by the master himself; the bacon was bred, killed, and cured on the premises; a small bullock was slaughtered and salted, and kept the family in beef for half a year; the wood-house and faggot pile contained the fuel grown in the adjacent copse, which supplied the place of coal. In the operations of husbandry the same general idea prevailed; everything was so managed as to be self-supporting—to require no extraneous aid. The very rotation of crops was so arranged as to preclude any exhaustion of the soil and consequent necessity for outlay in the purchase of manure. The only manure employed was the *débris* of old crops or the produce of cattle living on the farm. Everything was so contrived as to come in at its own proper season, and supply a want without recourse to foreign assistance. The tenancy was a kingdom in miniature: the master, his family and servants, its population—a population which often, by the bye, was born, married, and died within its narrow limits. To some extent this system survives at the present day. A large proportion of farmers, especially those of small or comparatively small holdings, enter upon their tenancies with very faint and ill-defined ideas of making money. That is not their immediate object, nor even their favourite anticipation. They look to get a house, and garden, and orchard—plenty of solid food, and full barrels in the cellar. For themselves, a certain independence, a sense of being master—that most delicious of all feelings—a certain positive position, a welcome in the hunting field; above all, a home—a home for their wives and children, a possible inheritance for one at least of them, and even if opportunity offers for second and third sons, for on some large estates to bear a particular *name* is a guarantee of getting a farm if time only is given.

The object of these men is not so much money. They do not look upon farming as a business in the same sense in which a merchant regards his trade. There is an amount of pleasure in contemplating such a picture as this; it is thoroughly English in its character. The home, the independent feeling, the good name serving as a passport to the children, the sturdy manliness of the central figure, is exceedingly attractive to the imagination, and even stirs some deeper chords in the heart; but it has its weak spot, and it is this weak spot that is fast driving it out of date. As they do not primarily look to make money, these men do not base their calculations upon the fundamental principles of pecuniary success. They begin business with too little capital: frequently men take farms of say 200, 250, or 300 acres with the goodwill of the landlord or his agent and £300 cash in hand of their own; the rest is borrowed, or the first rent days deferred by arrangement with the acting solicitor till the farm has grown its own stock, when the deficiency is made good with interest. If borrowing is resorted to, the bank holds a bill of sale or some similar instrument on the stock and implements purchased with its cash. Many a man has taken a farm with barely enough money of his own to pay the first year's labour bill. It was a well-known adage that if a competent man could but just put his foot in a farm he was sure of getting on. This practice was just successful and no more. If the conditions remained the same as they were at the first entering upon the tenancy, all went well; but the slightest derangement of those conditions pinched terribly. This explains the consternation and outcry caused by the labourers' demand for higher wages. It upset the balance. It further operated because in other matters more hard cash was wanted than formerly. The baker had superseded the family oven; the great brewer abolished the brewhouse; the sons required education; the daughters did not relish the dairy; the system of barter was gone—cash took its place. The farm was no longer entirely self-supporting. It was necessary to keep account books, a thing never done before. The words 'profit and loss' were introduced and began to be thoroughly understood. To make a 'profit' the farm must become a business; a business requires a certain amount of speculation; speculation means capital. These men had not got capital. A change, therefore, was imminent.

These were some of the internal causes which led up to the present transition state of farming. But there were other causes externally at work far more powerful than these. The principle was and still is the increase in the population, and the almost unaccountable increasing appetite for meat. This is a singular phenomenon. We are told that in one year the amount of meat consumed per head of the population increased from 98 lbs. to 102 lbs. Therefore the increase in population causes not only a larger *prima facie* demand, but also a higher ratio in the quantity consumed by the individual; and the result is an additional demand every year. The reason of this appetite for meat does not immediately concern the subject; it may arise from several causes combined, such as the great waste from the imprudent use of money by the artisan class, supplemented perhaps by the natural craving for a stimulant, a blood-producer, in those who are debarred from exercise and fresh air in large towns. This demand for meat was already exceeding the supply when the cattle plague and other contagious diseases destroyed the floating herds (so to speak) and compelled the dealers to fall back upon the reserve stock, and to anticipate the future returns by extending the slaughter of young cattle and sheep. The result has been that an entire recovery has never been attained from that shock, and prices then risen have never since declined. Nor does it seem probable that they will decline. The question is, how to prevent them from rising still higher, and even how to continue a sufficient supply at increased prices.

Up till comparatively recently the efforts of agriculturists towards enlarging the meat supply have been stimulated simply by the necessity, introduced by the internal causes already alluded to, to extend their operations, and with the view of making profits never thought of before. Many landlords were so far influenced as to modify their agreements; more capital was put in the soil in the shape of manure, and on the soil as improved implements for steam and deeper cultivation. The results of this system have been so remarkable in particular places that it is not surprising to find the enthusiastic individuals immediately concerned firm in the belief that a remedy had been found. In some counties it is stated that the meat production on one or two farms has reached £7. per acre, which is considered as an advance of £50. per cvnt. on the former yield. The calculation is now applied to the whole of England, and the result is so large as to prevent all fear of a meat famine. But a very little analysis will show the utter falsity of these calculations. There are, they say, 31,000,000 acres under all sorts of crops, which taken on the average yield 30 shillings per acre in meat. But if the system of high farming were applied to the whole of this area the produce would be at the rate of £5. to the acre, giving rather more than double the present. But the agricultural returns published by Government show that something like 40 per cent. of the cultivated soil of England consists of permanent pasture, i.e. nearly half. Now the increased supply of meat on the exceptional farms alluded to entirely arises from high farming, chiefly of arable land. How is it possible to farm pasture so as to produce double as much as at present? It cannot all either be broken up into arable, as some gentlemen propose, because hay must be had, and it is an awkward thing to import, to say nothing of the question of cost. Nearly half, then, of this wonderful calculation falls to the ground, and we may not unnaturally doubt its accuracy to a great extent as regards the remaining half. For instance, it is notorious that all land is not capable of an equal amount of cultivation—that would disturb the calculation materially; and, again, some land absolutely will not bear too high farming, it will go stale; and there are thousands of acres which nothing but a deposit of guano six inches thick would render fertile. The matter need not be examined further. What is evident is this: a system of high farming has been perfected, which in isolated positions and under favourable conditions will very largely increase the profit of the farmer. Given a landlord with a plastic mind, good soil, large capital, and plenty of time, no doubt money may be made. But nothing like a solution of the great problem of the national demand for meat has been arrived at. Upon this system nothing would meet it but the enforced employment of the whole Imperial revenue upon the soil.

But let it not be thought for a moment that any discouragement should be thrown upon high farming. On the contrary, the question is, can it still be further perfected, till it really does rise to something like a remedy? The immediate difficulty is to keep larger herds of cattle. Cattle are fed on cake, grass, turnips, &c., &c. These materials again are produced from manure. To begin with the grass—can the crop of grass be doubled? The agricultural world was amused a short time since with a plan for producing a continuous crop of grass by means of perforated hose for water—amused, because it looked so like a toy for a gentleman's park, and so little like a serious piece of machinery. It was intended to give a short but sweet crop of grass in a few days, which was then fed off by sheep, folded by patent hurdles so as to eat a certain portion at a time. Day by day the fold was moved a few yards farther: on returning in a circle to the same spot the crop was found ready again, simply by the application of water forced by steam in a spray over the soil. It answered so far, but it was in the summer. Would grass grow now in the early winter by such a process alone? Would it grow when the frost came by the application of water? And such a process must exhaust the soil sooner than anything that could be conceived. The strongest liquid manure would fail to keep up such a strain for any length of time. Besides, the plan was only a modification of the old water meadows. Water, too, is not always available.

A larger and more extended attempt was the use of sewage from towns. The most extraordinary results were at first reported from this, but latterly little has been heard of it. The fact is, it was found that after a certain time the land became so saturated that vegetation was killed by the excess of chemicals in it, or was so rank and so coarse that no sale could be got for it. In many places the application of sewage to grass has in consequence been abandoned, and arable land used instead. But this presents much difficulty. The cost of drainage, &c., is so heavy that a return upon the invested capital cannot be expected for some time. The crops grown upon land so treated are certainly gigantic—swedes, for instance, become of immense size and the leaves enormous. In a word, it is introducing the conditions, the soil, and forcing power of tropical climates into our own latitude. If the sewage could be applied in the spring only or during the summer, possibly it might succeed. But sewage only exists under peculiar conditions, one of which is that it flows perpetually and must be got rid of somehow in the winter too. But England has no tropical heat in the winter: it is producing the soil of a swamp without the burning sun. Such unnatural conditions cannot be expected permanently to succeed.

Then can the area under grass be largely extended so as to increase the grazing power? For cattle to be entirely supported and fattened on grass would require fields like prairies in extent. Larger numbers can be kept by the use of stalls and artificial food mingled with swedes, &c., and some hay. To produce these a proper proportion of land must remain arable. Sheep, too, require immense tracts of arable land. If anything, they are more important than cattle; for mutton is much more commonly consumed than beef. This restricts the area of pasture; and any very extensive alteration cannot be anticipated. Much, therefore, will evidently depend on the method of cultivating arable land. In such cultivation a rotation has to be observed—turnips, a favourite food for sheep, cannot be grown continuously. Wheat is one of the crops intervening; and wheat is the direct food of man. Foreign competition has not driven English wheat out of the market, but it has rendered wheat itself unprofitable. As a crop, it does not pay the cost of production, except in isolated instances. It appears once in a rotation of crops chiefly employed in feeding cattle: these pay, but the wheat crop when it comes only prevents a season of dead loss on that portion of the farm. What is wanted, then, is some new crop to take the place of wheat, and to fill up that gap with a yield of profitable animal food. This is a subject worthy the attention of chambers of agriculture throughout the country, and of agricultural stations on the Continent.

Without some such new and important vegetable, or some equally new and important manure, perhaps without the two together, it is useless to expect any very much larger amount of capital to be put on the soil, for the simple reason that present conditions prevent an adequate return for it. More than a given amount of capital could not be used on a farm at present, let the tenant farm never so highly. There is no scope for it, no material for it to work with. If it would pay capitalists to invest in cattle stalls and meat production, what is to prevent capital from being so invested now? No need for compensating clauses. An acre or two of land is not much to purchase and erect stalls on. The cattle could be fed on artificial food, which could be purchased. The fact is, artificial food is too dear and too scarce. If such a course were followed, it would be dearer and scarcer still. Looked at from such a stand-point, what is wanted is more artificial food, which means more manure, and manure means force. Where is the force to come from? Where is the steam, in a metaphorical sense—where are the chemicals, the material substances to be converted into living protoplasm? For animals are merely machines for converting matter into organic substance. Coal contains a force stored from the sun in ages past: where shall we find a cattle coal (if a phrase may be coined), to put life in, and supply the food of life to additional millions of shadowy herds of the future? Till some such vegetable or some such manure can be found, all that can be done is to smoothe away the difficulties attending the production of stock by the present methods; and the principle of these is, we are told, the want of compensatory clauses. But if there really was a necessity for such clauses, they would soon be forthcoming. If a tenant offered his landlord double the rent for complete compensation, he would get it. Considering the enormous advantages that the tenant expects to get by compensatory clauses, this would not be too much. But the tenants do not do that because they know that they could not increase the produce so largely as to warrant it. Yet unless the production is doubled the national demand will not be met, and this is the real question, and not the farmer's profit alone, as some gentlemen seem to forget. If the tenant did get such a piece of legislation, he would not be benefited by it. The class who agitate for reform never are immediately reached by it. If there was such a rush to invest capital in land, the tenant farmers as a body would be driven out of the field by competition, for, as a rule, they have not got large capital. With the discovery of some method of doubling the meat production profitably, with the introduction of some such cattle coal (as we may provisionally term it) in the shape of new foods and new manures, with compensatory clauses and so on, when farming will really give large returns for capital invested, there will undoubtedly arise a system which will almost abolish the tenant farmer.

We may then look to a time when farming will become a commercial speculation, and will be carried on by large joint-stock concerns, issuing shares of £10, £15, or £50 each and occupying from three to ten thousand acres. Such companies would, perhaps, purchase the entire sewage of an adjacent town. Their buildings, their streets of cattle stalls, would be placed on a slope sheltered from the north-east, but near the highest spot on the estate, so as to distribute manure and water from their reservoirs by the power of gravitation. A stationary steam-engine would crush their cake and pulp their roots, pump their water, perhaps even shear their sheep. They would employ butchers and others, a whole staff, to kill and cut up bullocks in pieces suitable for the London market, transmitting their meat straight to the salesman without the intervention of the dealer. That salesman would himself be entirely in the employ of the company, and sell no other meat but what they supplied him with. This would at once give a larger profit to the producer and a lower price (in comparison) to the public. In summer, meat might be cooled by the ice-house or refrigerator, which must necessarily be attached to the company's bacon factory. The great object, as everyone knows who has been in warm climates, is to get the meat thoroughly cool directly after slaughtering, to extract the heat of the flesh and juices, and then it will keep much longer and be more valuable to the retail butcher, who purchases from the salesman, as he need not force a sale. The slaughter would probably usually take place in the afternoon, and the transit by the evening train. There is not the least difficulty in this: it is done now from Scotland, and many of the butchers in country towns almost daily send up baskets of meat to the metropolitan salesman. Unfortunately they generally send their surplus stock, or unsaleable though not absolutely uneatable goods. Our company, on the contrary, having sufficient capital at command, would select their stock from the best strains, paying special attention to their meat-carrying power. It would be preferable to keep a smaller number of large animals than a larger of small-made beasts. The latter would require more buildings and more attention. Their stalls would contain a row of beasts, as their regular stock, equal in size, beauty, and meat-carrying power to those the public now see at long intervals exhibited at agricultural shows, but very seldom get a chance of tasting. Such animals as these are rarely driven along roads; and it would be a question whether the general adoption of the stall system and superior cattle might not materially diminish the spread of contagious diseases.

Except in particular districts it is hardly probable that the dairy would be united with the stock farm; but if so the ice-house would again come into requisition, and there would be a condensed milk factory on the premises.

In the fields the policy pursued by such a company would be similar. There would be no hedges—the waste of money paid for labour in hedging and ditching throughout the country is something enormous—the land would be as far as possible laid down level, for the use of the steam plough, the scarifier, and the drill. At present the length of time that intervenes between one crop and another is a dead loss. They might try the experiment, at least, of shortening this period, and thus increasing the number of crops produced in the year. Cucumbers, for instance, essentially summer plants, are grown by artificial means at all seasons, and almost continuously. Why should not cattle food be raised in the same way —always, of course, provided that it pay, which it probably would in the future? Heat and moisture are the primary causes of growth. Water is easily applied. Heat is more difficult of application; but, for the sake of illustration, say by iron pipes carrying hot air or steam. It may yet happen to us to find electricity employed as a means of forcing crops. It has been long well known that the effects of sending an electric current through plants are astonishing; and it has been often thought that the circumstance of a good or bad crop depends much upon the state of the electrical atmosphere; and this again is by some considered to depend upon the solar spots and phenomena. With respect to artificial crops, a great degree of heat would not be necessary, for cattle and sheep food does not always need to be brought to its full perfection; in other words, to seed. Sugar has recently been used to make the plant break ground quickly (seven or eight days is spoken of); the cheaper sorts are scarcely dearer than the high-priced artificial manures, and so large a quantity is not required. There is a cheaper sugar too in existence abroad, which it has not yet been found worth while to import. There is nothing strained in the idea of an artificial harvest: grass has already been dried into hay by blasts of hot air forced upon and through it by steam power. Haymakers know full well that a hot wind will make hay faster than a burning sun. The quantity of artificial manure used by such a company would be so large as perhaps to justify its manufacture on the spot.

Evidently, whatever is done in these ways, a larger amount of skilled labour will be required. Like the great factories and manufactures, companies such as these would run up a small street or so of four-roomed houses for their own artisans—they will scarcely be called labourers in the future. Men to drive the steam-plough, to manage the valuable stalls of cattle, to work the various and complicated machinery of such an establishment, will require to exhibit intelligence hitherto lacking—lacking, perhaps, principally for want of mental exercise. Such artisans must receive higher pay, in all probability about, or nearly equal to, the wages paid in factories—from £1 and 30 shillings to £2. This will be far better than the very awkward method of low pay and a share in the concern.

Would there be any danger in such circumstances as these of the men forming a union, and, in order to keep up their wages, insisting on restricting the output of meat, just as the colliers did that of coal? And what in such an event would be the policy of the Government? Of course the inevitable railway must accompany these new conditions; or, rather, a tramway from the nearest rail would be necessary to convey the daily baskets of meat for the metropolitan market, the wool, and other produce, and to bring back the coal, etc. There would be an office in London, and the shares would be quoted on the Stock Exchange. In one word, agriculture would become a commercial enterprise. Such are some of the developments possible upon the discovery of a new food, a new manure, rendering large profits for the investment of capital. Capital there is, enough and to spare, in the market. The immense debt of France was so eagerly subscribed for, it was said, because the capitalists had so much faith in the vitality of the country and its power of recouping. That might be; but not a little of the success of the loans was owing to the vast amount of capital lying unemployed for want of an opening large enough. There is no want of capital, and no real restrictions to its application to agriculture; the only drawback is, that at present it will not pay to invest it in the soil.

The returns are not quick enough.

It may not, however, be uninstructive to contemplate the possible position of the landlord of the future. If the legislation desired by the tenant farmers were to be carried to its logical conclusion, the landlord would be reduced to a lay figure with a rent-charge on the estate. Under the old system of farming the tenant divided the whole produce of the farm into four parts: one to pay rent, one for labour, one to live on, and the fourth to put away, unless, as too often happened, this last part was swallowed up in the payment of interest on borrowed capital.

Such a division as this seemed to indicate that a farm was much more profitable than generally supposed; and the landlord's share of the produce, considering that the largest part of the capital then invested was his, i.e. the latent capital of the soil, appeared scarcely proportionable.

This inequality has increased rather than decreased, for the yield is certainly very much larger, yet the share of the landlord still remains an arbitrary amount, very little indeed if the average produce in meat alone is to reach £5 per acre. The contemplated tenant-right legislation will still further reduce the landlord's interest in the farm; in fact, he will have nothing whatever to do with it, except to receive the rent. He will have practically no power over it, either legally or morally. At present it is an object with him to see that the tenant does not permit the farm to depreciate in value. The lease or yearly agreement is drawn up upon that principle, with special clauses to prevent the exhaustion of the soil; and his agents and solicitors are constantly on the watch to see that nothing of the kind takes place. But under a tenant-right Act, the landlord has no object except to receive his rent. He would know that if the tenant depreciates the value of the farm, the amount of that depreciation will be fixed by arbitration, and the tenant will have to recoup him. On the other hand, if the tenant increases the fertility of the soil, he knows that he will have to compensate him for these improvements, and to do so is exactly equivalent to a diminution of the rent. In other words, it acts like a graduated scale: if the tenant under-farms, the landlord is compensated and receives the equivalent of a higher rent; but if the tenant over-farms, the landlord has to compensate him, i.e. to do what amounts in practice to taking a lower rent. In fact, it is a premium to the landlord to get his land under-farmed: yet this is put forward as a certain method of doubling the meat supply! A more cumbrous method of modifying the position of the landlord can scarcely be conceived. It is based upon the theory of rent. Now under modern conditions it would appear that rent, in the present acceptation of the term, had much better be abolished altogether. It would be presumptuous to attempt to lay down an exact and complete plan for the solution of a question so complicated, and which must evidently undergo many changes. But some general idea may be safely indicated. In the first place, then, the landlord should retain the full and complete possession of the soil. It is nonsense to talk of tenant-right as a right, and to deny the landlord, because he is a landlord, and for nothing else, his right. Be it observed, that if the tenant has obtained his right by ten years' occupation, the landlord has obtained his often through as many generations. The promoters of this new right are very anxious to introduce commercial principles into the matter; but what would be thought in town society if an Act were passed at the instance of lodgers or tenants enabling them to retain possession of houses and to defy the real owner? It looks very much like a scheme for the gradual absorption, not to say confiscation, of the land by the tenants. But, while retaining the landlord's full possession, perhaps it might answer to make him a partner receiving a share which fluctuated with the losses or profits of the concern. This might be peculiarly suitable if any such developments as the agricultural company described above should come into existence. Let the landlord receive a certain fixed sum under all conditions, whether of profit or loss—amounting to a percentage say of one and a half per cent. upon his latent capital—upon the value of the soil, which he invests in the speculation. If the land was worth £60,000, this would be a fixed share of say £1,000 per annum, equal to a low rent. Then, over and above this, let him receive a percentage on the receipts of the tenants, which would produce a larger or smaller sum according as the year was one of profit or loss, and according as the land was well or ill cultivated. Such a plan would make it the obvious interest of the landlord to get his land as highly cultivated as possible, and might perhaps induce him to invest cash capital in the soil, a very great advance upon the present system; there would be no necessity whatever for compensatory legislation, and it would be a natural in preference to a forced solution to the question.

No stronger sign of the break-up of the old system of farming can be adduced, than the tendency to specializing. There are farms which are entirely occupied with the production of milk. The tenant of a dairy farm finds himself near a station on a great trunk line to London. The cost of labour in making butter and cheese is something considerable, especially if, as is often the case now-a-days, his wife comes from a better class, a higher social circle, and has no traditionary aptitude for the dairy. The returns are almost immediate—they fulfil the modern demand for small profit and quick returns—and there is a very small margin of loss. He therefore turns his attention to milk, and gradually eliminates all animals from his stock that do not give a good supply. The whole economy of the farm, the amount of hay harvested, and so on, is all directed in this one groove, towards this one special object. The farm becomes specialized as a milk-farm. In other districts where there is down-land, neither very fertile when broken up into arable, nor suitable for grazing, sheep are the staple, and all the energies of the place are concentrated upon them. Such a district is the Cotteswold of Gloucestershire, where there is not only a special form of farming, but a speciality in the production, i.e. the well-known Cotteswold sheep. Other farms, again, are entirely devoted to meat production, to grazing or stall-feeding; and of late there have been instances in which not a single animal has been kept on a large arable farm, the object being to grow food for the stall-feeders, or corn. The work on these farms is done almost entirely by steam, and exhaustion of the soil prevented, first, by extremely deep cultivation, and next by the use of vast quantities of artificial manure. To judge by statistics, these gentlemen make a very good thing of it. This tendency to specialise farms shows very plainly the altered and increased demand, and the efforts being made to meet it—efforts which may possibly result in unexpected future combinations, more improbable at present than an agricultural joint-stock company.

It would seem as if the farmers as a body can effect very little to ameliorate or alter their condition, or the circumstances which surround them. They depend almost entirely upon the mood of the population: if that mood is for meat, they must change their arrangements to supply it; if the cry were corn, they could not resist it. It follows that their trade combinations—if they may be called by that name—are very powerless. Their feeble cohesion, the want of the union of many in the idea of one, is aptly shown in the chambers of agriculture which were to do so much and have effected so little. The utmost, the most strenuous and enthusiastic member of a chamber can assert that they have accomplished is, that they have enlightened the public mind to some extent, that they have introduced a Bill into Parliament, and that the Government have once or twice lent half an ear to their deputations. They have achieved nothing practical—not even the suppression of the importation of live stock, and with it contagious diseases, which at one time menaced their very existence. As to enlightening the public, that public has a grave suspicion that the chambers are very one-sided in their discussions. That would, however, matter but little as far as the obtaining an end was concerned; but they are not only one-sided, they are not one-sided enough. If politics are eschewed, which would have given them a much more vigorous life, let a pecuniary interest be called to their assistance. If the subscription were £5 or even £10 per annum, they might do something yet, and the new class of farmers who are gradually supplanting the old would not hesitate to pay that amount if they saw a closely compacted body of men sternly bent on an object. But some of them now only require a 5 shilling-yearly subscription from their members. What can be expected for that? Who can expect to coerce the Government by the expenditure of one penny farthing per week? We hear from time to time of the immense crops yielded by new soil broken in America; of corn sown thirty times in succession, and yet still producing heavily. The chambers might profitably employ their money (if they have enough, which is doubtful) in causing an analysis and careful enquiry into these extraordinary statements to be made. Perhaps the most solid advantage they have afforded the tenant farmer has been that of the analysation of manures at a very low charge, thus securing them from imposition. Other than that it is difficult to see what influence they have exerted upon the future farm. The real pioneers of progress have been isolated gentlemen, who happen to combine in themselves capital and ingenuity. These have made the experiments, sustained the heavy preliminary losses, and their results now give us some data for predicting what may be done. Their conclusions cannot be adopted in full, but the service they have rendered agriculture is incalculable. It is just possible that the vexed question of capital and labour may find a portion of its solution in the future of agriculture. The tenant-right agitation is to some extent very similar to that supported by the labouring classes, and an attempt to meet the one will in some degree tend to meet the other. The tenant is the labourer; the landlord represents the capitalist. The tenant, it is true, has capital too; but that capital is the equivalent of the tools of the labourer. If he finds his own tools, the labourer invests a certain proportion of his capital.

In the development we have contemplated of an agricultural company, a share in the concern was not given to the artisans or labourers; but that would not preclude their having a considerable plot of ground attached to their houses, to be cultivated by themselves. For the cultivation of these allotments at least they would find their own tools and their own time, both of which are equal to a proportion of capital, and the resemblance between their case and that of the tenant farmer is here complete. If a labourer receives £50 per annum, that represents the interest on £1,000 at five per cent. His labour, to pay, must therefore result in the production of £20 per cent. on this £1,000 = £200, one-half of which is represented by the increased yield, and the other half represented by the skill and time he gives. So that the fact of his employing his skill upon the farm is equivalent to his investing £100 on the soil. This is a rough calculation, not made for exactitude, but for illustration. Here, again, he resembles the tenant farmer, because the tenant, in addition to his proportion of capital, invests his skill, his acquired knowledge of agriculture, and his time, in the cultivation of the soil. When the position of the tenant towards the landlord is determined, the position of the labourer towards the tenant is also adjusted in a great measure. It may be objected that this will not apply to manufactures, and therefore no settlement of the labour question will be arrived at, because in manufactures there are only two parties, the capitalist and the labourer, while in farming there is a third, the landlord. It may possibly be found necessary to create this third party, the landlord, in a modified form, before the difficulty in the manufacturing districts can be met.

The great use of the landlord is to preserve the balance. He would say to the capitalist, 'Take your share, and no more'; to the labourer the same; 'for if either predominates and tyrannises, my interest suffers, and I shall therefore take care to prevent that'. The landlord, in fact, represents the material itself—the interest of the public at large, who have no representative in the manufactories.

These are only suggestions, but it certainly does seem as if the new conditions of farming were making a step towards the solution of that most interesting problem which, like many other great questions, will probably be adjusted by a compromise rather than by a violent change or an entirely novel state of society. The political strength of a class may be estimated by the bids or no bids made for their support by the party who believe that they are approaching power. At the present moment the agriculturists are perfectly well aware that their solid ranks are relied upon to weigh down the scale in the coming general election. But, independently of any party whatever, it is evident that, as the increasing demand for meat concentrates the attention of the nation upon them, so in proportion must their political power advance.

As the population still further masses itself in huge towns and cities, and the margin of cattle stock lying in reserve narrows itself, any unforeseen disturbance in the order of things might without much difficulty produce a crisis, when for a moment at least, the agriculturists would hold the destiny of the country in their hands.

High Pressure Agriculture

1876

Although agriculture year by year approaches nearer and nearer in methods of practice to those employed in manufacture, as yet the winter is a season of inaction, a period of repose. It is as the earth wakes up in spring that the anxieties of the agriculturist commence. The amount of labour employed during the winter is small, and though it is a drag—for such labour does not yield any appreciable result—yet it is not serious. But the moment the year begins to open, the farmer must cast about for labour, and his weekly disbursements under that head gradually grow larger, till they reach the climax in harvest. With spring, therefore, he feels the returning difficulty of high wages. The rise or fall of the wages of coal miners to the extent of 10 per cent. only causes a disturbance in the trade. A reduction of 10 per cent. has more than once caused a strike; a rise to that amount, if it has not led to a lock-out, at all events produces an appreciable effect in the price of coal. The colliery owners have an immense advantage over the farmer in the matter of wages in this very way, i.e. that if they go up 10 per cent. they can at once put on a few shillings per ton, and so recoup themselves, or, what is practically the same thing, they can limit the output at any moment, and so force up the price and decrease their expenditure. The farmer has no resource of this kind; his business cannot be conducted or regulated according to a sliding scale. His output will not admit of regulation, it depends entirely upon nature for its fluctuations, and is beyond his control. It sometimes happens that the output, the crop of wheat for instance, is too large to yield a profit, because the price will not pay; and, on the other hand, a bad season does not give sufficient to pay at any price. The coal-owner is to a great extent a monopolist, not by legal restrictions, but from the circumstances of the case. Although cargoes were imported from Belgium during the height of the coal famine, they did not arrive in quantities sufficient to do him material injury; and without any desire to reflect upon their conduct, the fact is obvious and indisputable, that practically they are now in almost precisely the position the farmers

113

were before the repeal of the Corn Laws. The object of introducing these comparisons is to illustrate the pressure of the labour question upon the farmer, who is compelled to submit to a vast increase of wages without the resource of limiting his output, exposed to foreign competition in the shape of enormous importations of wheat, and unable to effect that kind of compromise which is arrived at by the aid of a sliding scale of wages. Whether at any time in the future the agricultural labourers will reach that stage of intelligent combination which now marks the miners and others, so as to admit of arbitrators fixing the rate of payment in proportion to the state of trade, is uncertain; but what is certain is that at present the farmer, with a decreasing profit and a fluctuating market, is obliged to submit to an increasing expenditure upon labour. Ten per cent. or 15 per cent. increase is enough to cause disturbances in the iron and coal trades, where the employers are men of large wealth. The percentage of increase in the farmer's case rises to 30 per cent. in winter, and fully 50 per cent. in harvest time. But he cannot limit his output without destroying himself, and the available capital in individual cases to withstand the strain is usually very small. The actual wages paid vary in different counties, but the principle is the same everywhere. Suppose, for instance, that a farmer formerly—and within a very recent period—paid his men 9 shillings per week in winter, and 12 shillings or 13 shillings per week in summer; he would now pay 12 shillings in winter, and as high as 18 shillings in summer. These may be for the purposes of illustration taken as the nominal wages; but as a matter of fact, the men would earn more. For in winter they could get jobs at piece-work, which there would be no time to do in summer; and in the corn harvest, or as a mower, a stalwart labourer might get as much as 25 shillings. So that if an agriculturist's winter labour bill was formerly £90., he would now pay £120.; and if his summer bill were once £120., he would now pay all of £180.; and a difference of £60., let it be remembered, represents the interest on a large sum of money. In addition, women's wages have risen from 9 pence a day to 1 shilling and 3 pence, which is a long way towards double the price. Boys' wages have also increased, and they now can earn what was not long since the wages of a man. These also must be added to the labour bill. Then it is found necessary to provide the labourer with better cottage accommodation. It is true that the landlord usually erects cottages, but the tenant has to pay a percentage upon the capital so invested, say 3 per cent.; and although this is supposed to be covered by the shilling or so a week rent, yet in reality coin does not pass, and the cottage is, to all intents and purposes, thrown in. Still further, there comes the cost of the beer supplied to the labourer. Despite the advice of those who are his proclaimed friends, the labourer is still firmly

114

U. L. Sieger '79

determined to have his beer. It is surprising what a quantity they require in harvest; and, like everything else, ale has increased in price, and as few now brew at home, it represents an additional money expenditure. Half-a-crown per week for each adult labourer would be a moderate estimate; and a brewer's bill of £50. for beer consumed in harvest would not be a large one under present conditions. The increase may reasonably be put down at 10 per cent. Take then a mean or average of 40 per cent. in the actual cost of labour, 3 per cent. for cottage accommodation and sundry little conveniences—as coal conveyed free of cost—and 10 per cent. for liquors, and there is a total of 53 per cent. or, in round numbers, 50 per cent. of increase in the labour expenditure all the year round.

As before, it must be remembered that the farmer cannot regulate his output. If the corn is so abundant as to be thrown to the hogs, or if the yield is so small as to cause an overwhelming importation, happen what may, he must still pay the same price for work done. It is easy to conceive that in a business where previously the profit and loss account was very evenly balanced, the addition of 50 per cent. extra expenditure upon labour may reduce the profit to absolutely nil. There are those who object that really the payment of a few shillings more or less to a poor cottager cannot affect the position of an agriculturist who may dispose of £500. worth of corn in a single day. But no one doubts that the addition of a very small percentage of expenditure may produce disastrous effects upon concerns whose dealings are on a gigantic scale. Thus it has been found that the railway passenger duty—an impost apparently insignificant in individual cases—causes a very appreciable diminution of returns, lowers the dividends of wealthy companies, affects the shares, forces up the fares, and creates a considerable agitation. The accounts of such companies are kept in decimals—a fact in itself proving the power of apparent trifles to mount up. What would the directors of such companies say in their half-yearly reports, if almost suddenly their labour expenditure went up 50 per cent.? Probably the report would state that, in view of the necessity of keeping up a certain reserve at the bank, it would be proper to reduce the dividend from 4½ to about 2 per cent. The agriculturist also feels it hard that he should be subjected to a great increase of expenditure without the means of defending himself, and without the possibility of rapid development of his particular industry; for, while nothing has so expanded of late years as the practice of agriculture, yet that extension demands the investment of capital, which means interest, and time has to elapse before a corresponding return is obtained. During that time such interest paid on capital is a dead loss.

From these considerations it follows that the agricultural labourer is much more master of the situation than the coal miner; for his employer has no escape from his demands, except by risking a lock-out, which may ruin him. The number of colliery owners is comparatively small, and combination amongst them easy; but the farmers are a numerous class, and are extended over such wide areas that a general resistance—the only resistance really effectual—is almost impossible. A partial lock-out like that which ended in the farmer's favour so recently is of no service. The fact is patent that, despite that successful attempt, wages are as high as ever, with every appearance of rising still higher. The failure of the union as a union has made no real difference. Every agricultural labourer in the country, whether he subscribes or not, is in point of fact a unionist still in the sense of doing his best to press the farmer for more money. There are ways other than those of a downright strike by which men who are one and all agreed upon that particular point can force their employers to give them additional wages. An employer does not like to see a discontented spirit prevailing among his men, he does not like to hear continued mutterings and grumblings; he would sooner pay a shilling or two more and have his men go willingly about their work. Still less does he enjoy the knowledge that, unless his eye be constantly upon them, his work is neglected and his time wasted. He would prefer to pay more. He hates to be continually changing his labourers—to have one come for a week or two, and then, just as he is growing useful, to leave. In every respect it is better for an employer to have a man who is accustomed to the place and to the cattle, who knows his ways and wishes, and may be depended upon to be always at his post. Hitherto, however, agriculturists have failed to secure such men by the increase of wages. On the contrary, they complain that the labourers are more discontented, more fond of rambling than ever, and that it is difficult, even by paying the highest price, to get a full day's work out of them. They complain also of a species of indefinite rebellion, a disinclination to obey orders, of insolence and off-hand behaviour, which in itself is a kind of pressure. The fact that large arable farms at this moment are difficult to let, is attributable in part to the heavy outlay which such holdings imply for labour. The rise of wages has also done its part towards the substitution of grass where practicable for corn, as pasture farms do not require so many men to work them. The labour question as it applies to the land is less noisy now, but its real pressure is more severely felt than ever.

The desire not only to lower the weekly expenditure upon labour, but to obtain a certain amount of independence by reducing the number employed, has accelerated the introduction of machinery. The reaping machine, for instance, does the work of a whole gang of reapers, and the employer has it under his control. But to purchase the machine a sum of money must be expended, and so it happens that, while the product is but little increased and the profit has decreased, the capital invested is heavier than previously. An agriculturist now who has any energy at all, or any desire of success, must be prepared to expend heavy sums upon implements. The theory is that thereby a saving is effected in labour; and doubtless this is partially true—the expense of maintaining horses is also reduced. But a steam traction engine can only be used for a few set purposes, therefore the capital invested in such a purchase practically lies idle three parts of the year. There is an advantage, of course, but it is only felt when the accounts of a series of years are compared. Nowadays, the pressure upon agriculture is so great that farmers can rarely afford to look forward so long. Yet they are compelled to employ machinery, compelled to adopt modern improvements, more or less, by the irresistible march of events. The very moment the wheat is cut and carried the threshing engine goes to work, and the new crop is thrown upon the market. In old days the farmer who began to thresh his wheat so soon was looked upon as in trouble, hard up for money; and the disappearance of a new wheat-rick was the sign of approaching bankruptcy. No one wishes to return to the old condition of affairs; but the fact remains that the agriculturist is forced by the necessity of obtaining ready cash to get his wheat into the market quickly. He requires ready cash, not because he is on the verge of bankruptcy, but on account of the commercial aspect which agricultural affairs have taken of late, money circulating so much faster, and the principle of small profits and quick returns having begun to force its way in. The labour used was of old partially paid for in kind—the custom of gleaning after the reaper still remains in places as an offshoot of that practice; but now the men are remunerated in coin, and coin must be had. Therefore everything that the agriculturist can send into the market at once he hastily despatches, unless indeed he is a man of large capital, and can afford to wait till prices rise. Even the large capitalist rarely carries this plan very far, for prices do not in these days often reach high enough to give sufficient interest upon locked-up and idle money. Hay is sometimes held back in this way, and with success, but rarely by the farmer himself. The dealer is always anxious to store up hay, for he knows full well that sooner or later the market will run up to a good figure. Heavy *coups* have been accomplished by such men, but the farmer does not share in their profit. Every day the cry in agriculture, as in every other business, is louder and louder for ready money. People cannot afford to wait. The agriculturist, in addition to his primary outlay upon stock, on seed, on carts, horses, and machinery, has also to meet the annual demand of the soil for artificial manure. Formerly, the stock upon the farm produced the manure required; but now this is not sufficient, or rather it does not arrive quick enough, and the manufacturer must be called in, and of course he wants his money. The men who lay down the drainage pipes upon the farm, must be paid. There is a constant wear and tear of machinery going on, which steals away cash in driblets, but these petty sums speedily become formidable. The stock used to be fed upon the hay grown in the fields of the farm; and labour being then cheap, this hay did not seem to cost much. Very little money left the farmer's pocket in a direct manner. But now those who do not wish to be left behind in the race of agriculture must call in the aid of cake, and once again the ready-money difficulty forces itself upon the farmer. Everybody wants coin from him, and will give him but short credit; but then on his side his own returns are slow, and cannot be hastened. So to say, he has to give the earth long credit, while the men with whom he deals will only extend short credit to him, and his landlord perhaps no time at all.

The earth is not fast enough to meet the demands made upon the agriculturist. Idle earth will not hurry itself—calmly it sleeps away half the year. Early in the autumn, immediately the corn is down, the ponderous steam traction engine tears up the soil and buries the close-cut stubble. The engine must be owned or hired. In either case it must be paid for, and the coal it consumes, and a horse must be employed all day to bring it water. Generally the land is ploughed twice, then the drill and the harrow come, and these, too, must be paid for, and the man who attends to them. Sometimes it happens, as it did in many instances last season, that after the soil is prepared bad weather intervenes, and the seed cannot be sown. Then in the spring the operations have to be repeated, and a double expense is incurred. As the year advances the crop has to be hoed and then guarded from the birds. Finally, after nearly six months, the crop is garnered in; but even then, before it can be turned into coin, the threshing machine must be paid for. In the case of root crops no money even yet reaches the hand of the farmer. He must wait till sheep or cattle have eaten, digested, and turned them into wool, beef, or mutton; and pay all the while for the attendance upon such stock. So that the agriculturist turns his money over but once a year; yet he is expected to keep pace in his payments with the trader, who turns it over perhaps once a month. If this is not putting high pressure upon agriculture, what can be called high pressure? The earth is so idle; like Nature in *Faust*,

> And what to yield she does not freely choose,
> You cannot wrest from her with wheels and screws.

Not only with wheels and screws, but with drugs and chemicals, superphosphates and what not, every effort has been made to stimulate the soil. The yield has been increased very considerably, but not the number of crops in a year. The few exceptional instances where irrigation by water or sewage has succeeded do not affect the position of agriculture generally. The fact that everything connected with agriculture is in a transitional state adds to the burden. The old practice of agriculture was as fixed as the course of the sun. But no man knows now whether or not, after a heavy outlay upon fresh machines or new manure, or buildings of a special class to breed a special stock, some novel process may spring up, or some other kind of stock come into favour; and where would he be then? The certain character of agriculture is exchanged for uncertainty. This does not affect the new blood, the younger men who are supplanting the old farmers; they are educated to meet it as far as it can be met, and rapid change does not appear disastrous to them. But the young blood has as yet only partially taken the place of the old. The greater number of farms are in the hands of men who are bewildered at the altered condition of affairs, so that some very real suffering is caused, and there are even symptoms that ere long there may ensue a crisis in agriculture, just as every now and then a crisis occurs in trade. Without a doubt, the country at large profits by the pressure upon agriculture, and agriculture itself will profit ultimately, but while the grass grows it is possible for the horse to get very lean.

The very lowest classes in the country have improved in manners, dress, and language; and the agriculturist is not exempt from this species of social pressure. He find it necessary to procure a good education for his sons and daughters, otherwise the sons cannot possibly get on in life, and his daughters will never marry. But it so happens that education to the agriculturist is exceptionally expensive—to a degree not easily realised by those who dwell in the vicinity of great towns. There every facility is afforded, cheap and quick communication, open libraries, classes of all kinds at an almost nominal charge, in addition to the numerous schools and academies. The farmer whose ready-money is very small compared with the sums daily handled by men of only moderate position in towns, finds it necessary to send his children a great distance to receive their education, and this distance means money. The difficulty of education is really seriously felt in some localities, and efforts have been made to meet it, but hitherto with very poor success. Of course, good schools and colleges are as open to the farmer's sons as to any others; but the farmer cannot afford to pay the sums demanded. Yet the rising generation of young agriculturists, to keep pace with the times and with the progress of their own calling, must not only be well-grounded in general knowledge, but must be thoroughly masters of science. The education of, say, a family of five, if it is carried out only moderately well, causes an expenditure which the farmer can but just bear.

The rise of rents, accompanying as it does so many other burdens, all growing heavier at once, is also a serious item. The rise is not altogether general, or rather it is general but not simultaneous in all places at once. It usually occurs on the termination of a lease, on the death or removal of an old and valued tenant to whom a certain amount of consideration was shown, and so it may often be found that alongside a farm rented at the top-most price there runs another which pays on the scale prevalent twenty years ago. But the tendency is everywhere upwards; nor can the landlord be blamed, seeing that land has increased in value. Yet it presses heavily upon the agriculturist, who sees the percentage of return upon his invested capital sink lower and lower. On the face of it a rise of rent can nearly always be justified; but in the case of farms where the soil is unkindly and requires special expenditure, the owner should remember that he may cripple his tenant, and prevent him from improving the estate by asking too much. The rise is perhaps, in part, caused by the great results achieved in a few places by modern agriculture conducted upon scientific principles, and without limit as to cost. When people see these results they naturally think their land more valuable than before, and expect more from it. To meet the increased rental the tenant must do something; he must put on more manure and grow a heavier crop, or he must introduce a special class of stock for which he can obtain a special price; so that rent again assists in forcing up agriculture to high-pressure pitch.

Undoubtedly, also, the vast demands of a population determined to live well, exercises an immense influence upon agriculture, but this is an influence almost wholly in the farmer's favour, and though it may cause changes that are expensive, yet it ultimately yields him a profit. But the social changes brought about by that population do not altogether suit the position of the agriculturist, at least not at present. In passing the Education Acts, Parliament practically decreed the education of the agricultural labourer. But it happened that the agricultural labourer could not wholly discharge the cost of the knowledge he was to acquire. So that, as schools had to be built, the cost, either in school-board rates or voluntary contributions, fell upon the farmer. As yet but few school-boards have been established in rural districts—although, curiously enough, now that most of the required schools are built, rural opinion is turning in favour of boards—but where there are not school-boards, voluntary rates are paid. Ten or twelve pounds a year upon a moderate-sized farm may not sound a large sum to contribute towards the education of the poorer classes engaged in agriculture; but when added to the increase in other items of expenditure, it swells the total considerably. Poor rates in country parishes are still high, often very high, compared with the rates paid in large towns where there are factories with sick clubs attached, and hospitals, and where in some mysterious way the old people seem to disappear, while in rural districts they linger on on public support. Half-a-crown in the pound is too much in this age: yet at present there does not appear to be any system devised by which material relief would be afforded. Some people think that rural parishes might maintain their poor cheaper and even more comfortably at home as it were, than by sending them all to a central establishment where large sums are spent upon officials. These school rates, whether voluntary or not, and poor rates, cause a certain dislike of the tithes paid to the clergy—their pressure is felt to be heavier. Lately the turnpike gates have been removed, and the repairs of the roads fall upon each parish, or if under highway boards upon the district, to which however each parish contributes its quota. This is likely to be a cause of loud complaint unless, indeed, some action is taken by the Legislature to lighten it.

Pressure of this kind coming from all quarters naturally makes the agriculturist more irritable about the damages caused by game than he would otherwise be. The amount of relief given by the Agricultural Holdings Act is as yet unfelt, whatever it may do in the future. Summing up these facts, it will be easily understood that the practice of agriculture at the present moment is conducted under very high pressure indeed.

The Size of Farms

1874

The term 'small farm' often conveys a somewhat inaccurate meaning to those who are not intimately acquainted with rural economy. A small farm is not necessarily a small holding, though such is the usual acceptance of the phrase. There are many farms which, judged by the number of acres, would be considered large, and yet which, when tested by their capabilities for maintaining stock, are really small. It is not uncommon, on open down land, to find farms of many hundred acres which are scarcely equivalent, in what may be called their produce power, to others of hardly a fourth of their size, situated in the vale. On downs of this character the soil is exceedingly thin, a mere crust, resting upon chalk and flint. The herbage growing upon such a substratum must, as a matter of course, be small in quantity, and it consequently requires a much larger extent of land to support a given number of stock. In fact, in some places a mile more or less of down land seems of very little importance, so cheaply is it held in estimation, and so small the profit per acre. It is, of course, almost useless to manure a soil of barely four inches thick, and it is probably this very fact that renders the breaking up of down land into arable fields of doubtful utility. For the first year or two there is a fair crop, and things look hopeful. The new soil, freshly turned up to the atmosphere, and the sun, after a repose of centuries, strengthened too by the ashes of the burnt turf, possesses an amount of latent vitality which leads the farmer to remember, wistfully, the accounts he has heard of the virgin soils of America. But it is quickly exhausted, and cannot be renovated. Deep ploughing is out of the question; there is nothing but chalk and flint to turn up. Manuring with artificial manures is equally impossible, first from the cost, and secondly because there is no depth of soil to assimilate them. So that in a season or two the crops grow 'spindly' and weak, the farmer is discouraged, and ceases to take much trouble with it, and the yield, deducting the expenses, does not appreciably exceed that of the unbroken down. The attempt to turn a naturally small farm (though numerically a large one) into a really

123

great farm, has failed. It is questionable whether there would be any arable land at all upon such downs as these were it not for the extraordinary increase in the value of sheep, which stimulates the hill farmer to grow roots. Now, roots do not require deep ploughing. They are very subject to the terrible 'fly', and it has been found that the less the land is ploughed the freer the turnips are from these insects. The manure for the extent of arable land required for roots is supplied by the sheep, who are folded on it, and if he gets a wet season the hill farmer is happy. The incessant downpour, which spoils the lowland crops, is a blessing to the farmer on the thirsty downs. His turnips look fresh and green and vigorous, free from the dreaded fly. The last few years have been a time of great prosperity for these gentlemen. Whether these miles and miles of down will ever be made to produce in a proper ratio to their extent, is a question. It has been suggested that the only way to render them fertile would be to plant them with trees, and after three generations cut down the timber and burn the stumps, thus increasing the depth of soil. This is probably the only method which could be devised: and this is impracticable. Another suggestion is to employ 'quartz-mills' in grinding up the flints. It has been found that the removal of the innumerable flints from arable down land—an experiment that has frequently been tried—instead of increasing the crops, actually caused a decrease. It is supposed that the slow decomposition of the flint furnishes a species of manure, and supplies the necessary silex in which the soil is otherwise deficient. If this is the case, the grinding up of the flints would render the process of disintegration and assimilation with the soil more rapid, and consequently more effectual. These varieties of soil render the calculations made by certain enthusiastic individuals of the possible amount of national produce under more favourable conditions, very fallacious. At the same time they render almost nugatory for practical purposes the statistics collected and published by Government, of the extent of land under various crops, and the average acreage of holdings. The controversy between large and small farms cannot be safely illustrated by references to these statistics. Under present circumstances it is natural to commence the investigation of the economy of small farms with the expenditure for labour. Experience has shown that the amount of labour, and the expenditure, is disproportionately great upon small farms. The ratio may be roughly put at three to two. If it required two labourers to conduct the operations upon a farm of a given size, then three men would be sufficient to work a farm of nearly double the extent, always, of course, provided that the land was of similar quality. Consequently the expense of labour presses very much more heavily upon tenants of small holdings; and they feel this, and complain of it greatly, especially as it is almost the rule for small holdings to be higher rented than large ones. The reasons why the number of men required upon a small farm is proportionately larger, are simple enough. If only ten cows, let us say, are kept, a man must be employed to milk and fodder them; but the same man could attend to twelve or fifteen almost as easily as to only ten. On a great farm there is always plenty for the men to do. On a small one there are times when it is difficult to find the labourers employment, and yet the staff must be kept up, and the expenditure is the same. The farmer himself could easily administer double the number of acres, but his labour is confined to so small an area that half his time and abilities are wasted. Not unfrequently the small farmer has to give higher wages by a shilling or two to his men because he has not got cottages and gardens for them, while there are few large farms without these conveniences. The personal relations between the small farmer and his labourers are not so satisfactory as on the larger holding. The labourer, from seeing his master work beside him in the fields, from daily conversation, and from seeing the shifts to which his employer is often put, loses a good deal of his respect, and becomes unpleasantly familiar. He feels that his master is to some degree under an obligation to him, and he is not restrained by any feeling of delicacy from making him see that fact. The labourer knows that if he were to suddenly leave, his master would be in the greatest difficulty, especially if it was a busy season. His place could not be immediately supplied, and the loss of two or three days may sometimes be very serious. But the large farmer, if a man goes, has only to draft a part of his staff employed on other duties to fill up his place till a successor arrives. The important tasks are continued; only the unimportant are neglected. Day by day the relations of the small farmer to his labourers grow more and more unpleasant. The pressure of the labour question falls very heavily upon him. As the number of men he employs is disproportionately great, so the rise of wages affects him comparatively much more than the large farmer. Instead of being independent of his men, he is dependent on them. He cannot order them to do this or that. He is forced to take them into his confidence, to ask their opinion if it would be better to do so-and-so today, or not, and very often gives way, and allows them to do what his judgement disapproves. This sounds almost absurd, but it is, nevertheless, strictly true. It is common to hear tenant farmers of small holdings complaining that they have to beg their men as a favour to do the work, to remonstrate with them, and point out the why and wherefore this or that should be done. The consequence is that, even when the men are got to work, they do it in an idle, listless manner, taking their time about it, pausing to look at the time and the weather. They have no fear of displeasing their employers, no fear of being discharged. This indifference to the work in hand is not characteristic of the labourers employed by the small farmer alone, it is the case with all, but it is felt more by him because he is forced into closer personal contact than the larger farmer. The complaint that the men will not work is common all over the country. The increase of wages has made no improvement: if anything, rather the reverse. They are slow to come in the morning; quick to go at night. They prolong the luncheon hour to its extreme limit, but they exact their wages to the uttermost farthing, whether earned or not. The Labourers' Union may have increased this idleness, but it is not altogether caused by the sense that there is a power in existence which will support them against their employer. In former times there was no work for the inhabitants of rural districts but on the farms, and there was, as a result, a plethora of labour. There were more men than the farmers could find full work for. They were only too glad, therefore, to get hired for a year. If that system only gave them low wages in summer and during harvest, it secured them against want in the winter, when employment was difficult to obtain. But now the railways, the collieries, the mines, the factories, and other great commercial enterprises at home and abroad, absorb the raw material of labour, and render the demand in the agricultural districts greater than the supply. Instead of having to search for an employer, the employer has to search for a man. The labourer knows that, if discharged, he can move a mile or two further on and find plenty of work. He therefore feels independent, and the stimulus to make himself valuable by exertion is removed. It is not in human nature to be otherwise, except under conditions of high moral and intellectual training. But in the labourer the primeval instincts are found in their broadest, most unabashed form. It is not a pleasant position for the small tenant farmer to have to meet this species of subdued insolence every day of his life. With the large tenant farmer it is different. He is not dependent upon a man or two. If he discharges one he has another working in a distant field to supply his place. He is better able to meet the altered conditions of agricultural life. His resources are more elastic. He can keep up a bold independent tone with his men, and they respect him all the more. He has two or three cottages, perhaps more, on his farm, with large gardens; these are always sought after, and give him the command of a permanent staff. The fluctuation of the labour market does not touch him so closely. Personally he escapes the annoyances of the altered tone of the labourer. There is an inherent instinct in the labourer to respect the tenant of a large farm. Let the tenant of a small one be a gentleman in his manner and way of life; let him be richer than his neighbour; still the prestige clings to the number of acres. The large farm is better for the labourer than the small one in many ways, and becomes more so daily as the labourer grows less a fixture, and contracts the habit of wandering and of migration. On a small farm, after the more important tasks are finished, after the busy season is over, there is little to do. But on the large one there is a constant succession of varied employment, and more piecework, that desideratum of the labourer. On a small farm he can only earn exceptionally high wages at one or two particular periods of the year; but on the large one there is almost always an opportunity of making extra money. Then there is the machinery used on a great holding—he becomes gradually acquainted with the method of managing that, and so of growing into a skilled workman. A great farmer usually has one or more bailiffs; besides head men, head carters, head shepherds, &c. All these offer opportunities of rising in life, especially the place of bailiff. It is not uncommon to find a bailiff, who was nothing but a day labourer at first, living in a farmhouse and having the sole charge of several hundred acres. In the process which has so long been going on of absorption of small farms, it often happens that the annexation of a small farm to a large one leaves a farmhouse unoccupied. Then a bailiff is placed in it, and takes charge of the land which was originally a separate holding. He is well paid, has some perquisites, and saves a little money. He not unlikely marries a dairymaid—no bad match, however lowly it may sound. The dairymaids of these days are not the dairymaids of old. They receive first-rate wages, even as high as £40 a year. They are well treated in the family, and are often women of a superior class. They almost always save money. From the union of a bailiff and a dairymaid have sprung many well-to-do farmers, whose sons are in farms now. But when the bailiff becomes a farmer, then he finds the utility of small farms. He has neither the capital nor the interest to obtain a large one. He goes into a small one for the present. Large farms are therefore, on the whole, better for the labourer than small ones. The simple labourer has a chance of earning more extra money upon them, there are more positions of trust and emolument, and there is a road to the goal of his ambition. But the small farms have their use in enabling men, who could not otherwise enter the list of farmers, to become their own masters. Whether this is for the advantage of the community is another matter.

The small farmer who trots into market on his cob, or drives in in his trap, has to take a subordinate position at the market ordinary. His place is not near the chairman—his seat is not fixed: and, secondly, it is not reverently kept waiting for him till it suits his convenience. He has to find room where he can. The landlord does not watch for his appearance to issue the order to remove the covers. It is not unlikely that his cheque would be honoured for a larger amount than that of the gentleman who sits at the head of the table; but a thousand pounds do not go so far with him as five hundred with the other in attracting the respect of his fellows. The broad acres tell. There is a prestige, a lingering remnant of the importance attached to the land in feudal times, hovering round the tenant of a great farm. Commonly, too, he is regarded as the *alter ego* of his landlord, the squire, and not seldom of the peer. He has easy access to the mansion of the landed proprietor as the principal tenant. He enters freely into conversation with that magnate, is invited to dinner parties, sometimes even shoots in the same company. At election times he goes round canvassing with the candidate himself. At the hunt he is recognized by the gentry. The clergyman dines with him. He is an agriculturist. A small tenant is only a farmer. There is a vast difference in the meaning of these two words. If a chamber of agriculture is formed the large tenant is elected as the chairman; the small tenant is only asked to be a member. As chairman the 'agriculturist' perhaps waits on the Chancellor of the Exchequer as one of a deputation, and exchanges a few words with the Minister. He may even keep a racehorse (steeplechaser) without incurring the charge of extravagance from his fellows. The line is as marked between him and the small farmer as between the latter and the labourer. The small farmer naturally aspires to this sort of distinction. Yet most small farmers declare that they regard the increase of large farms, and the decrease in the number of small ones, with much regret. But the paradox resolves itself easily into this: the more small farms there are, the less the influence and social superiority of the large farmer.

Small farms are almost always rented higher than large ones, supposing the quality of the land to be equal. A similar fact is that small freehold farms sell at more per acre than those of double the size. The larger the farm the cheaper it is rented, even in hard cash, and there are circumstances not recognized in the agreement which make small farms dearer still. It is only lately that tenant farmers have taken to keeping account books. To a person accustomed to commercial enterprises, with the profit and loss sharply defined, the accounts, say of a small dairy farm, would prove utterly unintelligible. He might find the tenant apparently prosperous, putting by a small sum yearly, the land itself in good condition, and yet when he came to reckon up the expenditure and the income, they would, nine times out ten, but just balance each other. How, then, he would ask, is the profit made? First, there is the house and garden and orchard rent free. Then there are an innumerable number of small economies too minute to be put on paper, and an equally innumerable number of small sources of income which it is almost impossible to keep an account of. One year, perhaps, there is an extra crop of hay, of which the tenant is permitted to sell a considerable amount. Another, by careful management, he contrives to fatten two or three good beasts for the butcher at Christmas, on what might be termed the leavings of the place, supplemented with a little oilcake. The profits are somehow squeezed in. The primary idea is to manage so that the farm shall be self-supporting, and then the little extras go to profit. How to strictly define these no one can exactly tell. But they certainly do exist. On a small farm the margin of these extras is exceedingly contracted. With the increasing size of the farm under consideration they enlarge in a geometrical ratio. The buttermilk and general leavings of a small farm will only keep a few pigs; on a large farm a great number can be kept without adding a penny to the expenditure. When hay is sold it is in quantities that add a heavy figure to the income. All the little economies and the little sources of income swell up to a large sum. Yet the large farm is more cheaply rented than the small one. So that really two or three shillings per acre ought to be added to the nominal rent of a small farm when its in-comings and outgoings are compared with a large one. On arable farms, where profit and loss are more sharply defined, the same thing takes place. The very waste of a large farm will keep almost as much stock as a small one. Comparatively it takes more capital to stock a small farm than a great one. The occupier of a small farm does not enter upon life with any equal chance. His neighbour of a great holding, though at first he began with scarcely any more capital, soon begins to turn over heavy sums. When such sums pass through the hands every year, some amount is sure to remain in the fingers if only a little ordinary care is taken. Somehow, earth seems more generous cultivated in extensive areas. The small farmer can rarely employ machinery. His capital is not large enough, nor indeed, if he had the capital, his holding is not large enough to warrant him in sinking a thousand or two in steam-ploughing tackle. If he is well off he can generally hire a steam-plough, it is true; but then, unfortunately, the majority of small farmers are anything but well off. They commence life with capital barely sufficient to stock their farms. Here and there a farm may be found which, however poorly cultivated, is so rich in its soil that the occupier cannot help but gradually improve in his circumstances. But there are scores of other farms which, with ordinary cultivation, only just pay their way. If they were highly cultivated they, too, could pay fairly. But the tenant has no capital. He cannot even afford to hire the steam-plough. He can only use artificial manures in the most sparing manner. At the end of twenty years he is just where he began; with this difference, he has a wife, and perhaps half-a-dozen children. The case is perfectly hopeless for him, and he knows it. It weighs on him. No amount of work, of care, of self-denial, can stave off that thickening cloud of debt which

130

gathers slowly around him. He moves about his place in a dull, listless manner. He cannot properly educate his children. There are no good middle-class schools within the reach of his income. The so-called middle-class schools are far above him. He could, perhaps, pay £40 per annum for one boy, but not for two or three. Then there are the girls. He must have a governess for them, or let them run wild. Education is a serious problem to the small tenant farmer. He feels it more and more day by day. Illness in his family would eat up the whole profits of a prosperous year. His boys have no chance of entering farms when they grow up. In the first place, he cannot advance them any capital nor borrow any, for the local bank perfectly well knows what difficulties he is floundering into. Neither can he get them farms by personal interest with influential men. There is an odour of ill-success about him—it clings to his name. Landlords like successful men. Tenant farmers in this position feel it bitterly. They complain that they are ground up between two mill-stones. There is the landlord and the inexorable rent upon the one side; there is the ever-increasing cost of labour upon the other. To add to the burden comes the question of education and the high price of every necessity of life. It is hard, while struggling under these oppressive burdens, to hear themselves abused as wallowing in the wealth that they wring by tyranny from the sweat of the labourer's brow, to be accused of drinking champagne while the labourer starves. Those who live in agricultural districts, and are acquainted with the circumstances of tenant farmers, have only to look around them to see that six out of nine small tenants are in a state of insolvency. They keep on from year to year, and, after a fashion, pay their way; but if their assets were reckoned up they would fall short of their liabilities. It is very questionable whether small farms are a national advantage. It may be said that if more capital was employed on them they would be as good as large ones. Unfortunately, however, more capital never will be employed on them. Men who have any amount of capital at command will not settle down on a small farm. It does not pay sufficient interest on the outlay. If they farm at all they take large farms, where there is scope for enterprise and high cultivation. Men of capital, too, naturally look to take a certain social position. It may be merely a prejudice; but prejudices are very powerful, and they know that social status attaches to the great tenant, and not to the small one. In a merely mechanical sense the small farm offers obstacles to high cultivation. There cannot be large fields on a small farm. Without large fields the steam-plough is comparatively of little use. Everything militates against small holdings in these days. The primary idea of farming in former times was economy. The tenant endeavoured to expend as little money as possible upon his farm. He bought no manure;

131

all he used was produced on his own premises. He made money by saving, by the practice of the severest utilitarianism, by a system of paring and scraping. Now, the primary idea is speculation—the laying out of money with a view to its return with interest. It can hardly be called speculation, for in its present meaning that word has an insecure sound, and these enterprises are, with common care and ordinary circumstances, sure to be successful. The outlay of an additional £1 per acre on manure, or better cultivation, is certain to be repaid. It is, therefore, speculation in its most legitimate sense. The small farm gives no scope for enterprise of this kind. It is, essentially, a business of small economies—the modern practice cannot be profitably applied to it. Yet there is probably no land in England so highly cultivated as the allotment grounds let out to the labourers, and these are the smallest farms in the world. They are rented at very small sums, yet they return more per acre to the landlord than the extensive areas leased by the rich farmer. The amount of produce they bring forth in a year is nearly double that of the ordinary farm.

If all England was cultivated on the allotment system, there would be no fear of famine, let the population increase in what ratio it pleased. Some even think that in the end it will come to this: that nothing less will meet the imperative demand for food. Why, then, if this is the case, are small farms not so useful as large ones? The small farm is too large to be cultivated with the spade, and to receive that minute attention which is bestowed upon the allotment garden; but at the same time it is too small to be treated with the steam-plough, the expensive manure, and general high cultivation system. Looked at, therefore, from the point of view of the increasing population, it becomes a question whether England will have to be turned into a vast allotment-ground, or will be thrown into a comparatively small number of hands, and cultivated on what may be called the steam-plough system. In either case the small farm falls through. There will be no place for it, except, perhaps, in the neighbourhood of cities, where a small farm is a species of market-garden. The produce of the steam-plough system is, per acre, nearly equal to that of the spade, and it is much more manageable, more in accordance with the spirit of the times.

It would, however, be foolish to prophesy the prevalence of any method. Time was when there was nothing so changeless, so fixed and unalterable, as farming: nothing so conservative. Now there are few occupations which alter so much in a few years' time. New plans, new inventions and discoveries, follow each other in constant succession. The capabilities of agriculture seem inexhaustible. The number of clever and intellectual men who turn their attention to it multiplies daily. It has its colleges, its professors, its students. Mind is at work devising new forms of machinery to develop the resources of nature. It would require a great volume to describe the machinery alone that has been contrived of late years, and is now in the market. The chemistry of agriculture would fill many more such volumes. Geology, botany, entomology, almost all the sciences, are pressing forward to its aid. What developments may be in store no man can safely foretell, though the direction of the stream can be indicated. The small farm appears doomed. There are places, of course, where a small farm may be preferable. Take say a hundred acres of marshy pasture land under a wood overrun with rabbits and choked with coarse furrow-grass; put a sturdy, half-educated, rude man of the old school in charge of it. By denying himself everything but the commonest necessities, working like a slave, regardless of personal comfort, he may, in the course of twenty years, if he remains single, put by a small sum for his old age, together with a plentiful provision of rheumatism. Perhaps this *may* be preferable. But surely it would be better to drain the marsh, grub the wood, destroy the rabbits, and keep a good stock, by throwing such a tenantry into connection with an adjoining farm. It is said that the advantage of small holdings is, that they foster a band of independent and yet not wealthy men, the yeomen of England, and pride of the nation. It may have been so in former times. Men will not take a small farm now, unless compelled to do so by their circumstances. Consequently, most small farms are in the hands of men little better than labourers, as ignorant and as prejudiced against improvement.

The size of a useful farm may be put at 250 acres at the lowest, and so upwards, 300, 350, 400. Such farms are within the reach of men of any capital—they are large enough for the introduction of most modern improvements, and they are within the management of a single person. They may be properly termed useful holdings. A tenant with 350 acres of fair land, with a reasonable rental and proportion of capital, ought to produce highly, and so be a beneficial member of society, and to put by considerable sums. Over 400 acres the capital required for full development of the soil rapidly increases in amount. The labour bill rises, because more head-men, bailiffs, carters, shepherds, etc., must be employed, and these very properly receive higher wages as trusted servants. The tenant cannot be his own bailiff, he cannot be master and foreman too. At 800 acres an area is reached which will allow of farming on the very highest and noblest scale. From this to 1200 or 1500, the agriculturist can use his own steam-plough, and feel that he has invested capital in the purchase of such expensive implements, with profit to himself as well as benefit to his land. He employs a number of labourers and other hands, and such a tenantry approaches more nearly to the manufactory in the good it does to the neighbourhood. The utility of bringing up a race of students instructed in chemistry, geology, entomology, mechanics, etc., in agricultural colleges, with the assistance of professors, if they are afterwards to be placed on small farms, is a matter of much doubt; they would have no room for the exercise of their attainments. Not many years ago a cry was raised that the nation would be ruined, if the process of throwing small farms together so as to make one large one was continued. Farm-houses, it was stated, would be found empty in all parts of the country—the hearth cold, no smoke rising from the chimney—quite a pathetic picture. But the abolition of the race of men who dwelt in these farm-houses, most of them, by-the-by, mere cottages, is a boon to agriculture. They were a race who did as their fathers did before them; who let the rich liquid manure from the cowyards trickle out into the first natural hollow, and there accumulate in ponds before their very doors, festering and poisoning the air, instead of spreading it out upon the land, and doubling the yield of grass. These were the men who were hard to their labourers, stinting their pay to the lowest fraction, exacting the uttermost farthing. They are nearly gone now, vanished from the face of the earth. Their successors with double the number of acres employ more than double the number of labourers, and pay them nearly twice as much, while producing far more for the community at large. There is not the slightest cause for real alarm in the tendency to group small farms; no comparison whatever, as has been attempted, with the state of rural Italy in the latter days of Imperial Rome, when the soil was owned by a few lords, and cultivated by gangs of slaves. Our labourers have shown that they have not the remotest intention of allowing themselves to become slaves, and they are in reality more free and independent under a system of large than of small farms. There is not so much chance of prying interference with their habits and conduct out of the master's time. The great farmer is so far removed above their level that he has no time nor inclination to keep a minute record of their actions, their intermarriages, and quarrels. The old style of small farmer was so little removed from their own sphere that he took a lively interest in their personal proceedings, which at times was capable of being resolved into a tyrannical interference. It is the large farmer who builds new and good cottages for his labourers, or who induces his landlord to do so. From a national point of view the chief object is to get the full value out of the soil. Let anyone take a train through an agricultural county, and mark the difference, the striking contrasts every mile almost will reveal. Here is a network of small fields of all shapes, triangular, with corners in which it is difficult to make hay for the shadow and damp, and enclosed with great hedges, thick as small copses, and which, if measured, would amount to a fourth the size of the ground: this is the small farm. Further on is a broad expanse of open land, level as a die, well-drained, without hedges to shelter birds and occupy the valuable space: this is the large farm.

The small farmer is almost always a dairyman. There are very few arable farms small in the sense of a small dairy farm. There are scores of dairy farms under forty acres, and not a few less than twenty. But arable farming would be almost impossible under such conditions. The arable farm is essentially a large one. The pasture is rented much higher than the arable, yet the latter generally produces most, not, perhaps, in the tenant's profit, but in food. This is because there is a succession of crops. The pasture land has but one crop. Efforts have been made recently to produce more than one in a season by manure, or by sewage, and they are successful in a measure; but they cannot be universally applied. The amount of labour employed in a pasture farm is much smaller than on an arable one: this, too, is in favour of the arable, so far as the labourers are concerned. Pasture farms never, or scarcely ever, reach the size of arable. Scarcely any improvements in agriculture or in stock have originated or been perpetuated upon pasture land. The high-bred short-horns could not be carried to their perfection on pasture alone; they require the products of the arable farm. The magnificent Cotswold sheep are bred in an arable district. The steamplough, the artificial manure, the hundred inventions of modern times, are applicable to the arable, not the pasture farm. The small-pasture tenantry remains pretty much where it was twenty years ago. In a few instances sewage has been applied, and on the more extensive holdings there has been an attempt at draining. Some have ambitiously applied the stall system, and many more have so far retrograded, that they sell their milk to the London dealers, and even let out their cows to a middleman. This may pay for the time, but it does not look like the improvement which results in an increased produce. For the rest, they are where their forefathers were before them; the same old routine of foddering, milking, hedge-cutting; haymaking—nothing new, or likely to yield a pound's weight more meat for the increasing population. But the arable farmer, even though the extent of his holding is comparatively small, is compelled to advance, or he would be driven off the ground entirely. He must drain a little, plough a little deeper, use a little artificial manure, let him be never so poor. It is questionable whether many of the old stock of small farmers, who contrived to amass money, did so purely and simply by farming. This applies, of course, to the period succeeding the repeal of the Corn Laws. Previously to that, a man might make money on a small farm. Since then, however, the small farmers who have made money have a reputation for having done so in a way little suspected by the townsman who envies their prosperity, and looks with a longing eye upon the lowing herds and green fields. They were nothing more nor less than usurers, many of them. They lent the little money they had got to their neighbours at exorbitant interest. As soon as a farmer, by scraping and small economies, had saved up a few hundreds, he looked round him, and soon saw a man struggling against a bad season, ill-luck, or a large family, and lent him money as the dreaded rent-day drew on. Thus the few hundreds grew at heavy interest. Under the small-farm system there was never a time when a borrower was not forthcoming. With the small farmers there can be little cause for the cry for compensation for unexhausted improvements, because they never make improvements. Very few indeed have leases: it is generally a yearly tenancy.

A man is said to farm the revenue, to farm the customs or tolls: that is, he gives a certain price for them, and makes his profit by minute economies, by personal labour, and from chance accidents in his favour. This is the primary meaning of farming. In this sense it is almost certain that the days of farming are numbered. The very agitation for compensation for unexhausted improvements implies that the farm is taken with the view of increasing its productiveness; and to do that requires expenditure.

There will be no farmers, in the old sense of the word, after a while. The tenant under the modern method becomes the landlord for the time being. He wishes to till the land as if it was his own, and that he or his descendants would reap the benefit in after years. But the small farmer is essentially a man of economies—of parings. He wishes to get his profit out of it without putting anything in it first. Certain men have an unenviable reputation for this. They take a farm on the year's-notice-to-quit method. They neither manure it, nor dig it, plough it, nor keep it clean. They employ scarcely any men. It is their profit to reduce the expenditure. They get all they can out of it, and then, after half-a-dozen years, when the land shows signs of exhaustion, they leave it and go elsewhere. If the tenant requires protection against the landlord, the landlord requires protection against such tenants as these. They usually favour small farms, because removal from a large farm is a serious matter, and the obscurity of a small tenancy allows their nefarious designs to pass comparatively unnoticed till it is too late.

A great deal has often been said about the sturdy independent British farmer, whose freedom from interference and contempt of tyranny was matter for admiration and envy. The facts are rather different when he is the tenant of a small farm, and living on borrowed capital, as seven out of ten are. Small debtors are always more worried than large ones—over whom a certain amount of paternal care is exercised—and he is a small debtor. The bank looks after him sharp, so does the landlord's agent, who thinks the rent risky; so do the tradesmen. If the landlord's agent is at all a disagreeable person, his lot is indeed happy, almost as enviable as that of a 'toad under a harrow', to use an old agricultural simile. The margin between profit and loss is extremely small and rigid. But a large farm, on the contrary, is wonderfully elastic. If there is a falling off on one side, there is something to make it up on the other. Even if the rent be behindhand, the landlord will be cautious how he proceeds to extremities. It is not so easy to get a suitable tenant for a great farm. Allowances have to be made on both sides.

Whether it be considered from the tenant's own side, or from the labourer's, or from the landlord's, the balance of argument appears to be indisputably in favour of large farms. To the nation, to the ever-increasing population, the large farm offers a greater present produce, and possibilities of still further development. The political economist, who judges the prosperity of an occupation by the amount of capital attracted towards it, must also decide in its favour, for capital will never flow into small farms.

Weather and Wages in the Country

1879

In the last days of July the wheat has begun to show some trace of colour. Looking across a field, upon a slope where the glance can travel along the tips of the ears, a faint change of hue is visible. The yellow, indeed, has not yet come, but the green is going. Hard by, the barley, too, has altered and grown a little whiter as it waves in the breeze. Some few hours of sunshine at intervals have effected this, and given hope not only to the farmer but to the agricultural labourer. For two months those who every year look forward to haymaking for the extra money then paid have been waiting and despairing under almost continuous rain. Many men, women, and indeed whole families, who have travelled by road long distances from home to districts where hay crops are usually forward, have had to live for weeks without work. Just as the wheat and barley in more favoured districts begin to show signs of ripening, the hay harvest has at last commenced; and not till now. Here in the meadows the mowers are as busy as they usually are early in June. These travelling labourers have had to endure much hardship—hardship that has driven numbers of them away, unable to wait till the sun shone. The practice of travelling about for employment has much increased of late years among agricultural labourers, so that the suffering from this cause has been widespread. Again, the aged men in the villages who cannot work much look forward to spring and summer as a time when many tasks fall to them, and so supply some change of food and other necessaries. But they have this year had nothing to do. All the early spring the frost and severe weather prevented them working in the fields. Since then the rain has driven them back. The usual hoeing and weeding could not be done; and these poor old men, who live a hard life at the best of times, lost their usual opportunity. The same thing happened with the women who go haymaking, and who for the past two months have been watching for the rain to cease. Although far fewer women now work at harvest in the field, yet to those who still continue to do so the weather has been a serious matter. It is these people—the fringe as it were of the

138

agricultural labouring class—who have hitherto suffered most. The travelling families, the old men and women, have lost months of time, and of course the equivalent in money.

The regular agricultural labourers who work from year's end to year's end on the same farms have felt the stress of the weather, but in a different way. They have received their wages, but these wages have not been so profitable, for the following reasons. The extreme length of the winter caused the cottager to expend much of his slender store, or to mortgage his future harvest money, for fuel, food, or clothes. Then the frost destroyed his hope of a good garden crop of green vegetables. The labourer is a large consumer of such vegetables, and that is why a garden or an allotment is of so much importance to him and his family. To those who possess a good income the scarcity of garden produce in the spring and its high price was only a thing to grumble about. It meant a little more money to pay the greengrocer, but it did not mean deprivation. The cottager, however, had to suffer privation, and indeed still has at this moment, in one of his principal supports. Though meat and bacon are more largely consumed now than formerly, yet bread and vegetables are still of the utmost importance. The garden spring crops failed, and now it is by no means certain that disease will not destroy the potato yield. To those who have families this loss is not easily supplied. Such of the children, too, as had passed the school age could not find employment, but were compulsorily idle. In these indirect ways the regular labourer has had to endure a certain amount of discomfort. But what concerns him most is the question of the future. Will wages—not harvest but regular and winter wages—continue at their present rate? If landlords are compelled to lower their rents, if farmers have in so many cases been obliged to give up business altogether, if the price of cattle, sheep, produce, and even milk declines, can wages remain unaffected? It is too early yet to form a decided opinion; but it would seem against the obvious drift of circumstances if wages do not fall. Of course while the harvest impends farmers will retain their men at any sacrifice. It is also a point in favour of the labourer that in seasons of this kind machinery is of less avail. Farmers will have therefore to rely more upon manual labour when the weather clears. This fact probably had an adverse influence upon the business done by the implement exhibitors at the Kilburn Show. Agriculturists who could foresee the state of their crops would scarcely invest with such a prospect, knowing that they must put more hands on. If these delicious gleams of sunshine continue it is not at all impossible that there may be for a short time quite a demand for men. But, if we look forward to the time that must come after harvest, it scarcely seems likely that the recent high rates of wages can be maintained. The

harvest protects the labourer from the stress that has fallen upon the farmer, and in a sense upon the landlord. But the approach of winter may put a different aspect upon the case. Then comes the question of food. How fortunate it has been for the labourer that the foods upon which he relies—excepting garden produce—have been so cheap and abundant. Bread has been cheap; bacon and cheese cheap—so cheap that the English farmer can hardly produce either of these things without a loss at present prices. But if wheat rises, bread of course must rise with it; and this at once goes home to the cottage, where the loaf is all-important. It is even possible that the expected rise may prove temporary only; for we have not yet learned the power of America to supply us when once the dollar tempts the shipper. Cheap food will still come; but if the cottager has not the money to pay for it, a difficulty arises in that way. He has as yet had no opportunity of accumulating the usual summer savings.

The farmer has this season had to pay for profitless labour. Week after week, and even month after month, he has been obliged, by the necessity of retaining his men, to pay almost the same amount of money as if his work had been going on satisfactorily; whereas all the while little or nothing has been done. His ingenuity, indeed, has been taxed to the utmost to invent odd jobs—that might as well never have been thought of—to keep his men from idleness. Naturally, when the harvest is over the farmer will think seriously of reducing his expenditure on labour.

Altogether, it seems clear that towards the fall of the year the labourer will begin to feel in a direct way a full share of the pressure now weighing upon his employer.

The Gentleman-Farmer

1877

He comes striding over the fallow, a gun on his arm, a pipe in his mouth, and a dog at his heels. A tall loose-jointed young fellow—for his bones are not yet 'set', and the country air prolongs the period of growth—with plentiful indications of whiskers and moustache. His trousers are turned up (your old-fashioned farmer always wore gaiters) to preserve them from getting soiled; his cuffs are somewhat wrinkled, but he will change them before dinner; and 'There's the bell, by Jove!'—for his tutor, the big tenant-farmer, or rather agricultural capitalist, sits down at six, rings in his guests, and has a man-servant to wait at table and fill his pupil's glass with wine. If the new novels have not come up from Messrs. Smith & Son's bookstall and library at the station—whither the groom rides daily to fetch them—and if the squire or the rector has not sent round a pressing invitation, the pupil mounts his bicycle, and takes a 'run' into the market-town. As he glides along the smooth road (which, by the bye, in a year or two will not be quite so smooth, now the turnpikes have dropped in, and the parish has to repair it) a ploughman remarks to his master, a *working* farmer—observe that—as they lean against a gate,

He be a spruck un!
Ay, ay, John; I allers zed it 'ud come to no good when um zet up a aggericulturul college!

At the market-town our friend meets a few choice spirits at the billiard-table, and 'knocks the balls' about at pool. At a quarter-past eleven, when the house by law should be shut, he quits the green cloth for the bar, where the favoured *habitués* are sipping the sweetest, i.e. forbidden, glass of the evening; and after glancing at the sporting-paper, consults in a corner with the landlord, who is a bookmaker on a pretty extensive scale under the rose. Having made an entry or two in a certain small pocket-book, chaffed the barmaid, and gallantly lifted his hat to the buxom landlady (who pronounces him '*such*' a gentleman!') he starts for home as the church-clock tolls midnight, while the policeman on the beat carefully looks round the corner the other way, mindful of many a fee. Slipping in by a latchkey, our studious pupil finishes his pipe in bed, and drops off to sleep, perhaps dreaming of the old song,

'We be all jolly fellows what follows the plough!'

Breakfast about ten—the raw mists have rolled away by then—in his own special corner by the bay-window looking out on the lawn and flower-beds. His letters are there on a silver salver, and the morning paper, unopened and smelling of printer's ink, lies beside them. His host's daughter is there, and laughingly pours out his coffee, and contrives to make it precisely to his fancy. There are the breast of a pheasant, some kidneys, a ham, and a few other trifles to pick from, or pitch at Jip, who sits at his feet and 'yaps,' if his lips are dry and palate parched after last night. A glance at the sporting correspondent's news, a yawn or so, and then—to business. Throwing the breechloader over his shoulder, he stalks through the turnips, zigzagging towards a noise of panting and puffing, and a column of black smoke yonder. Bang, bang! right and left, by Jove! Picking up the partridges with a passing thought of bread-sauce, he makes his way to where the steam-ploughing engines are at work, and, choosing a comfortable sheltered corner under an oak, sits down upon the dry bank in the warm sunshine to study the operations. There is something very soothing in the hum of the flywheels, and gradually the scene fades out of sight; sweet slumber settles upon him, till a tall greyhound dashes up and licks a fly off his nose, and a jovial voice cries, 'Now, Tom; lunch-time, my boy!' So they stroll home together, Tom and his master, who tells him a sly story, and jerks his thumb in his ribs, while they shout with laughter, and the startled rooks rise with a loud 'Caw!'

After lunch Tom thinks he will stretch the mare on the downs; and returning about four finds lawn-tennis in full swing, and three or four ladies charmingly attired, who form a very pretty foreground to the ancient rambling, red-tiled, and ivy-hidden house. There is some decent champagne at dinner; and, on the whole, things are tolerably comfortable. You would hardly think, if you sat at that well-appointed table and glanced at the furniture and the pictures on the walls and the silver prize-cups yonder, sipping your champagne and trifling with fish or game, that agriculture was going to the dogs. But you might perhaps begin to realize that the big agricultural capitalist is a latter-day plant, which his landlord, even though he have a title, finds it necessary to cultivate skilfully and conciliate socially. Tom, having just returned from his holiday ramble to Paris, or some other continental pleasure centre, has plenty to talk of, and presently is in request at the piano, and does not acquit himself badly.

When these things come to pall a little the season grows cooler, and the scent begins to lie, and our friend becomes very busy indeed, for he has to attend a meet of the hounds almost every morning. The capitalist, his tutor, has three or four, or even six, hunters in his stable, and Tom has to keep them up to their work; the tutor rides a stone or so too heavy for the younger horses. Besides which Tom has a mare of his own, which he is 'making', and which he risks his neck to show off, with a shrewd notion of selling and clearing a fifty before long. For although an idle dog in the eyes of the working farmers round about, our pupil is far sharper in the ways of this modern world than they are, and is wide awake to the advantage of making a circle of acquaintances at the Hunt who may be useful to him hereafter. Should frost interfere with these pursuits, there are the snipes to be knocked over in the water-meadows, and that woodcock they flushed in the double mound, where the spring bubbles up and does not freeze, to be looked after. Or better still, there is the rabbit-ferreting going on in the squire's covers, which affords first-class practice, and plenty of it. There are few places more lively than the end of a great sandy bank riddled with burrows when three or four 'pugs' are busy inside, with their red eyes and somewhat butcher-like tastes. The bunnies come tumbling out here, there, and everywhere—popping from one hole to the other, darting across to the wood there, slipping up the ditch, dodging behind trees and stumps and boulder-stones, and doing everything, in fact, except give you time to take aim. The keeper stands on one side of the hedge, Tom watches the other, two assistants are in the ditches attending to 'pug', and the firing is something to listen to—a perfect Plevna for the brown-coated creatures. In the rear, note a mighty jar of October ale, and altogether, even in frosty weather, Tom contrives to keep himself warm.

But it is not all play. You should see him in a slop-jacket, with a black face, and a bundle of cotton-waste in one hand, driving the traction engine with the greatest *sang-froid*, fetching up a load of coal in the wagon behind from the railway-station, or working the ploughing tackle; and in the interim, while his engine is slacking, i.e. the wire-rope uncoiling and the plough travelling towards the opposite engine, cracking filberts with the spanner. You should see him at the annual sale of shorthorns or ram-lambs, or whatever the speciality of the place may be, busy with the dinner-tickets, showing the big men over the pens, and hinting confidentially that this ram or that bull is 'a splendid thing, sir, and sure to make your money twice over'. Then behold him rising at the inevitable dinner to propose the toast of 'the buyers', and rolling out well-balanced periods, which make the company feel what a thing it is to have 'eddication'. To be able to hold forth glibly, and strike the popular nails on the head with a

sprinkling of jocularity, is an essential accomplishment to the 'coming' agriculturist. Without a good speech or two nothing can be done. Upstairs in his room Tom has a box crammed full of scientific knowledge—books on geology, botany, mathematics (!) physiology, &c., which he had to scan pretty closely at 'college', and which are supposed to fit youth for the plough and the cattle-stall, but which box has never been opened since he arrived on the farm. He looks upon them with intense scorn, and prides himself on being a 'practical' man. He sees that good sherry well plied has an amazing influence on the price of shorthorns. He notes that a brace of pheasants or a hare judiciously left at the local newspaper-office is usually followed by 'extensive' accounts of the wonderful animals or extraordinary crops to be found at a certain spot. Free champagne has been known to oil quills with a wider scope than that of the local editor; and the agricultural capitalist who would get a cosmopolitan fame and bring bidders from the United States and Australia must keep open house to the press. Tom has a shrewd idea that certain pieces of oblong paper with a stamp on them are continually passing between his tutor, the auctioneer (who should in these days rather be called the agricultural stockbroker—not punningly either) and the Bank. The meaning of which is that these great concerns of three and four thousand acres require a good deal of 'financing', and also that more money is made by judicious speculation—buying and selling and making a price with advertising—than by the simple husbandry of sowing the seed and waiting till it ripens. Nor does he forget to observe that a 'silver tongue' and good address will get a young fellow a first-class farm much more surely than any solid experience. For though the squire's lady may sneer at his lack of pedigree, and so forth, yet somehow there is more pleasure in seeing a tall, well-dressed, gentlemanly young man, who can talk and knows how to behave, in the pew at church every Sunday than the cumbrous old style of rude and yet sheepish tenant-farmer. So Tom is by no means such a fool as he may seem to the slow-coaches of the parish. He has a note-book, in which he jots down briefly and in cipher these and similar observations upon the ways of mankind; and when he draws on his snow-white cuffs and gold links, and adjusts a stray curl over his forehead before he goes down to dinner, where he will meet somebody from 'the Hall', he is wiser in his generation than those crotchety college-tutors with their jargon of superphosphates. To all the rectors' daughters (who seldom have curates to keep up to their duty) round about, to the big gentlemen farmers' girls, and even to the ladies at 'the Hall', bored to death half their time, Tom and his kind are a positive blessing. As for his hunting and shooting, a heavy sum has been paid as a premium, and a stiff amount annually for his board, &c., and why should he not have it out of the soil?

These youths of late years have become quite a feature in rural society. Who are they? It would be hard to say, as they are drawn from so many sources. When men have accumulated great fortunes in trade or commerce, as the years go on they find their boys growing up, and what is to be done with them? One is destined to carry on the City concern; another goes into the Church or the Army or the Bar, places once only filled from the country gentlemen's families; and the third—'Well, he's fond of out-door exercise, let's make him a farmer!' That is the history in many cases; but occasionally the pupil is a cadet from a higher social grade—a grade which sees the necessity of putting the fellows to do something to get money or at least their living, and yet cannot overcome the repugnance to trade. Now in the position of the big agriculturist there exists a certain parallelism, as it were, with the gentry; there is nothing degrading or pettifogging about it, and so this new profession powerfully recommends itself. And the free open-air life is a great inducement.

These young men not infrequently go off to the colonies after they have finished their time, and grow into mighty sheep-masters in Australia, or own a hundred thousand acres in Natal, and so do good work in the world. For the young fellow who gets through his billiards and petty bookmaking, stable propensities, and so forth, early in life, is generally found to possess more knowledge of men and to succeed better than the mere studious book-worm or milk-sop, who is ever at the edge of a petticoat, cannot soil his boots after a hare, and thinks croquet an exciting game.

John Smith's Shanty

1874

He was standing in the ditch leaning heavily upon the long handle of his axe. It was a straight stick of ash, roughly shaved down to some sort of semblance of smoothness, such as would have worked up an unpractised hand into a mass of blisters in ten minutes' usage, but which glided easily through those horny palms, leaving no mark of friction. The continuous outdoor labour, the beating of innumerable storms, and the hard, coarse fare, had dried up all the original moisture of the hand, till it was rough, firm, and cracked or chapped like a piece of wood exposed to the sun and weather. The natural oil of the skin, which gives to the hand its beautiful suppleness and delicate sense of touch, was gone like the sap in the tree he was felling, for it was early in the winter. However the brow might perspire, there was no dampness on the hand, and the helve of the axe was scarcely harder and drier. In order, therefore, that the grasp might be firm, it was necessary to artificially wet the palms, and hence that custom which so often disgusts lookers-on, of spitting on the hands before commencing work. This apparently gratuitous piece of dirtiness is in reality absolutely necessary. Men with hands in this state have hardly any feeling in them; they find it difficult to pick up anything small, as a pin—the fingers fumble over it; and as for a pen, they hold it like a hammer. His chest was open to the north wind, which whistled through the bare branches of the tall elm overhead as if they were the cordage of a ship, and came in sudden blasts through the gaps in the hedge, blowing his shirt back, and exposing the immense breadth of bone, and rough dark skin tanned to a brown-red by the summer sun while mowing. The neck rose from it short and thick like that of a bull, and the head was round, and covered with a crop of short grizzled hair not yet quite grey, but fast losing its original chestnut colour. The features were fairly regular, but coarse, and the nose flattened. An almost worn-out old hat thrown back on the head showed a low, broad, wrinkled forehead. The eyes were small and bleared, set deep under shaggy eyebrows. The corduroy trousers, yellow with clay and sand, were shortened below the knee by leather straps like garters, so as to exhibit the whole of the clumsy boots, with soles like planks, and shod with iron at heel and tip. These boots weigh seven pounds the pair; and in wet weather, with clay and dirt clinging to them, must reach nearly double that.

In spite of all the magnificent muscular development which this man possessed, there was nothing of the Hercules about him. The grace of strength was wanting, the curved lines were lacking; all was gaunt, angular, and square. The chest was broad enough, but flat, a framework of bones hidden by a rough hairy skin; the breasts did not swell up like the rounded prominences of the antique statue. The neck, strong enough as it was to bear the weight of a sack of corn with ease, was too short, and too much a part, as it were, of the shoulders. It did not rise up like a tower, distinct in itself; and the muscles on it, as they moved, produced hollow cavities distressing to the eye. It was strength without beauty; a mechanical kind of power, like that of an engine, working through straight lines and sharp angles. There was too much of the machine, and too little of the animal; the lithe, easy motion of the lion or the tiger was not there. The impression conveyed was, that such strength had been gained through a course of incessant exertion of the rudest kind, unassisted by generous food and checked by unnatural exposure.

John Smith heaved up his axe and struck at the great bulging roots of the elm, from which he had cleared away the earth with his spade. A heavy chip flew out with a dull thud on the sward. The straight handle of the axe increased the labour of the work, for in this curiously conservative country the American improvement of the double curved handle has not yet been adopted. Chip after chip fell in the ditch, or went spinning out into the field. The axe rose and fell with a slow, monotonous motion. Though there was immense strength in every blow, there was no vigour in it. Suddenly, while it was swinging in the air overhead, there came the faint, low echo of a distant railway whistle, and the axe was dropped at once, without even completing the blow. 'That's the express,' he muttered, and began cleaning the dirt from his shoes. The daily whistle of the express was the signal for luncheon. Hastily throwing on a slop hung on the bushes, and over that a coat, he picked up a small bag, and walked slowly off down the side of the hedge to where the highway road went by. Here he sat down, somewhat sheltered by a hawthorn bush, in the ditch, facing the road, and drew out his bread and cheese.

About a quarter of a loaf of bread, or nearly, and one slice of cheese was this full-grown and powerful man's dinner that cold, raw winter's day. His drink was a pint of cold weak tea, kept in a tin can, for these men are moderate enough with liquor at their meals, whatever they may be at other times. He held the bread in his left hand and the cheese was placed on it, and kept in its place by the thumb, the grimy dirt on which was shielded by a small piece of bread beneath it from the precious cheese. His plate and dish was his broad palm, his only implement a great jack-knife with a buckhorn handle. He ate slowly, thoughtfully, deliberately; weighing each mouthful, chewing the cud as it were. All the man's motions were heavy and slow, deadened as if clogged with a great load. There was no 'life' in him. What little animation there was left had taken him to eat his dinner by the roadside—the instinct of sociality—that if possible he might exchange a word with someone passing. In factories men work in gangs, and hundreds are often within call of each other; a rough joke or an occasional question can be put and answered; there is a certain amount of sympathy, a sensation of company and companionship. But alone in the fields, the human instinct of friendship is checked, the man is driven back upon himself and his own narrow range of thought, till the mind and heart grow dull, and there only remains such a vague ill-defined want as carried John Smith to the roadside that day.

He had finished his cheese and lit a short clay pipe, and thrust his hands deep in his pockets, when there was a rustling noise in the hedge a little farther down, and a short man jumped out into the road—even jumping with his hands in his pockets. He saw Smith directly and came towards him, and sat himself on a heap of flints used for mending the road.

'What's thee at today?' asked John, after a pause.

'Ditching,' said the other laconically, pushing out one foot by way of illustrating the fact. It was covered with black mud far above the ankle, and there were splashes of mud up to his waist—his hands, as he proceeded to light his pipe, were black, too, from the same cause.

'Thee's bin in main deep,' said John, after a slow survey of the other's appearance.

The fellow stamped his boot on the ground, and the slime and slush oozed out of it and formed a puddle. 'That's pretty stuff to stand in for a man of sixty-four, yent it, John?' With a volubility and energy of speech little to be expected from his wizened appearance, the hedger and ditcher entered into details of his job. He began work at six that morning with stiff legs and swollen feet, and as he stood in the mingled mire and water, the rheumatism came gradually on, rising higher up his limbs from the ankles, and growing sharper with every twinge, while the cold and bitter wind cut through his thin slop on his chest, which was not so strong as it used to be. His arms got stiff with the labour of lifting up shovelful after shovelful of heavy mud to plaster the side of the ditch, his feet turned cold as 'flints', and the sickly smell of the slime upset his stomach so that when he tried to eat his bread and cheese he could not. Through this speech John smoked steadily on, till the other stopped and looked at him for sympathy.

'Well, Jim, anyhow,' said Smith, 'thee hasn't got far to walk to the job;' and he pointed with the stem of his pipe to the low roof of a cottage just visible a few hundred yards distant.

'Ay, and a place it be to live in, that,' said Jim. There were only two rooms, he explained, and both downstairs—no upstairs at all—and the first of these was so small he could reach across it, and the thatch had got so thin in one place that the rain came through. The floor was only hard mud, and the garden not big enough to grow a sack of potatoes, while one wall of the house, which was only 'wattle and daub' (i.e. lath and plaster) rose up from the very edge of a great stagnant pond. Overhead there was an elm, from the branches of which in wet weather there was a perpetual drip, drip on the thatch, till the moss and grass grew on the roof in profusion. All the sewage and drainage from the cottage ran into the pond, over which at night there was almost always a thick damp mist, which crept in through the crevices of the rotten walls, and froze the blood in the sleepers' veins. Sometimes a flood came down, and the pond rose and washed away the cabbages from the garden, leaving a deposit of gritty sand which killed all vegetation, and they could only keep the water from coming indoors by making a small dam of clay across the doorway. There was only a low hedge of elder between the cottage and a dirty lane; and in the night, especially if there happened to be a light burning, it was common enough for a stone to come through the window, flung by some half-drunken ploughboy. A pretty place for a human being to live in: and again he looked up into Smith's face for comment.

'Thee built 'un thee-self, didn't 'ee?' said John, in his slow way.

'Ay, that I did,' continued Jim, not seeing the drift of the remark. He not only built it, but he brought up nineteen children in it, and fourteen of them lived to grow up, all the offspring of one wife. And a time she had of it, too. None of them ever fell in that pond, though he often wished they would; and they were all pretty healthy, which was a bad thing, because it made them hungry, and if they had been ill the parish would have kept them. All that he had done on 12 shillings a week, and he minded the time when it was only 9 shillings, ay, and even when it was 6 shillings, and 'twas better then than it was now with 15 shillings. That was before the Unions came about, in the time of the old workhouses in every parish. Then the farmers used to find everybody a job. Every morning they had to go round from one farmer to the other, and if there was no work then they went to the workhouse, or sometimes to the vestry-room in the church, where every man had a loaf of bread for every head there was in his family, so that the more children he had the more loaves of bread, which was a capital thing when the children were small. He had known a man in those times sent seven miles with a wheelbarrow to fetch a barrow load of coal from the canal wharf, and then have to wheel it back seven miles, and get one shilling for his day's work. Still they were better times than these, because the farmers for their own sake were forced to find the fellows something to do; but now they did not care, and it was a hard thing to find work, especially when a man grew old, and stiff about the joints. Now the Boards of Guardians would not give any relief unless the applicants were ill, or not able-bodied, and even then they were often required to break stones, and he was very much inclined to throw his spade in that old pond and go to the Union with the 'missis' and all the lot for good. He had the rheumatism bad enough. It would serve them right. He had worked 'nigh handy' sixty years; and all he had got by it he could put in his eye. They ought to keep him now. It was not half so good as the old times for all the talk; then the children could bring home a bit of wood out of the hedges to boil the pot with, but now they must not touch a stick, or there was the law on them in a minute. And then the coal at the price it was. Why didn't his sons keep him? Where were they? One was a soldier, and another had gone to America, and the third was married and had a hard job to keep himself, and the fourth was gone nobody knew where. As for the wenches, they were no good in that way. So he and his 'missis' muddled on at home with three of the youngest. And they could not let them alone even in that. He did go into the Union workhouse for a bit, a while ago, when the rheumatism was extraordinary bad, but some of the guardians smelt out that he had a cottage of his own, and it was against the law to relieve anybody that had property; so he must pay back the relief as a loan or sell the cottage. He was offered £25 for the place and garden, and he meant to have taken it, but when they came to look into the writings it was not clear that he could sell it. It was quit-rent land, and although the landlord had not taken the rent for twenty years, yet he had entered it in his book as paid (out of good nature) and the lawyers said it could not be done. But as they would not let him sell it, he would not turn out, not he. There he would stop—just to spite them. He knew that nook of his was wanted for cattle stalls on the new principle, and very handy it would be with all that water close at hand, but he had worked for sixty years, and had had nineteen children there, and he would not turn out. Not he. The parson's 'missis' and the squire's 'missis' came the other day about that youngest boy of his. They wanted to get him into some school up in London somewhere, but he remembered how the squire had served him just for picking up a dead rabbit that laid in his path one hard snow time. Six weeks on gaol because he could not pay the fine. And the parson turned him out of his allotment because he saw him stagger a little in the road one night with rheumatism. It was a lie that he was drunk. And suppose he was? The parson had his wine, he reckoned. They should not have his boy. He rather hoped he would grow up a bad one, and bother them well. He minded when that sharp old Miss— was always coming round with tracts and blankets, like taking some straw to a lot of pigs, and lecturing his 'missis' about economy. What a fuss she made, and scolded his wife as if she was a thief for having that fifteenth boy! His 'missis' turned on her at last, and said, 'Lor, miss, that's all the pleasure me an' my old man got.' As for this talk about the labourers' Unions, it was all very well for the young men; but it made it worse still for the old ones. The farmers, if they had to give such a price, would have young men in full strength: there was no chance at all for an old fellow of sixty-four with rheumatism. Some of them, too, were terribly offended—some of the old sort—and turned off the few pensioners they had kept on at odd jobs for years. However, he supposed he must get back to that ditch again.

This long oration was delivered not without a certain degree of power and effect, showing that the man, whatever his faults, might with training have become rather a clever fellow. The very way in which he contradicted himself, and announced his intention of never doing that which a moment before he was determined on, was not without an amount of oratorical art, since the turn in his view of the subject was led up to by a variety of reasons which were supposed to convince himself and his hearer at the same time. His remarks were all the more effective because there was an evident substratum of stern truth beneath them. But they failed to make much impression on Smith, who saw his companion depart without a word.

The fact was, that Smith was too well acquainted with the private life of the orator. In his dull, dim way, he half recognized that the unfortunate old fellow's evils had been in great part of his own creating. He knew that he was far from faultless. That poaching business—a very venial offence in a labourer's eyes—he knew had been a serious one, a matter of some two-score pheasants and a desperate fight with the gang. Looking at it as property, the squire had been merciful, pleading with the magistrates for a mitigated penalty. The drunkenness was habitual. In short, they were a bad lot—there was a name attached to the whole family for thieving, poaching, drinking, and even worse. Yet still there were two points that did sink deep into Smith's mind, and made him pause several times that afternoon in his work. The first was that long family of nineteen mouths, with the father and mother making twenty-one. What a number of sins, in the rude logic of the struggle for existence, that terrible fact glossed over! Who could blame—what labourer at least could blame—the ragged, ill-clothed children for taking the dead wood from the hedges to warm their naked limbs? What labourer could blame the father for taking the hares and rabbits running across his very path to fill that wretched hovel with savoury steam from the pot? And further, what labourer could blame the miserable old man for drowning his feelings, and his sensation of cold and hunger, in liquor?

The great evil of these things is that a fellow-feeling will arise with the wrong-doer, till the original distinction between right and wrong is lost sight of entirely. John Smith had a family too. The other point was the sixty years of labour and their fruit. After two generations of hardest toil and rudest exposure, still dependent upon the seasons even to permit him to work, when that work could be obtained. No rest, no cosy fireside nook: still the bitter wind, and the half-frozen slime and slush rising above the ankle. In an undefined way Smith had been proud of his broad, enormous strength, and rocklike hardihood. He had felt a certain rude pleasure in opening his broad chest to the winter wind. But now he involuntarily closed his shirt and buttoned it. He did not feel so confident in his own power of meeting all the contingencies of the future.

Thought without method and without logical sequence is apt to press heavily upon the uneducated mind. It was thus that these reflections left a sensation of weight and discomfort upon Smith, and it was in a worse humour than was common to his usually well-balanced organization that he hid away his tools under the bushes as the evening grew too dark for work, and slowly paced homewards. He had some two miles to walk, and he had long since begun to feel hungry. Plodding along in a heavy, uneven gait, there overtook him a tall, raw young lad of eighteen or twenty, slouching forward with vast strides and whistling merrily. The lad slackened his steps and joined company!

'Where bist thee working now, then?' asked Smith.

He replied, evidently in high spirits, that he had that day got a job at the new railway that was making. The wages were 18 shillings a week—3 shillings a day—and he had heard that as soon as the men grew to understand their work and to be a little skilful, they could get 24 shillings easily, up by London. The only drawback was the long walk to the work. Lodgings close at hand were very dear, as also was food, so dear as to lower the actual receipts to an equality, if not below that of the agricultural labourer. Four miles every morning and every night was the price he paid for 18 shillings a week.

Smith began in his slow, dull way to reckon up his wages aloud against

154

this. First he had 13 shillings a week for his daily work. Then he had 1 shilling extra for milking on Sundays, and two good meals with beer on that day. Every week-day he had a pint of beer on finishing work. The young navvy had to find his own liquor. His cottage, it was true, was his own (that is, he only paid a low quit-rent of 1 shilling a year for it) so that that could be reckoned in as part of his earnings, as it could with many other men. But the navvy's wages were the same all the year round, while his in summer were often nearly double. As a stalwart mower he could earn 25 shillings a week and more, as a haymaker 18 shillings, and at harvesting perhaps 30 shillings. If the season was good, and there was a press for hands, he would get more. But, looking forward there was no prospect of rising higher in his trade, of getting higher wages for more skilful work. He could not be more skilful than he was in ordinary farm work; and as yet the call for clever men to attend to machinery, &c., was very limited; nor were such a class of workmen usually drawn from the resident population where improvements were introduced. The only hope of higher wages that was held out to him was from the gradual rise of everything, or the forced rise consequent upon agitation. But, said he, the navvy must follow his work from place to place, and lodgings are dear in the towns, and the farmers in country places will not let their cottages except to their own labourers—how was the navvy even with higher wages to keep a wife? The aspiring young fellow beside him replied at once sharply and decisively, that he did not mean to have a wife, leastways not till he had got his regular 30 shillings a week, which he might in time. Then John Smith made a noise in his chest like a grunt.

They parted after this. Smith went into the farmhouse, and got his pint of beer, drinking it in one long slow draught, and then made his way through the scattered village to his cottage. There was a frown on his forehead as he lifted the latch of the long low thatched building which was his home.

The flickering light of the fire on the hearth, throwing great shadows as it blazed up and fell, dazed his eyes as he stepped in, and he did not notice a line stretched right across the room on which small articles of clothing were hanging to dry in a row. A damp worsted stocking flapped against his face, and his foot stumbled on the uneven flag stones which formed the floor. He sat down silently upon a three-legged stool—an old milking-stool—and, putting his hands on his knees, stared into the fire. It was formed of a few sticks with just one knob of coal balanced on the top of them, evident care having been taken that not a jot of its precious heat should be lost. A great black pot with open lid swung over it, from which rose a slight steam and a bubbling noise; and this huge, gaunt, bareboned, hungry man, looking into it, saw a large raw swede, just as from the field, with only the greens cut off, simmering for his supper. That root in its day of life had been fed well with superphosphate, and flourished exceedingly, till now its globe could hardly go into the pot. Down the low chimney there came the monotonous growl of the bitter winter wind, and a few spots of rain fell hissing on the embers.

'Is this all thee has got?' he asked, turning to a woman who was busied with some more damp clothes in a basket.

She faced round quickly—a short, narrow, meagre creature, flat-chested and square-shouldered, whose face was the hue of light-coloured clay, an almost corpse-like complexion. Her thin lips hissed out, 'Ay, if thee takes thee money to the pothouse thee won't get bacon for supper.'

Smith said nothing in reply, but stared again into the fire.

The children's voices, which had lowered the moment there seemed a coming quarrel between their parents, rose again. There were three of them—the youngest four, the eldest seven—playing on the stone flags of the floor, between whose rough edges there were wide crevices of hardened mud. With a few short sticks and a broken piece of earthenware for toys, they were happy in their way. Whatever their food might have been, they showed no traces of hard usage. Their red 'puddy' fists were fat, and their naked legs round and plump enough. Their faces were full and rosy, and their voices clear and anything but querulous. The eager passions of childhood come out fierce and unrestrained, and blows were freely interchanged, without, however, either cries or apparent hatred. Their naked knees were on the stone-flags, and the wind, creeping in a draught under the ill-fitting door, blew their ragged clothes about.

'Thee med well look at 'em, John,' said the woman, seeing Smith cast a sideway glance at the children; and rapidly manipulating the clothing, her thin nervous lips poured forth a torrent of words upon the silent man. They had had nothing but bread that day, and nothing but bread and lard the day before, and now the lard was gone, and the baker would not trust any more. There were no potatoes because the disease had destroyed them, and the cabbages were sold for that bit of coal; and as for the swede, she took it out of Mr ____'s field, and he was a cross-grained man, and who knew but what they might have the constable on them before morning? Jane W. and Sarah Y. went to prison for seven days for stealing swedes. All along of that cursed drink. If she were the squire she'd shut up all the pothouses in the county. The men went there, and drank the very shirts off their backs, and the clothes off their children, ay, and the shoes off their feet; and what was the use of their having more money when it only went into the publican's pocket? There they sat, and drank the bread out of the babies' mouths. As for the women, the most of them, poor things, never tasted beer from one year's end to another. Old Carter handed her a pint that day, and when she tasted it she did not know what it was. He might smile, but it was true though: no more did Jane W. and Sally Y.: they did not know what it tasted like. And yet they had to be out in the fields at work at eight o'clock, and their washing to do before that, and perhaps a baby in their arms, and the tea as weak as water, and no sugar. Milk, they could not get milk for money—he knew that very well; all the milk went to London. A precious lot of good the higher wages had done them. The farmers would not let them have a drop of milk or a scrap of victuals, and talked about rising the price of the allotment grounds. Allotment did she say? and how did he lose his allotment?—didn't he drink, drink, drink, till he had to hand over his allotment to the landlord of the pothouse, and did not they take it away from both as soon as they heard of it? Served him right. They had not got a pound of potatoes, and the children did use to lick up the potato-pot liquor as if they liked it.

Smith asked where Polly was, but that was only a signal for a fresh outburst. Polly, if he'd a looked after her she would have been all right. (Smith turned a sharp glance at her in some alarm at this.) Letting a great girl like that go about at night by herself while he was a drink, drink, drinking, and there she was now, the bad hussy, gone to the workhouse to lie in. (Smith winced.) *She* never disgraced herself like that; and if he had sent the wench to service, or stopped her going down to that pothouse with the fellows, this would not have happened. She always told him how it would end. He was a good-for-nothing, drunken brute of a man, and had brought her to all this misery; and she began sobbing.

After twelve long hours of toil, including the walk to and fro, exposed to the bitter cold, with but a slice of cheese to support the strength of that brawny chest, this welcome to his supper was more than the sturdy, silent man could bear. With a dull remembrance of the happy sunlit summer, twenty years ago, when Martha was a plump, laughing girl, of sloe-black eyes and nut-brown complexion—with a glimpse of that merry courting time passing across his mind, Smith got up and walked out into the dark rainy night. 'Ay, thee bist agoing to the liquor again,' were the last words he heard as he shut the door.

It was too true. But what labourer, let us ask, with a full conception of the circumstances, would blame him? Here there was nothing but hard and scanty fare, no heat, no light, nothing to cheer the heart, nothing to cause it to forget the toil of the day and the thought of the morrow, no generous liquor sung by poets to warm the physical man. But only a few yards farther down the road there was a great house, with its shutters cosily

157

closed, ablaze with heat and light, echoing with merry laughter and song. There was an array of good fellows ready to welcome him, to tell him the news, to listen eagerly to what he could tell them, to ask him to drink, and to drink from his cup in boon companionship. There was a social circle in which his heart and intellect could expand, at least for a while, till the strong liquor mounted up and overcame his brain; and then, even then, there was the forgetfulness, the deep slumber of intoxication, utterly oblivious of all things—perhaps the greatest pleasure of all. Smith went there, and who of his own class would blame him? And if his own class did not, of what use is it for other and higher classes to preach morality to him? It is a man's own comrades, his own class, whose opinions he dreads and conforms to. If they condemned him for going there, he would avoid the public-house. But they would have called him a fool if he avoided it. In their logic who could say they were wrong? A man who is happy is a long while getting drunk, he talks as much as he drinks; but Smith was dull and silent, and drank steadily. It was not late, but when the house closed he could but just keep his feet. In the thick darkness and the driving rain he staggered on, unconscious of the road he was taking, but bearing roughly towards home. The cold air rather more stupefied him than brought him to himself. Insensibly he wandered with uncertain steps down a lane which led by a gentle slope out into the fields, the fall of the ground guiding his footsteps, and then stumbling over the root of an ash-tree, fell heavily on the wet grass. His eyes, half-shut before, closed as if by clockwork, and in a moment he was firm asleep. His hat had fallen from his brow, and the grizzled hair was blown about by the wind as it came in gusts through the hedge. His body was a little sheltered by the tree, but his chest was open and bare half-way down his waistcoat; and the heavy drops fell from the boughs of the ash on his stalwart neck, gradually saturating his shirt. It may have been that the cold numbed him and rendered him more insensible than he otherwise would have been. No star shone out that night; all was darkness, clouds, and rain till the dawn broke.

Soon after dawn, the young navvy, going to his work by a short cut, found Smith still asleep, and shook him till he got up. He was stupid beyond all power of words to express; but at last came to a dim idea that he must get home. Then the young navvy left him, anxious about being late at his employment, and John Smith slowly *felt* his way to his own door. His wife, already up, opened it. 'Thee varmint! thee never gi'ed I that shilling last night for the baker.' Smith felt hopelessly in his pocket, and then looked at her vacantly. 'Thee drunken, nasty old ____,' said the infuriated woman, almost unconsciously lifting her hand. Perhaps it was that action of hers which suggested the same to his mind, which was in a mechanical state. Perhaps the stinging words of last night had at last sunk deep enough to scarify his self-esteem. Perhaps he did not at that moment fully remember the strength of his own mighty arm. But he struck her, and she fell. Her forehead came in contact with the cradle, in which the youngest boy was sleeping, and woke him with a cry. She lay quite still. Smith sat stupidly down on the old milking-stool, with his elbows on his knees. The shrill voice of his wife, as she met him at the door, had brought more than one female neighbour to the window; they saw what happened, and they were there in a minute. Martha was only insensible, and they soon brought her to, but the mark on the temple remained.

Five days afterwards John Smith, agricultural labourer, aged forty-five, stood in the dock to answer a charge of assaulting his wife. There were five magistrates on the Bench—two large landowners, a baronet in the chair, and two clergymen. Martha Smith hung her head as they placed her in the witness-box, and tried to evade kissing the Book, but the police saw that that formality was complied with. The Clerk asked her what she had to complain of. No answer. 'Come, tell us all about it,' said the eldest of the magistrates in a fatherly tone of voice. Still silence. 'Well, how did you get that mark on your forehead?' asked the Clerk. No answer. 'Speak up!' cried a shrill voice in the body of the court. It was one of Martha's cronies, who was immediately silenced by the police; but the train had been fired. Martha would not fail before another woman. But she did not commence about the assault. It was the drink she spoke of, nothing but the drink; and as she talked of that she warmed with her subject and her grievances, and forgot the old love for her husband, and her former hesitation, and placed that vice in all its naked deformity and hideous results in plain but burning words before the Bench. Had she been the cleverest advocate she could not have prepared the ground for her case better. This tale of drink predisposed their minds against the defendant. Only the Clerk, wedded to legal forms, fidgeted under this eloquence, and seized the first pause: 'But now, how about the assault? Come to that,' he said sharply. 'I'm coming, sir,' said Martha; and she described Smith coming home, stupid and ferocious, after staying out all night, and felling her to the ground because she asked him for a shilling to buy the children's daily bread. Then she pointed to the bruise on her forehead, and a suppressed murmur of indignation ran through the Court, and angry looks were directed at the defendant. Did she do or say anything to provoke the blow? asked the Chairman. No more than to ask for the shilling. Did she not abuse him? Well, yes, she did; she owned she did call him a drunken brute afterwards; she could not help it. These women, with their rapid tongues, have a terrible advantage over the slower-witted men.

Had the defendant any questions to ask his wife? Smith began to say that he was very sorry, sir, but the Clerk snapped him up short. 'That's your defence. Have you any questions? No; well, call your witnesses.' Martha called her witnesses, the women living next door. They did not do her case much good; they were too evidently eager to obtain the defendant's condemnation. But, on the other hand, they did not do it any harm, for in the main it was easy to see that they really corroborated her statements. Smith asked then no questions; the labouring class rarely understand the object of cross-questioning. If asked to do so they almost invariably begin to tell their own tale.

'Now, then,' said the Clerk, 'what have you got to say for yourself—what's your defence?' Smith looked down and stammered something. He was confused; they checked him from telling his story when his mouth was full of language, now it would not come. He did not know but that if he began he might be checked again. The eldest magistrate on the Bench saw his embarrassment, and, willing to assist him, spoke as kindly as he could under the circumstances. 'Speak up, John; tell us all about it. I am sorry to see you there.' 'He's the finest, most stalwart man in my parish,' he continued, turning to the Chairman. Thus encouraged, John got out a word or two. He was very sorry; he did not mean to hurt her; he knew he was tipsy, and 'twas his own fault; she had been a good wife to him; she asked him for money. Then all of a sudden John drew up his form to his full height, and his chest swelled out, and he spoke in his own strong voice clearly now that he had got a topic apart from his disgrace. These were his words, a little softened into more civilized pronunciation to make them intelligible:

'She asked I for money, she did, and what was I to gi'e her? I hadn't a got a shilling nor a sixpence, and she knew it, and knowed that I couldn't get one either till Saturday night. I gets thirteen shillings a week from Master H., and a shilling on Sundays, and I hev got five children and a wife to keep out of that—that's two shillings a week for each on us, that's just threepence halfpenny a day, look 'ee, sir. And what victuals be I to buy wi' that, let alone beer? and a man can't do no work wi'out a quart a day, and that's fourpence, and there's my share, look 'ee, gone at onst. Wur be I to get any victuals, and wur be I to get any clothes an' boots, I should like for to know? And Jack he gets big and wants a main lot, and so did Polly, but her's gone to the work'us', wuss luck. And parson wants I to send the young 'uns to school, and pay a penny a week for 'em, and missis she wants a bit o' bacon in the house and a loaf, and what good is that of, among all we? I gets a slice of bacon twice a week, and sometimes narn. And beer—I knows I drinks beer, and more as I ought, but what's a chap to do when

he's a'most shrammed wi' cold, and nar a bit o' nothin' in the pot but an old yeller swede as hard as wood? And my teeth bean't as good as 'em used to be. I knows I drinks beer, and so would anybody in my place—it makes me kinder stupid, as I don't feel nothing then. Wot's the good—I've worked this thirty year or more, since I wur big enough to go with the plough, and I've a knowed they as have worked for nigh handy sixty, and wot do 'em get for it? All he'd a got wur the rheumatiz. Yer med as well drink while 'ee can. I never meaned to hurt her, and her knows it; and if it wurn't for a parcel of women a-shoving on her on, her would never a come here agen me. I knows I drinks, and what else be I to do? I can't work allus.'

'But what are you going to say in your defence—do you say she provoked you or anything?' asked the Clerk.

'No, I don't know as she provoked I. I wur provoked, though, I wur. I don't bear no malice agen she. I ain't a got nothin' more for to say.'

The magistrates retired, and the Chairman, on returning, said that this was a most brutal and unprovoked assault, made all the worse by the previous drinking habits of the defendant. If it had not been for the good character he bore generally speaking (here he looked towards the elder magistrate, who had evidently said a word in Smith's behalf), he would have had a month's imprisonment, or more. As it was, he was committed for a fortnight, and to pay the costs, or seven additional days; and he hoped this would be a warning to him.

The elder magistrate looked at John Smith, and saw his jaw set firmly, and his brow contract, and his heart was moved towards him.

'Cannot you get better wages than that, John?' he said. At the railway they would give you eighteen or twenty.'

'It's so far to walk, sir, and my legs bean't as lissom as they used to be.'

'But take the missis and live there.'

'Lodgings is too dear, sir.'

'Ah, exactly. Still I don't see how the farmers could pay you more. I'll see what can be done for you.'

Smith was led from the dock to the cell. The expenses were paid by an unknown hand; but he underwent his fortnight's imprisonment. His wife and children, with an empty larder, were obliged to go to the workhouse, where also his daughter was at the same time confined of an illegitimate child. This is no fiction, but an uncompromising picture of things as they are. Who is to blame for them?

Who is to blame for clerks in merchants' offices marrying on 30s. or £2 a week, and rearing a large family in shabby gentility, pinched for food, for fuel, for clothing? Is the merchant at fault for that? The truth is that the fault lies with no class, it is the natural outcome of our whole social system; and how can we expect any social system, however generally perfect, to be free of all defects? And is there not a certain amount of fault in the parties themselves? But upon this it is not to any man's taste to dwell: it is barely possible to admit there was a fault, but no farther. For every man feels that he has a natural right to marry, and that the system which would deprive him of that right is wrong. He has a right to have a home. Then, taking it for granted that there is a defect somewhere in the system, what remedy is there? It does not appear that any radical and sweeping change can be applied. As the evil has not its origin in any one particular state of things, but from the concentration of many causes, so it must be attacked from several quarters. It has been so attacked during the last few years, and the results are beginning to show themselves, producing at first, as all great changes do, a state of transition. No better proof of the gradual change that has been going on can be adduced than the scarcity of lads ready to commence such a career as John Smith's. The adventurous young men either emigrate or become navvies on the railways and other works, and, if at all intelligent, are soon put in charge of machinery. At the present day, in some localities, the farmers cannot get boys to lead the horses at plough. They are either not to be found, or when found refuse that employment as not worth their while. The result is that old men of sixty-five and past may be seen tottering along the furrows, leading the plough horses, as they did two generations ago, in their first childhood. Not able-bodied enough for full work, they are glad of the job. Nor will the boys, as a rule, undertake the menial duty of bird-keeping; so that, as these employments were usually given to very young children, the provisions of the Agricultural Children's Act are already practically complied with. The men now to be found at work on the farms are principally of the middle-aged class, or verging onwards to that stage of life, and, as a rule, married and with families. They have been farm labourers from boyhood, and it is now too late to change, nor, indeed, could they stand the wear and tear of a navvy's life, while their experience enables them to get fair wages, with the advantage of cheap cottages and allotments. To them there is, in fact, little temptation to move; and every year, as labour grows scarcer, their earnings increase. Some of these get to be bailiffs, and to be put in charge of valuable stock and even machinery. But they, of course, die out gradually, and who is to supply their place? The present rising generation will not, unless, perhaps, the modification in the mode of farming—the introduction of machinery and a more commercial spirit—result in the necessity of employing a more intelligent class of men, with higher wages and opportunities of rising in life. It is very evident that an increase of wages must have come whether there had been any agitation on the subject or not. In many places it had come, and in these places the agitation has not raised them a shilling. Nor do the farmers object to higher wages, at least not those who are conforming themselves to the modern system of agriculture; only they require good value for their money; in other words, they will have able-bodied and intelligent employees. All this tends to improve the position of the labourers. Many of them are now firmly impressed with the value of education—in itself a very great advance—and most anxious to avail themselves of it. The old-fashioned labourers were very ignorant. Some four out of seven could neither read nor write; and a large proportion who could do so, did it imperfectly. This applies to the middle-aged and aged men now working in agriculture. But they are all eager that their children should learn. How many times have we heard them proudly say, while confessing their own inability to read or write, 'But our "Jack" can read th' paper'! Compulsion is not wanted to make them send their children to school. Without discussing the merits or demerits of the Education Act, it is certain that it came at a most opportune moment. The clergy had indeed established schools in many places, but their efforts were badly seconded. Now, when there is an objection to a School Board, great efforts are made to do without it, and the consequence is an effective school. A very large proportion, too, of the agricultural poor are Dissenters, and they could not be persuaded to send their children to the clergyman's school; but now they see the school supported by Government, and framed to meet the requirements of every child in the parish, they feel that they have a right there, and that it is not sectarian. The result is a good attendance without any compulsion. In another year's time it would be almost safe to predict that there will not be an agricultural labourer's child to be found who has not some rudiments of education. This is greatly to be rejoiced at, because as intelligence increases brutality diminishes. The educated labourer will not be so ready to beat his wife, because the opinion of his intelligent fellow-workmen will be against it. Higher wages may give him for a time greater temptation to drink; but there will be a diminution in the number of confirmed sots. He will not sit soddening himself night after night with the quart cup, his aroused intelligence will be too restless for that. But we would look for the greatest improvement to take place through the agency of the women. If the agricultural labourer was ignorant, the agricultural woman was painfully so. Marriage between them seemed rather like the union of two over-grown children than of rational human creatures. It is needless to go into details—one instance will illustrate this statement. Above all things a mother might be supposed to be solicitous for the honour of her daughter. But not so, in too many cases. If the daughter disgraced herself with a man in her own position of life, she was made to feel the full wrath of parental indignation. But if it was with someone who could afford to support the child, it was another thing. Mothers have frequently been heard to say, 'Ay, an' if she did have a baby 'twas wi' one as can pay for 'n.' There was no degradation if only it could be paid for. This horrible doctrine was instilled into the girls, and naturally led to the very worst consequences. Its outcome was the constant practice of appealing to the local petty sessions to establish the parentage of the child. Such an enquiry, however carefully conducted by the magistrates, could not fail to be terribly opposed to all feelings of female modesty. Every detail of it was, of course, repeated a hundred times afterwards, and tended to harden the girls in a career of immorality. This still continues. But gradually an improvement is taking place: women are not now employed (as a rule) in the coarser out-door labour. They do not milk, or attend on cattle. The work on arable land is not in any way degrading. Of the girls, a considerable proportion go out to service in towns, where they are in much demand. In service they are to some extent imbued with the higher tone of their employers, until they would shrink from such a public exposure as has been alluded to. They, in fact, get social education. When they marry, this in its turn reacts upon the men, and upon their offspring, who are brought up with better moral ideas. Here again the improved school comes in, and teaches them self-respect. It cannot but be that the improvement of the women must have a great effect upon the men.

One more cause of a higher tone among the female sex is undoubtedly the larger and more commodious cottages now coming into use. The greatest curse to the labourer was his ability to squat on a piece of waste land, and put up such a shanty as we have described above, consisting of lath and plaster walls and two small rooms, often on the most unhealthy spot that could possibly be chosen. There he lived like an animal, or rather as no animal but a pig could live. Grown-up persons of both sexes, and sometimes more than one family, slept in the same crowded apartment, outraging all decency. This had the most disastrous results with the female offspring. Now, however, this practice is almost entirely put an end to. That such cottages exist is a fact which cannot be denied; but it is only on sufferance, often as a shelter for aged people, who must otherwise go to the workhouse; but no new ones are built. Landlords and farmers prefer to have cottages of their own for their men, usually close to their occupation. These cottages are sufficiently large and commodious. It is a delicate thing to say, but it really would seem that the better class of agriculturists, who are now gradually superseding the old, have a most beneficial effect upon the labourer. They are themselves well educated, and their wives and daughters set an example which must be felt. As stated above, it is an object with them to have cottages of their own in their occupation. These are visited by their wives and daughters, who naturally take an interest in the labourers' children. It is very certain that a decrease of crime has taken place. Poaching in particular has diminished, though there was never so much game preserved as at present, and it was never so valuable, and consequently so tempting.

In wages there will probably be very little alteration for the present. As above stated, there were places where wages had risen before the agitation, and in many parts of the South of England they have not materially increased. This is a test which would seem to show that there is a natural ratio between the rate of wages and the income of the employers of labour; a ratio which cannot permanently be disturbed. As the income of agriculturists from better cultivation increases, so will the wages of their labourers insensibly rise. Doubtless there may come a time when pay that would seem out of the question now may be common enough; but that time will not come with a sudden leap. Attempts to force it can only result in reactionary ruin. On the whole it was wise of the agriculturists not to combine against the labourers' agitation. The momentary irritation stirred up against them is fast fading away before the substantial fact that the farmers are willing and ready to pay for good work. The forbearance they have shown has done much to restore confidence. The threatened wholesale exportation of agricultural labour to America has caused no dismay in agricultural quarters; for farmers very pertinently ask themselves, 'Where are these thousands of agricultural labourers to come from, in order to be exported? We cannot find them at any price. The higher the wages we pay, the greater the scarcity of labour seems to become. That thousands of emigrants may be scraped up we do not doubt, but we question if one-tenth of them will be *bona fide* agricultural labourers.'

Such success as did attend the agitation was almost entirely due to the fact that it taught the labourers to use the improved means of locomotion. Until a year or so ago how few agricultural labourers ever travelled by rail; and, one might almost say, none by steamer. They did not understand how to avail themselves of the easy means of communication, nor conceive the advantages it placed within their reach. In one county there might be a superfluity of labour, in another, fifty miles distant, a scarcity; but they did not seem to grasp the idea that it was possible to travel there, and procure the premium on labour. But the agitation showed them that this was possible, and educated them up to partially understand the law of supply and demand. The agitation did not cause a demand. On the contrary, by transporting bodies of men from one part of the country to another where they were wanted, it tended to equalize the condition of things—to equalize wages everywhere. The ignorance which even now prevails amongst the rural population of what is going on in the next county is surprising. Even in the largest agricultural villages (excepting, of course, among the higher class, who are few in number) there is scarcely a daily paper to be found. The immense circulation of the penny dailies certainly does not depend upon the agricultural districts. Now and then the *Telegraph* and *Daily News* may be found at the inns and beer-houses, but scarcely ever in a labourer's cottage. This, of course, arose to a great extent from their inability to read; but the rising generation can, and they are getting eager after news. Papers now not infrequently insert advertisements of labour wanted. This is perfectly legitimate, and likely to do far more solid good than the most crowded and enthusiastic meeting, or the most perfect union organization. On all hands it is clear that matters are in a transition state with the agricultural labourer, and they seem to indicate a much more promising future. His wages are increasing; his children have opportunities of education at a nominal charge; and as they grow older are in great demand for employment. His dwellings are larger, more decent, and healthy. The female section possesses a higher moral tone, and his daughters easily get situations. It does not seem that anything more can be done for him from the outside. His future now depends on himself. If he chooses, and has sufficient natural calibre, such scenes as we depicted in the early part of this paper will become impossible. They were pictures drawn from reality, but from a reality which is fast becoming a thing of the past. When once his natural intelligence is thoroughly aroused—and education is fast arousing it—long lives of one and two generations in extent, spent as has been described, will be utterly out of the question, and such changes must be for the advantage of the whole community.

Women in the Field

1875

Those who labour in the fields require no calendar, no carefully compiled book of reference to tell them when to sow and when to reap, to warn them of the flight of time. The flowers, blooming and fading, mark the months with unfailing regularity. When the sweet violet may be found in warm sheltered nooks, and the sleepy snake first crawls out from under the brown leaves, then it is time to gather the couch or roots after the plough, and to hoe the young turnips and swedes. This is the first work of the year for the agricultural women. It is not a pleasant work. Everyone who has walked over a ploughed field remembers how the boots were clogged with the adhesive clay, and how the continuous ridges and furrows impeded progress. These women have to stoop and gather up the white couch roots, and the other weeds, and place them in heaps to be burnt. The spring is not always soft and balmy. There comes one lovely day, when the bright sunlight encourages the buds and peeping leaves to push out, and then follows a week or more of the harsh biting east wind. The arable field is generally devoid of hedges or trees to break the force of the weather, and the couch-pickers have to withstand its cutting rush in the open. Dwellers in cities as they cower near the fire and listen to the howl of the storm in the chimney, and see from the window the smoke driven in all directions, remark to each other, 'What wretched weather. The east wind penetrates one to the bones'. Gentlemen hurry along the pavement wrapped in huge greatcoats, ladies with shawls and comforters and sealskin muffs. But what do these know of the real force of an east wind? Well-fed—there is nothing like good food to fortify the frame against cold—well clothed, with roaring fires to rush home to, and brilliantly-lit apartments impervious to draught, what conception can they form of the misery of standing all day without the slightest shelter, exposed to the rude northern blast? The cold clods of earth numb the fingers as they search for the roots and weeds. The damp clay chills the feet through thick-nailed boots, and the back grows stiff with stooping. If the poor woman suffers from the rheumatisms so common

among the labouring class, such a day as this will make every bone in her body ache. When at last four o'clock comes she has to walk a mile or two miles to her cottage and prepare her husband's supper. In hilly districts, where sheep are the staple production, it follows, of course, that turnips and swedes as their food are the most important crop. Upon the unenclosed open downs the cold of early spring is intense, and the women who are engaged in hoeing feel it bitterly. Down in the rich fertile valleys, in the meadows, women are at work picking up the stones out of the way of the scythe, or beating clots about with a short prong. All these are wretched tasks, especially the last, and the remuneration for exposure and handling dirt very small. But now 'green grow the rushes', and the cuckooflower thrusts its pale petals up among the rising grass. Till that grass reaches maturity the women in meadow districts can find no field employment. The woods are now carpeted with acres upon acres of the wild hyacinth, or bluebell, and far surpass in loveliness the most cultivated garden. The sheen of the rich deep blue shows like a lake of colour, in which the tall ash poles stand, and in the sunset each bell is tinged with purple. The nightingale sings in the hazel copse, or on the hawthorn bough, both day and night, and higher up, upon the downs, the skies are full of larks carolling at 'Heaven's gate'. But the poor woman hears them not. She has no memories of poetry; her mind can call up no beautiful thoughts to associate with the flower or the bird. She can sign her name in a scrawling hand, and she can spell through simple print, but to all intents and purposes she is completely ignorant. Therefore, she cannot see, that is, appreciate or feel with, the beauty with which she is surrounded. Yet, despite the harsh, rude life she leads, there works up to the surface some little instinctive yearning after a higher condition. The yellow flowers in the cottage garden—why is it that cottagers are so fond of yellow?—the gilly flower, the single stock, marigolds, and such old-fashioned favourites, show a desire for ornament; still more so the occasional geranium in the window, specially tended by the wife.

> The ousel-cock, so black of hue,
> With orange tawny bill,

moves restlessly to and fro in his great wicker-work cage beside the door, and depend upon it, it is the woman who supplies him regularly with food. The sun grows hotter now, and the dog-rose blooms, sign of June and haymaking. The women with their prongs begin 'tedding', i.e., throwing the grass about which the mowers have cut, spreading it from the swathe equally over the ground. They also turn it; but now the hay-making machines are so general their chief work is with the rake. Even this has been almost superseded upon large farms by the horse-rake. Hay-making is the pleasantest time for the agricultural woman. The heat is better than the cold winds, the work light, and varied, and the wages higher. But much mischief is done by the indiscriminate mixing of the sexes, and the language in a hay-field is not that of pastoral poetry. Now the small creeping convolvulus with pink-streaked petals winds along the edge of the corn-field, and the beautiful 'blue-bottle' lifts its head among the wheat and barley. At three o'clock in the morning the women rise to clean the cottage, and wash the linen, and at five set out for the harvest-field. Often they walk two miles carrying the baby, and then leave it in charge of a girl while they reap. The wheat is bent back with a curved stick held in the left hand called a 'fagging-stick', and the right hand chops with the sharp sickle against the straw. Through the blazing heat of the long summer day, till night, and sometimes under the pale light of the harvest-moon this labour continues. Its effects are visible in the thin frame, the bony wrist, the skinny arm showing the sinews, the rounded shoulders and stoop, the wrinkles and lines upon the sunburnt faces. Many women labour thus while still suckling their infants; and at night carry home heavy bundles of gleanings upon their heads. This work is done by the piece—so much per acre—and they rely upon these extraordinary exertions to supply them with clothing or pay the rent. Already the leaves of the lime tree are turning colour, the acorns on the oak are enlarging, and the berries of the bryony ripening. The robin commences to sing again, and other birds are silent. The wailing sound of the threshing-machine rises and falls with the wind, and the women are busy 'sheening' as they call it, that is feeding the thresher. Others are preparing the straw for the thatcher. The strong traction-engine drags the plough through the hard soil where so lately the tall wheat stood, and women are again employed cleaning the land. Their condition is so much better than it was that they do not milk; and that is nearly all. Their labour is too hard, and in too exposed places; and yet they cannot get sufficient of it, for machinery has taken their employment away. From earliest childhood they are inured to the coarse ways and rough talk of rude men, and the saddest results, in a moral sense, ensue. They dwell among the flowers, but the flowers are not for them. It is difficult to reach them; but one thing may be done. The young girls are now being taught in schools, why should not some organization be set on foot by ladies, both in town and country, to receive them after leaving school, and provide them with situations as domestic servants, for whom there is an increasing demand.

Cheese-Making in the West

1877

The enrolment of a cheese show on the list of annual exhibitions in London cannot be regarded as a mere accidental event. There are other signs besides this that the art of cheese-making in England is beginning to be studied with a zeal hitherto unknown, and is this year attracting a larger proportion of the national industry. One of these signs may be found in the agricultural returns recently published, by which it appears that the pasture lands of Great Britain have again increased greatly during the past twelve months, while the number of live stock has decreased, showing thus that the addition made to the grass lands has not been made with the view to fattening more beasts for the market, but for dairy purposes. Accordingly, it is remarked that not only in London, but in all the western counties where cheese shows and cheese fairs are held, they have been better attended both by buyers and sellers than in any former year. The farmer who pays his rent by the sale of his cheeses is becoming a more important person. He finds ready customers for them at a remunerative profit; but he will soon have to keep his wits about him to make sure that his neighbour does not outdo him in the quality of his produce.

The elementary principles of the cheese-making art are pretty well known to all except the most thorough-going cockneys. The processes by which the milk is first consolidated, then separated into curds and whey; by which the curds are first broken up, then heated, then ground up again, and lastly packed up and crushed together in the press; are familiar to almost every one who has ever stayed a fortnight in the West of England. That which is less known and less well understood is the semi-instinctive skill which directs the process through all its apparently simple stages. Yet the buxom dame who is charged with this duty is as justly proud of her vocation and as full of busy importance as the manager of a brewery in October or the major-domo of a baronial hall on Christmas Eve. She is proud not only of her art itself, but of her particular interpretation thereof. Her own method is unique—either elaborated out of her own inner con-

172

sciousness and her own experience or learnt from some ancestor who so inaugurated it; and in its own way it is a branch of scientific knowledge which the proprietress will stoutly uphold against all rivals in the world. 'The learning is a fine thing,' she will admit, 'and they do say that more is to be made with the head than with the hands.' But then the men of letters could never understand 'all the mysteries there is in the making of a cheese' and this real or supposed inability on their part appears to the good soul at least quite as reprehensible as her own incapacity to write a philosophical essay. After all, perhaps, the laugh is not all on our side. If the man who makes two blades of grass grow where only one grew before deserves more praise than the winner of many battles, surely those who convert the said blades of grass into such food as Stilton or Cheddar are entitled to greater honours than the pamphleteers and orators who set by the ears Turks and Russians on the one hand and Republicans and Monarchists on the other.

Cheese-making is especially, and it may almost be said essentially, a connubial occupation. It may be doubted whether a widow or a widower could ever make a good cheese; and as for an old maid, it is a maxim beyond dispute in the West country that the milk would turn sour under her eye. In the Saturnian age it is clear that all mortals were married in their teens, and this is why pastoral poets sing as much of love and matrimony as of milk-pails and cheese-presses. The whole science of cheese-making seems to be naturally based upon the assumption that the chief agents are man and wife. The husband and the wife are almost as necessary personages on the scene as the parson and clerk in a church, or the driver and fireman on a locomotive engine. One half of the performance devolves as naturally upon the lady as the other does upon the man; and the two parts, in which each takes a separate and legitimate pride, cannot be either interchanged or confused together without mischief and injury. Thus it is that the strong arm of Meliboeus carries in the pails of steaming milk, and pours the contents with steady accuracy into the strainer arranged for them; while the neat hands of Phyllis direct the wooden ladle, and with calm complacency stir and mix the matchlessly pure white sea as it slowly circles round its shining tin vat. Then it is the dame who measures out and adds the just proportion of rennet and of sour whey, while the emptying of the refuse whey, or rather the transportation of it to the region of the styes, falls naturally within the province of her more athletic lord. After the interval allowed for breakfast the same division of labour is continued, the hard work being assigned to him, and the light or head work devolving upon her. The task of gently crushing the curd when it is first formed is obviously a female occupation, and the bare arms of the performer in the at-

titude of executing this figure is one of the most familiar to those who have ever visited a dairy. To grind the curds when coagulated into harder masses requires generally a more muscular arm, and the duty of turning the cheeses in the cheese room is clearly one which no woman ought to be called upon to undertake. This duty alone is no light one when the shelves have begun to groan beneath the whole weight of the summer produce. A hundred cheeses, averaging 56 pounds a piece in weight, are not taken up from their several places and set down again bottom upwards in the same place without some physical exertion; and some of our athletes who distinguish themselves at Lillie Bridge or the German gymnasium would be puzzled to 'turn' a whole room full of cheeses as quickly and neatly as a stumpy little farmer from 'Zomerzet'. Besides this, there is other work to be done in the cheese room in adjusting the linen garments of the inmates. Each cheese, during the first days and weeks of its existence wears veritable 'stays', the lacing of which is in itself an art worthy of a Bond-street dressmaker; and this lacing up of stays is perhaps the only one of all the operations which in the cheese room, as elsewhere, may be assigned at will either to Meliboeus or Phyllis, or to the two together.

Throughout the whole of these processes it is clear to the philosophic mind what should be the relation of the principal actors to one another. If they are to hope for success they must be united in the staid and homely bonds of conjugal felicity. Neither the passions nor the jealousies of lovers must trouble the cool atmosphere of the dairy; flirting would interfere fatally with the regular order of the day. Each of the actors must stand on the strict level of equality which marriage presupposes, and be allowed an exactly fair proportion of responsibility and credit. Thus it is the man who discusses all subjects of interest between him and his landlord. It is the wife who conducts negotiations with the purchaser of the cheeses. All her efforts lead up to a successful interview with the dealer when he comes on his autumn rounds, or, if she is of more ambitious spirit, to a place of honour at the fair. The dealer knows to which of the pair praise or blame is justly due, if the purchase turns out to be above or below the average of former years; and the connoisseur in cheeses will admit, if he has any fairness, that a *chef d' oeuvre* from Frome or Beeby reflects about equal proportions of credit on the farmer and the farmer's wife.

Agricultural Labour

1872

To the Editor

Sir,—I wish to lay before you a few facts illustrating the comparative position of the agricultural labourer and of the mechanic, which, in this district, are brought into sharp relief, in consequence of the neighbourhood being agricultural, while the town is the workshop of the Great Western Railway. The subject naturally opens with the following advertisement, copied from the *Daily Telegraph*:

LABOURERS,—Will any employ agricultural labourers out of work? Will gladly work at 9 shillings per week. Address, 'Relieving Officer, Cranborne, Dorset.' North country papers please notice this.

The ordinary labourer in this district receives 9 shillings or 10 shillings a week, as the circumstances vary, regularly. Last summer I am assured by a large farmer that he paid men 30 shillings a week. The same gentleman employs a shepherd at 11 shillings a week, with £2 over at Michaelmas, and £1 for lambing; making an average of 12 shillings per week all the year round.

Nine or ten shillings a week is the regular pay. In addition to this, in the spring there is hoeing, in the summer mowing, in the autumn reaping, and hoeing again. As I have stated above, in the height of the harvest 30 shillings a week is sometimes, and not unusually, paid.

To compensate for the loss of these extras in the winter there must be added the convenience of a cottage at an extremely low and often nominal rent; and the advantage of a garden, sometimes as much as 20 lugs; and representing a supply of vegetables. The wages, therefore, of the agricultural labourer are, taking the whole year round, as nearly as possible equal to those of the labourer in the factory in actual hard cash; and taken in another light, more than equal, for the mechanical labourer is usually unable to find lodgings in the town near to his work from their high price, and is, therefore, obliged to take a cottage in some village at the distance of two or three miles. More than 100 of the employees in the Great Western Railway's works at New Swindon walk every morning to their work from Wroughton, four miles, and home again at night, altogether eight miles. In

176

U. L. Sieger '79

one extreme case which came under my observation a boy, employed in the rail mill, walked from Wootton Bassett, six miles, every morning, and six at night. The labour and time expended in this walking are equal to half a day's work, so that the mechanical labourer really, for the same money, works a day and a half, as compared with the agricultural labourer. Half his time in the winter the agricultural labourer only works from eight till four or five. The mechanic is completely under the control of his employer; but of late years, at least, the agricultural labourer, and especially in the summer, goes his own way pretty much, or as one farmer very appositely expressed it, 'We have to pray them to work as well as pay them'.

The rent of small houses in the town adjacent to the factory varies from 5 shillings to 6 shillings and 8 shillings per week—a price too high for the great majority of mechanics to pay. The result, consequently, is that two or three families live, or rather 'pig', in one house—one takes it as nominal tenant and the rest pay him; so that really the overcrowding in houses tenanted by mechanics is worse and more common than in purely agricultural villages, with this additional evil, that in a town the effect in inducing disease is not modified by the action of plenty of free air as in the country.

On the whole, therefore, the agricultural labourer appears to be in, at the very least, an equivalent position to that of the mechanical labourer, if not in many cases superior. I have advisedly used the term 'mechanical labourer', because a comparison cannot fairly be instituted between the unskilled agricultural labourer and the superior mechanic or skilled workman, who earns £2, £3, or even £4 a week. The comparison is only proper when the mechanical labourer, working under the skilled mechanic, is considered.

In conclusion, a remark may be made upon the system which prevails in too many agricultural districts, of the large landlords letting the cottages which were originally designed for the labourers employed on the farms where the cottages stand to mechanics, for the sake of an extra 2 shillings or 3 shillings a week. The consequence often is that the agricultural labourer has to walk some distance, is dissatisfied, and justly so. The cottages upon farms should be strictly confined to agricultural labourers, who would then be more satisfied, and would better appreciate their advantages. The Duke of Marlborough, owner of a large number of cottages in this district, sets a laudable example in this matter. They are let only to agricultural labourers.—I am, Sir,

yours faithfully,
Richard Jefferies
Coate Farm, Swindon.   Feb. 28.

Notes

P. 21

The Wiltshire Downs and its three companion pieces, *In a Pine-Wood* (P. 28), *The Commonest Thing in the World* (P. 32), and *The Old Mill* (P. 36), appeared in *The Graphic*, an independent illustrated weekly newspaper started in 1869. Famous novelists of the day, among them Thomas Hardy and Rider Haggard, had their work serialized in the paper, which was a rival to the older and more renowned *Illustrated London News*. Shorter pieces in *The Graphic* often accompanied and enlarged upon the illustrations. Jefferies' essays here fulfil both functions, being word-pictures of a kind in which the more mature Jefferies was to excel.

P. 25

A Summer Day in Savernake Forest and *Village Hunting* (P. 41), are both aimed at a predominantly urban and suburban audience. They were written for *The Globe*, a London evening newspaper. At the time they appeared Jefferies was spending most of his time in or around the city, and it is interesting to note the exaggerated contrasts he makes between the noisy, expensive, hasty urban scene and a countryside made as attractive as possible to lure the urban 'pioneer'. Jefferies returns to the Fung-shuy theme in Chapter XVII of *Wild Life in a Southern County*.

P. 45

The Contents of Ten Acres—May. A mature Jefferies' essay which was published in *Forestry*, a journal for estate managers, those concerned with arboriculture, and country matters generally. It is the only contribution which he made to this periodical. The connection with it probably arose through its editor F. G. Heath. In the early 1870s Heath, then a journalist with the *Morning Advertiser*, examined the problems of the agricultural labourer in great detail for his newspaper and published two books on the subject. Though he took a distinctly different view of the causes of their difficulties, the flourish with which this essay is introduced in the magazine suggests that the editor was pleased to have such a renowned author contributing. This essay is contained in Jefferies' manuscripts for reprinting.

P. 53

Butterfly Corner is one of the most recent and interesting of the newly-discovered essays. It was published nine days after Jefferies' death, but internal evidence suggests that it was written in the summer of 1886. A notebook entry for August 15, 1886 states, 'Rubytail, logs. Butterfly corner'. The precision of description and patient cataloguing of the insects' movements over a long period are hallmarks of much of Jefferies' writing.

P.59

Flowers and Fruit was published in *The Globe* during Jefferies' Sydenham days. Its greatest significance lies in the picture which he sketches of 'a farm in the west', probably an idealization of Coate Farm. This, along with two other pieces from *The Globe* are mentioned for possible reprinting.

P.63

Birds of Swindon. Jefferies contributed several pieces to the *Swindon Advertiser*, including this letter. It provides the first published evidence of Jefferies as an observer of wild-life in the North Wiltshire area. Some of this material was used over eight years later in Chapter XX of *Wild Life in a Southern County*. This is not, as one would expect, Jefferies' best work, much of it consisting of a regurgitation of field notes. There is, nevertheless, sufficient evidence in the linking of folklore to the habits of birds and the painstaking thoroughness of observation to hint at later developments.

P. 70

The Future of Country Society and *The Size of Farms* (P. 139), both signed, appeared in the *New Quarterly*, avowedly 'a High-Class Literary and Social Periodical' meant for the educated reader. It was owned and edited by a friend of Jefferies, Oswald Crawfurd. The fact that this periodical avoided major contentious issues of the day has not deterred Jefferies from discussing some of the outstanding rural problems, though his treatment and proposed solutions are sufficiently balanced and non-controversial to satisfy the demands of the magazine.

P.99

The Future of Farming, High-Pressure Agriculture (P. 113), and *John Smith's Shanty* (P. 148), were all contributed to *Fraser's Magazine*, one of the first magazines to publish his work. In all, twelve articles and essays, the majority on agriculture, appeared in *Fraser's*. The magazine was edited up to 1874 by the historian and author J. A. Froude, of whom Leslie Stephen commented that 'He was hardly the man likely to attract eager young liberal writers'.[1] The implications of the initial part of *John Smith's Shanty* are, nevertheless, fairly radical. A part of this essay was published in the collection *The Toilers of the Field* in 1892, five years after Jefferies' death. The need for the essay to be published in its entirety seems to me to be two-fold. Firstly, it is an artistic whole and was printed as such in *Fraser's*. Secondly, the part omitted from *The Toilers of the Field* collection is more cautious and general in its approach, and adds balance to an essay which would otherwise appear atypical of Jefferies' writing of this period.

P.138

Weather and Wages in the Country appeared in the *Pall Mall Gazette* at the nadir of the Great Depression and captures well the problems faced by all sections of farming at this time. The *Gazette* was edited at this time by Frederick Greenwood, a friend of Jefferies and a major influence on his nature writing.

P.142

The Gentleman Farmer rightly belongs to the series, *Hodge and His Masters*, but, as it appeared in *The World* and not *The Standard*, some complications may have arisen, when this book was published. *The World* was edited at this time by the somewhat tempestuous Edmund Yates. Jefferies wrote several essays for this newspaper, mostly 'society' pieces. This is the only contribution with an agricultural theme, and, it should be noted, even this is concerned with the upper class of rural society.

[1] —*Some Early Impressions,* (London, 1924), p. 137.

P.168

Women in the Field was first printed in *The Graphic*. It was the first essay which he contributed to this newspaper, and the only one dealing with the agricultural workers' problems. It fits in well with *The Graphic's* avowed emphasis on social realism and shows, in the juxtaposition of the beauty and abundance of nature and the poverty and ugliness of human existence, one of Jefferies' favourite themes.

P.172

Cheese-Making in the West was contributed to *The Globe*. At this time (1877), Jefferies concentrated much of his writing on the dairy industry of the south-west, and particularly on the cheese producing part of it.

P.176

Agricultural Labour was published in *The Wiltshire and Gloucestershire Standard*. The subject matter was taken up again in letters to *The Times* eight months later. This letter shows that the 'Labour Question' had occupied his mind for some time, and that subsequently expressed opinions were not spontaneously offered.

Bibliography

WORKS BY JEFFERIES

1. *Books and Pamphlets*
   This section contains all Jefferies' published books and pamphlets, all books to which he contributed during his lifetime, and all anthologies of his work. The order is that of chronology of publication.

Reporting, Editing, and Authorship. London: John Snow, 1873 (pamphlet).

Jack Brass, Emperor of England. London: T. Pettitt, 1873 (pamphlet).

A Memoir of the Goddards of North Wilts, Compiled from Ancient Records, Registers and Family Papers. London: Simmons and Botten, 1873.

The Scarlet Shawl: A Novel. London: Tinsley, 1874.

Restless Human Hearts. 3 vols. London: Tinsley, 1875.

Suez-cide!! Or How Miss Britannia Bought a Dirty Puddle and Lost Her Sugar-plums. London: John Snow, 1876 (pamphlet).

World's End: A Story in Three Books. 3 vols. London: Tinsley, 1877.

The Gamekeeper at Home; or, Sketches of Natural History and Rural Life. London: Smith Elder, 1878.

Wild Life in a Southern County. London: Smith Elder, 1879 (an American reprint [1903, 1904] was re-titled *An English Village).*

The Amateur Poacher. London: Smith Elder, 1879.

Greene Ferne Farm. London: Smith Elder, 1880.

Hodge and His Masters. 2 vols. London: Smith Elder, 1880 (one English reprint [1946] was retitled *A Classic of English Farming).*

Round About a Great Estate. London: Smith Elder, 1880.

Wood Magic: A Fable. 2 vols. London: Cassell, 1881 (an American abridgment [1899, 1900] was retitled *Sir Bevis: A Tale of the Fields).*

Bevis: The Story of a Boy. 3 vols. London: Sampson Low, 1882 (English abridgments [1937, 1940] were retitled *Bevis at Home* and *Bevis and Mark* respectively).

Nature Near London. London: Chatto & Windus, 1883.

Society Novelettes. By Various Authors. 2 vols. London: Vizetelly, 1883 (Jefferies contributed two short stories, 'Kiss and Try' in volume I, 'Out of the Season' in volume II. Volume I was reprinted in 1886 as *No Rose Without a Thorn, and Other Tales,* volume II as *The Dove's Nest, and Other Tales).*

The Story of My Heart: My Autobiography. London: Longmans, 1883.

Red Deer. London: Longmans, 1884.

The Life of the Fields. London: Chatto & Windus, 1884.

The Dewy Morn. 2 vols. London: Bentley, 1884.

After London; or, Wild England. London: Cassell, 1885.

The Open Air. London: Chatto & Windus, 1885.

WHITE, GILBERT. *The Natural History of Selborne [1789].* With an introduction by RICHARD JEFFERIES. London: Walter Scott, 1887.

Amaryllis at the Fair. London: Sampson Low, 1887.

Field and Hedgerow: Being the Last Essays of Richard Jefferies, Collected by His Widow. London: Longmans, 1889.

The Toilers of the Field. London: Longmans, 1892.

Thoughts from the Writings of Richard Jefferies. Selected by H. S. H. WAYLEN. London: Longmans, 1896 (anthology).

The Early Fiction of Richard Jefferies. Edited by GRACE TOPLIS. London: Simpkin, Marshall, 1896.

Jefferies' Land: A History of Swindon and Its Environs. Edited by GRACE TOPLIS. London: Simpkin, Marshall, 1896.

T. T. T. Wells: A. Young, 1896 (short story).

Jefferies' Nature Thoughts. Edited by THOMAS COKE WATKINS. Portland, Maine: T. Mosher, 1904 (anthology).

Passages from the Nature Writings of Richard Jefferies. Selected by A. H. HYATT. London: Chatto & Windus, 1905 (anthology; the third impression was issued as *The Pocket Richard Jefferies Anthology,* 1911).

The Hills and the Vale. With an introduction by EDWARD THOMAS. London: Duckworth, 1909.

Selections from Richard Jefferies. Made by F. W. TICKNER. London: Longmans, 1909 (anthology).

Out-of-Doors with Richard Jefferies. Edited by ERIC FITCH DAGLISH. London: Dent, 1935 (anthology).

Richard Jefferies: Selections of His Work, with Details of His Life and Circumstance, His Death and Immortality. Edited with an introduction by HENRY WILLIAMSON. London: Faber, 1937 (anthology).

Jefferies' England. Edited by SAMUEL J. LOOKER. London: Constable, 1937 (anthology).

Readings from Richard Jefferies. Edited by RONALD HOOK. London: Macmillan, 1940 (anthology).

The Nature Diaries and Notebooks of Richard Jefferies, with an Essay 'A Tangle of Autumn', now printed for the first time. Edited by SAMUEL J. LOOKER. Billericay, Essex: Grey Walls Press, 1941.

Jefferies' Countryside. Edited by SAMUEL J. LOOKER. London: Constable, 1944 (anthology).

Richard Jefferies' London. Edited by SAMUEL J. LOOKER. London: Lutterworth Press, 1944 (anthology).

A Richard Jefferies Anthology. Selected by GEORGE PRATT INSH. London: Collins, 1945.

The Spring of the Year. Edited by SAMUEL J. LOOKER. London: Lutterworth Press, 1946 (anthology).

Summer in the Woods. A selection from the works of Richard Jefferies, with four drawings by S. H. de Roos. Amsterdam: Type Foundry, 1947 (anthology).

The Essential Richard Jefferies. With an introduction by MALCOLM ELWIN. London: Jonathan Cape, 1948 (anthology).

The Jefferies Companion. Edited by SAMUEL J. LOOKER. London: Phoenix House, 1948 (anthology).

Beauty is Immortal (Felise of the Dewy Morn), with Some Hitherto Uncollected Essays and Manuscripts. Edited by SAMUEL J. LOOKER. Worthing: Aldridge Brothers, 1948.

The Old House at Coate, and Other Hitherto Unprinted Essays. Edited by SAMUEL J. LOOKER. London: Lutterworth Press, 1948.

The Nature Diaries and Note-Books of Richard Jefferies. Edited by SAMUEL J. LOOKER. London: Grey Walls Press, 1948.

Chronicles of the Hedges, and Other Essays. Edited by SAMUEL J. LOOKER. London: Phoenix House, 1948.

Field and Farm: Essays Now First Collected, With Some from MSS. Edited by SAMUEL J. LOOKER. London: Phoenix House, 1957.

To this list must be added the privately printed volume:

'Jefferies Unpublished Manuscripts'. by SAMUEL J. LOOKER in Victor Bonham-Carter (ed.), *The Bryanston Miscellany*. Bryanston School, Dorset: 1958.

AND

'Richard Jefferies: Man of the Fields, a Biography and Letters' (Appendix I). by SAMUEL J. LOOKER and CHRICHTON PORTEOUS. London: John Baker, 1965.

2. Serializations

This contains all serial contributions to newspapers and magazines. It supplements and completes the list of individual essays contained in the following section. Where a paper which was not originally intended to form part of the scheme was later included in the published volume, the entry is given in parenthesis and also listed with the essays.

The Amateur Poacher, in *Pall Mall Gazette.* (1877: Nov. 16); 1879: March 1, 8, 14, 25, 29; April 3, 10, 16, 23, 26; May 6, 10, 17, 23, 31; June 10, 18, 21, 25; July 1, 5, 7.

The Gamekeeper at Home, in *Pall Mall Gazette.* (1877: Dec. 12, 14, 29); 1878: Jan. 4, 9, 12, 18, 22, 26, 31; Feb. 2, 8, 12, 16, 23; March 2, 12, 15, 19, 26, 28; April 1, 5, 9, 12, 17, 24.

Greene Ferne Farm, in *Time.* One chapter each month from April 1879 to February 1880.

History of Cirencester, in *Wilts and Gloucestershire Standard.* 1870: March 12, 26; April 4; May 7, 28; June 11; July 2, 9, 30; Aug. 6; Oct. 29.

History of Malmesbury, in *North Wilts Herald.* 1867: April 20, 27; May 4, 11, 25; June 1, 15, 22, 29; July 6, 13, 20, 27; Aug. 3, 10, 24, 31; Sept. 14, 21, 28.

History of Swindon and Its Environs, in *North Wilts Herald.* 1867: Oct. 5, 12, 19, 26; Nov. 2, 9; 1868: Jan. 4; Feb. 29. (Subsequently published as *Jefferies' Land: A History of Swindon and Its Environs.*)

Hodge and His Masters, in *Standard.* (1878: Sept. 24; Oct. 9, 17, 30; Nov. 14); Nov. 19, 26; Dec. 4, 12, 19, 25; 1879: Jan. 2, 8, 17, 28; Feb. 4; (March 31; April 15); Aug. 16, 22, 26; Sept. 2, 8, 15, 23, 30; Oct. 7, 14, 21, 28; Nov. 4, 12, 18; Dec. (16), 26, 30; 1880: Jan. 5, 12. (Published in the *Standard* as two serials: *Hodge at His Work*, Nov. 19, 1878 to Feb. 4, 1879; *Hodge's Masters*, Aug. 16, 1879 to Jan. 12, 1880.)

The Rise of Maximin, Emperor of the Occident, in *New Monthly Magazine.* 1876:

Oct., Nov., Dec.; 1877: Jan., Feb., March, April (two contributions), May, June, July.
Round About a Great Estate, in *Pall Mall Gazette.* 1880: Jan. 13, 19, 21, 24, 29; Feb. 5, 11, 14, 18, 24; March 2, 11, 17, 22, 29; April 2, 10, 14, 26, 28.
Wild Life in a Southern County, in *Pall Mall Gazette.* 1878: May 9, 13, 17, 22, 28; June 1, 6, 11, 14, 19, 21, 27; July 1, 6, 10, 16, 19, 22, 27; Aug. 1, 6, 10, 13, 16, 21, 23, 26; Sept. 5, 7, 11, 14, 19, 21, 25, 30; Oct. 7, 12, 16, 19, 24, 28; Nov. 2, 9, 16, 25; Dec. 4.

3. *Essays and Published Letters*

These are listed alphabetically under title, followed by the place and date of first publication in newspaper or magazine, and finally the location in collected volumes.

'About the Hedges.' *Standard,* Oct. 9, 1878. Later incorporated into *Hodge and His Masters.*
'Acorn-Gatherer, The.' *See* 'Bits of Oak-Bark.'
'After the County Franchise.' *Longman's Magazine,* Feb. 1884. *The Hills and the Vale.*
'Agricultural Affairs.' *Pall Mall Gazette,* June 5, 1880. Uncollected.
'Agricultural Book-Keeping.' *St. James's Gazette,* Aug. 15, 1884. Uncollected.
'Agricultural 'Capital Account', The.' *Live Stock Journal,* Sept. 7, 1877. Uncollected.
'Agricultural Heraldry.' *Live Stock Journal,* Dec. 7, 1877. *Field and Farm.*
'Agricultural Labour.' Letter to *Wilts and Gloucestershire Standard,* March 9, 1872. *Landscape and Labour.*
'Agricultural Labourer's Vote, The.' *Pall Mall Gazette,* May 24, 1877. Uncollected.
'Agricultural Side of the Water Question, The.' *Live Stock Journal,* April 5, 1878. Uncollected.
'Agriculture and the Water Congress.' *Live Stock Journal,* May 31, 1878. Uncollected.
'America and the Meat Market.' *Live Stock Journal,* Jan. 5, 1877. Uncollected.
'American Views on the Meat Traffic.' *Live Stock Journal,* March 2, 1877. Uncollected.
'Among the Nuts.' *Standard,* Aug. 23, 1886. *Field and Hedgerow.*
'Anthills. Adders.' *See* 'Heathlands.'
'April.' *See* 'Picture of April.'
'April Gossip.' *St. James's Gazette,* April 19, 1886. *Field and Hedgerow.*
'Art of Shooting, The' (editor's title). *The Field,* March 15, 1947. *Field and Farm.*
'At Coate Farm.' *See* 'The Cattle Shed at Coate.'
'August Out-of-doors.' *Pall Mall Gazette,* Aug. 28, 1879. *Chronicles of the Hedges.*
' 'Autonomy' and What It Means.' *Cassell's Family Magazine,* Feb. 1877. Uncollected.
'Autumn Fairs, The.' *Live Stock Journal,* Oct. 19, 1877. Uncollected.
'Average of Beauty, The.' *World,* April 26, 1876. Uncollected.
'Average Servant, The.' *Cassell's Family Magazine,* Jan. 1878. Uncollected.

'Backwoods, The.' Not published. *Beauty is Immortal.*

'Backwoods of London.' *Globe,* Sept. 21, 1877. *Chronicles of the Hedges.*

'Bad Harvests in Sussex.' *The Times,* Sept. 21, 1881. *Chronicles of the Hedges.* (This paper is the final paragraph of 'Some Uncultivated Country: Downs.' as it first appeared in *The Times.* It was later omitted when the essay was collected under the title 'Downs.' in *The Open Air.*)

'Barn, A.' *Standard,* Sept. 23, 1880. *Nature Near London.*

'Bathing Season, The.' *Pall Mall Gazette,* July 28 and Aug. 8, 1884. *The Open Air.*

'Bath Show Yard, The.' *Live Stock Journal,* June 15, 1877. Uncollected.

'Battle of 1866, The' (poem). *North Wilts Herald,* June 30, 1866. *The Early Fiction of Richard Jefferies* (Preface).

'Beatrice and the Centaur' (editor's title). Not published. Uncollected. (*See* Samuel J. Looker, 'Jefferies Unpublished Manuscripts.')

'Beauty in the Country.' Not published (?) *The Open Air.*

'Beauty of the Fields, The.' *See* 'Notes on Landscape Painting.'

'Beauty of the Trees, The' (editor's title). *See* 'Fir, Larch, and Sycamore, Near London.'

'Benediction of the Light, The (editor's title). *See* 'Thoughts in the Fields.'

'Ben Tubbs' Adventures.' Not published. Uncollected. (*See* notes on sales in *Times Literary Supplement,* May 29, 1959. The MS. was sold at Hodgson's, 24 April 1959.)

'Bill-Hook, The.' *See* 'Chronicles of the Hedges.'

'Bird Catchers.' *Pall Mall Gazette,* Oct. 26, 1880. Uncollected.

'Bird Notes in June' (editor's title). Not published. *Field and Farm.*

'Birds Climbing the Air.' *St. James's Gazette,* July 28, 1883. *The Life of the Fields.* (Published in *St. James's Gazette* under the title 'Climbing the Air.')

'Birds of Spring.' *Chambers' Journal,* March 1, 1884. *The Hills and the Vale.*

'Birds of Swindon.' Letter to *Swindon Advertiser,* April 24, 1871. *Landscape and Labour.*

'Birds' Nests.' *St. James's Gazette,* April 19, 1884. *Field and Hedgerow.*

'Bits of Oak Bark.' *Longman's Magazine,* March 1883. *The Life of the Fields.* (This overall title includes 'The Acorn-Gatherer,' 'The Legend of a Gateway,' and 'A Roman Brook.')

'Both Sides of the Meat Question.' *Live Stock Journal,* Feb. 9, 1887. Uncollected.

'Breeze on Beachy Head, The.' *Standard,* Sept. 6, 1881. *Nature Near London.*

'Brook, A.' *Standard,* Sept. 30, 1880. *Nature Near London.*

'Buckhurst Park.' *Standard,* Aug. 19, 1886. *Field and Hedgerow.*

'Butterfly Corner.' *Standard,* Aug. 23, 1887. *Landscape and Labour.*

'By the Exe.' *Standard,* Sept. 25, 1883. *The Life of the Fields.* (In the collected version, 'The Otter in Somerset' [q.v.] is added to the original text, plus a new passage concerning otters near London.)

'Castle Shed at Coate, The' (editor's title). *Countrygoer,* Winter 1948. *Field and Farm.* (This fragment should form part of 'The Old House at Coate', but was only discovered after that essay was published. Published in *Countrygoer* under the title 'At Coate Farm.')

'Chaffinch, The.' *See* 'Chronicles of the Hedges.'

'Changes in Country Habits.' *Pall Mall Gazette,* Aug. 28, 1877. *Field and Farm.*

'Cheese.' *Pall Mall Gazette,* Nov. 30, 1877. Uncollected.

'Cheese-Making in the West.' *Globe,* Oct. 9, 1877. *Landscape and Labour.*

'Choosing a Gun.' Not published. *The Hills and the Vale.* (Some of the material was used in the final chapter of *The Amateur Poacher.*)

'Christmas: Then and Now.' *Live Stock Journal Literary Supplement,* Dec. 21, 1877. *Field and Farm.*

'Chronicles of the Hedges.' *Land,* Feb. 12, 19, 26; March 19; April 2, 23; May 14, 21, 1881. *Chronicles of the Hedges.* (This overall title includes 'The Bill-Hook,' 'The Chaffinch,' and 'The Meadow Gateway.')

'Clematis Lane.' *Standard,* Sept. 12, 1883. *The Life of the Fields.*

'Climbing the Air.' *See* 'Birds Climbing the Air.'

'Coming of Summer, The.' *Longman's Magazine,* Dec. 1891. *The Toilers of the Field.*

'Coming Woman, The.' *World,* June 28, 1876. Uncollected.

'Commonest Thing in the World, The.' *Graphic,* Aug. 11, 1877. *Landscape and Labour.*

'Conforming to Environment.' *St. James's Gazette,* June 24, 1886. Uncollected.

'Contents of Ten Acres—May, The.' *Forestry,* May, 1883. *Landscape and Labour.*

'Contrasts Between Town and Country' (editor's title). Not Published. *Chronicles of the Hedges.*

'Cost of Agricultural Labour in 1875, The.' *Standard,* Oct. 1, 1875. Uncollected.

'Cottage Ideas.' *Chambers' Journal,* May 8, 1886. *Field and Hedgerow.*

'Cottage Society and County Suffrage.' *Pall Mall Gazette,* Nov. 6, 1877. *Field and Farm.*

'Country Curate, The.' *Standard,* Dec. 16, 1879. Later incorporated into *Hodge and His Masters.*

'Country Girls.' *Standard,* Oct. 30, 1878. Later incorporated into *Hodge and His Masters.*

'Country Literature.' *Pall Mall Gazette,* Oct. 22, 29; Nov. 5, 22, 30, 1881. *The Life of the Fields.*

'Country Places.' *Manchester Guardian,* Jan. 4, 11, 1887. *Field and Hedgerow.*

'Country Readers.' *Pall Mall Gazette,* Dec. 22, 1877. *Field and Farm.*

'Countryside: Sussex, The.' *Manchester Guardian,* Aug. 24, 31, 1886. *Field and Hedgerow.*

'Country Sunday, The.' *Longman's Magazine,* June 1887. *Field and Hedgerow.*

'Crows, The.' *Standard,* Nov. 12, 1880. Nature Near London.

'Dairy District, A.' *Live Stock Journal,* Oct. 5, 1877. *Field and Farm.*

'Dairy Factory System, The.' *Live Stock Journal,* Feb. 15, 1878. Uncollected.

'Danger to Dairymen, A.' *Live Stock Journal,* Nov. 9, 1877. *Field and Farm.*

'Dangers of Hunting, The.' *Live Stock Journal,* Jan. 12, 1877. Uncollected.

'Dawn, The.' Not published. *The Hills and the Vale.*

'Decline of Breeding, The.' *Live Stock Journal,* Jan. 4, 1878. Uncollected.

'Decline of Partridge Shooting.' *Pall Mall Gazette,* Aug. 31, 1878. *Chronicles of the Hedges.*

'Defence of Sport, A.' *National Review,* Aug. 1883. *Chronicles of the Hedges.* (Part of this essay, omitted from *Chronicles of the Hedges,* had already been published by Jefferies as 'Sport and Science' in *The Life of the Fields.*)

'Dinner at the Farm.' *The Bryanston Miscellany.* Samuel J. Looker, 'Jefferies Unpublished Manuscripts.' Uncollected.

'Ditch and the Pool, The' (editor's title). Not published. *Chronicles of the Hedges.*

'Domestic Rook, The.' *Live Stock Journal*, Feb. 1, 1878. *Chronicles of the Hedges.*

'Downs.' *The Times*, Sept. 21, 1881. *The Open Air.* (Published in *The Times* under the title 'Some Uncultivated Country: Downs.' *See also* 'Bad Harvests in Sussex.')

'Dream of Landseer's Lions, A.' Not published. Uncollected. (An early draft of 'The Lions in Trafalgar Square.' *See* Samuel J. Looker, 'Jefferies Unpublished Manuscripts.')

'Early Autumn.' *Pall Mall Gazette*, Oct. 20, 1879. *Chronicles of the Hedges.*

'Early in March.' *Standard*, March 31, 1879. Later incorporated into *Hodge and His Masters.*

'Earth Prayer, The' (poem, editor's title). Not published. *Chronicles of the Hedges.*

'Eggs and Poultry.' *St. James's Gazette*, Nov. 17, 1880. Uncollected.

'Economic Value of Game, The.' *Live Stock Journal*, Nov. 30, 1877. Uncollected.

'English Agricultural Chemists.' *Live Stock Journal*, May 17, 24, 1878. Uncollected. (There is some doubt whether this essay is by Jefferies. *See* Looker's note in *Field and Farm*, 186.)

'English Animals Abroad.' *Live Stock Journal*, April 20, 1877. *Field and Farm.*

'English Deerpark, An.' *Century Illustrated Magazine*, Oct. 1888. *Field and Hedgerow.*

'English Homestead, An.' *Fraser's Magazine*, Nov. 1876. *The Toilers of the Field.*

'Entered at Stationer's Hall.' *Cassell's Family Magazine*, Oct. 1877. Uncollected.

'Essay on Instinct.' Not published. Uncollected. (*See* Samuel J. Looker, 'Jefferies Unpublished Manuscripts.')

'Extinct Race, An.' *Longman's Magazine*, June 1891. *The Toilers of the Field.* (In *Longman's Magazine* this fragment was included in Andrew Lang's miscellany, 'At the Sign of the Ship.')

'Fallacy of Prices, The.' *Live Stock Journal*, May 4, 1877. Uncollected.

'Farmer at Home, The.' *Fraser's Magazine*, Aug. 1874. *The Toilers of the Field.*

'Farmer's Stores in London: An Opening for Young Agriculturists.' *Live Stock Journal*, July 12, 1878. Uncollected.

'Farm Prospects in the West of England.' *St. James's Gazette*, May 5, 1881. Uncollected.

'Farms Out of Cultivation.' *The Times*, Sept. 3, 1881. *Field and Farm.*

'February Day in Stanmer Park, A.' *St. James's Gazette*, Feb. 17, 1883. *Chronicles of the Hedges.*

'Fictitious Manure.' *Live Stock Journal*, April 18, 1878. Uncollected.

'Field and Farm.' *St. James's Gazette*, March 30, 1883. *Field and Farm.*

'Field-Faring Women.' *Fraser's Magazine*, Sept. 1875. *The Toilers of the Field.*

'Field-Play, The.' *Time*, Dec. 1883. *The Life of the Fields.* (This essay consists of two parts: 'Uptill-a-Thorn' and 'Rural Dynamite.')

'Field Sports in Art.' *Art Journal*, April 1885. *Field and Hedgerow.*

'Field Words and Ways.' *Pall Mall Gazette*, Nov. 25, 1886. *Field and Hedgerow.*

'Fields in April, The.'' *Pall Mall Gazette*, May 2, 1879. *Chronicles of the Hedges.* (In *Chronicles of the Hedges* this essay forms Part 2 of 'In the Fields. April.')

'Fields in May, The.' *Pall Mall Gazette*, June 3, 1879. *Chronicles of the Hedges.*

'Fine Lady Farmer, The.' *Standard*, Oct. 17, 1878. Later incorporated into *Hodge and His Masters.*

'Fir, Larch, and Sycamore, Near London.' *The Field*, June 7, 1947. *Chronicles of the Hedges.* (In *The Field* this fragment was entitled 'The Beauty of the Trees.'

Both are editor's titles.)

'Flocks of Birds.' *Standard*, Nov. 18, 1880. *Nature Near London.*

'Flowers and Fruit.' *Globe*, July 19, 1877. *Landscape and Labour.*

'Flowers of the Grass.' Not published. *Chronicles of the Hedges.*

'Flying Dutchman, The (A Legend of the Great Western Railway).' Not published. Uncollected. (Manuscript offered for sale by a Chicago bookseller, 1970.)

'Footpaths.' *Standard*, Nov. 3, 1880. *Nature Near London.*

'Forest.' *The Times*, Sept. 24, 1881. *The Open Air.* (Published in *The Times* under the title 'Some Uncultivated Country: Forest.')

'Future of Country Society, The.' *New Quarterly*, July 1877. *Landscape and Labour.*

'Future of Farming, The.' *Fraser's Magazine*, Dec. 1873. *Landscape and Labour.*

'Future of the Dairy, The.' *Live Stock Journal Almanack*, 1879. Uncollected.

'Gambling Farmer, The.' *Standard*, Sept. 24, 1878. Later incorporated into *Hodge and His Masters.*

'Game and Tenants' Leases.' *Live Stock Journal*, Oct. 11, 1878. Uncollected.

'Game as Property.' *Live Stock Journal*, March 8, 1878. *Field and Farm.*

'Game for Bicycles, A.' Not published. Uncollected. (*See* Samuel J. Looker, 'Jefferies Unpublished Manuscripts.')

'Game Question, The.' *Live Stock Journal*, March 1, 1878. Uncollected.

'Gaudy as a Garden.' *Graphic*, Aug. 26, 1876. *Chronicles of the Hedges.*

'Genesis of *The Story of My Heart*' (editor's title). Not published. *Field and Farm.*

'Gentleman Farmer, The.' *World*, Nov. 21, 1877. *Landscape and Labour.*

'Getting to Market.' *Live Stock Journal*, June 29, 1877. Uncollected.

' "Gilt-Edged" Butter.' *Live Stock Journal*, Nov. 23, 1877. Uncollected.

'Gold-Crested Wren, The.' *Longman's Magazine*, June 1891. *The Toilers of the Field.* (In *Longman's Magazine* this fragment was included in Andrew Lang's miscellany 'At the Sign of the Ship.')

'Golden Brown.' *Pall Mall Gazette*, Aug. 27, 1884. *The Open Air.*

'Great Agricultural Opportunity, A.' *Live Stock Journal*, Aug. 9, 1878. Uncollected.

'Great Agricultural Problem, A.' *Fraser's Magazine*, March 1878. Uncollected.

'Greater Gardens.' *Globe*, April 19, 1877. Uncollected.

'Great Grievance, A.' *Live Stock Journal*, March 8, 1878. *Field and Farm.*

'Great Snow, The' (editor's title). *The Field*, March 22, 1947. *Beauty is Immortal.*

'Green Corn, The.' *Good Words*, May 1883. *The Open Air.* (In *The Open Air* this essay becomes the last four paragraphs of 'Out of Doors in February.' *See* also 'Vignettes from Nature.')

'Grouse and Partridge Poaching.' *Pall Mall Gazette*, Aug. 13, 1880. Uncollected.

'Harvest, The.' *Pall Mall Gazette*, Aug. 23, 1880. Uncollected.

'Harvest Field, The.' *Live Stock Journal*, Aug. 16, 1878. Uncollected.

'Haunt of the Hare, The.' *Standard*, Nov. 14, 1884. *The Open Air.*

'Haunts of the Lapwing.' *Good Words*, Jan. and March 1883. *The Open Air* (The second part of this essay also forms the first part of 'Vignettes from Nature' [q.v.].)

'Hay Harvest Notes.' *Live Stock Journal*, June 15, 1877. *Chronicles of the Hedges.*

'Haymaking by Artificial Heat.' *Live Stock Journal*, July 5, 1878. Uncollected.

'Heart of England, The., or The Farmer and His Man.' Not Published. Uncollected. (A fragment of a proposed book. *See* 'Richard Jefferies: Man of the Fields', [Appendix I].)

'Heathlands.' *Standard*, Dec. 23, 1880. *Nature Near London.* (Published in the *Standard* under the title 'Rural London: Anthills. Adders.')

'Hedge and the Smell of Hops, The' (editor's title). Not Published. *Chronicles of the Hedges.*

'Hedge Miners.' *Land*, Aug. 6, 1881. *Chronicles of the Hedges.*

'Hedgerow Sportsman, The.' *St. James's Gazette*, Jan. 28, 1882. *Chronicles of the Hedges.*

'Henrique Beaumont' (short story). *North Wilts Herald*, July 21, 28; Aug. 4, 1866. *The Early Fiction of Richard Jefferies.*

'Herbs.' *Standard*, Oct. 15, 1880. *Nature Near London.*

'High-Pressure Agriculture.' *Fraser's Magazine*, August 1876. *Landscape and Labour.*

'History of Cirencester.' *See* 'Serializations.'

'History of Malmesbury.' *See* 'Serializations.'

'History of Swindon and Its Environs.' *See* 'Serializations.'

'Horse as a Social Force, The.' *Live Stock Journal*, July 20, 1877. *Field and Farm.*

'Horses in Relation to Art.' *Magazine of Art*, May and October 1878. *Beauty is Immortal.*

'Hours of Spring.' *Longman's Magazine*, May 1886. *Field and Hedgerow.*

'House Martins.' Not Published (?). *Field and Hedgerow.*

'Hovering of the Kestrel, The.' *St. James's Gazette*, Feb. 22, 1883. *The Life of the Fields.*

'How to Read Books.' *Cassell's Family Magazine*, Aug. 1876. *Beauty is Immortal.*

'Humanity and Natural History.' *Knowledge*, Jan. 5, 1883. Uncollected.

'Hyperion' (editor's title). Not published. *Beauty is Immortal.*

'Idle Earth, The.' *Longman's Magazine*, Dec. 1894. *The Hills and the Vale.*

'Imitation Cheeses.' *St. James's Gazette*, June 17, 1882. Uncollected.

'Improved Cars for Cattle.' *Live Stock Journal*, June 28, 1878. Uncollected.

'In a Pine-Wood.' *Graphic*, May 19, 1877. *Landscape and Labour.*

'In Brighton' (editor's title). Not published. *Beauty is Immortal.*

'Increasing Importance of Horse-Breeding.' *Live Stock Journal*, July 13, 1877. Uncollected.

'In Summer Fields.' *St. James's Gazette*, June 7, 1886. Uncollected.

'Intermixed Agriculture.' *Live Stock Journal*, Nov. 2, 1877. Uncollected.

'In the Fields: April.' *St. James's Gazette*, April 20, 1881. *Chronicles of the Hedges.* (In *Chronicles of the Hedges* the essay 'The Fields in April' is included as a second part under the same title.)

'In the Fields. March.' *St. James's Gazette*, March 12, 1881. *Chronicles of the Hedges.*

'In the Hop-Gardens.' *St. James's Gazette*, Sept. 23, 1880. *Chronicles of the Hedges.*

Introduction to Gilbert White's *Natural History of Selborne*. Camelot Classics, 1887. *The Spring of the Year.*

'January in the Sussex Woods.' *Standard*, Jan. 22, 1884. *The Life of the Fields.* (In the *Standard* the title was 'January in the Woods.')

'January Notes.' *Pall Mall Gazette*, Jan. 31, 1880. Uncollected.

'Jockeying Pheasant Preserves.' *Live Stock Journal*, June 1, 1877. Uncollected.

'John Smith's Shanty.' *Fraser's Magazine*, Feb. 1874. *The Toilers of the Field.* (Only the first part of this essay appeared in *The Toilers of the Field.*)

'Joint-Stock Agriculture.' *Pall Mall Gazette*, March 16, 1877. Uncollected.

'Joy of the Wind, The.' Not published. *Chronicles of the Hedges.*

'July Grass, The.' *Pall Mall Gazette*, July 24, 1886. *Field and Hedgerow.*

'Just Before Winter.' *Chambers' Journal*, Dec. 18, 1886. *Field and Hedgerow.*

'Kilburn Show, The.' *Pall Mall Gazette*, July 4, 1879. *Field and Farm.*

'King of Acres, A.' *Chambers' Journal*, Jan. 5, 12, 1884. *The Hills and the Vale.*

'Kiss and Try' (short story). *London Society*, Feb. 1877. *Society Novelettes I.*

'Labourer and His Hire, The.' *Live Stock Journal*, Aug. 30, 1878. Uncollected.

'Labourer's Daily Life, The.' *Fraser's Magazine*, Nov. 1874. *The Toilers of the Field.*

'Larger Thought of London, The.' Not published. *Chronicles of the Hedges.*

'Last of a London Trout, The.' Not published. *The Old House at Coate.* (Not to be confused with 'A London Trout.')

'Lawn Preserves.' *Globe*, May 9, 1877. Uncollected.

'Leafy November, A.' *Pall Mall Gazette*, Nov. 25, 1879. *Chronicles of the Hedges.*

'Left Out in the Cold.' *St. James's Gazette*, Dec. 30, 1884. *Field and Farm.*

'Legend of a Gateway, The.' *See* 'Bits of Oak-Bark.'

'Leicester Square.' Not published. *Chronicles of the Hedges.*

'Lesser Birds, The' (editor's title). *See* 'Thoughts in the Fields.'

'Lesson in Lent, A.' *Live Stock Journal*, March 30, 1877. *Chronicles of the Hedges.*

'Less Stock, Less Wheat.' *Live Stock Journal*, Oct. 26, 1877. Uncollected.

'Let Me Think.' *Cassell's Family Magazine*, Oct. 1876. *Beauty is Immortal.*

'Life of the Soul, The' (editor's title). Not published. *The Old House at Coate.*

'Lions in Trafalgar Square, The.' *Longman's Magazine*, March 1892. *The Toilers of the Field.*

'Locality and Nature.' *Pall Mall Gazette*, Feb. 17, 1887. *Field and Hedgerow.*

'Local Taxation' (letter). *Wilts and Gloucestershire Standard*, Jan. 1, 1876. Uncollected.

'London Bridge Station.' Not published. *Chronicles of the Hedges.*

'London Contrasts' (editor's title). Not published. *Chronicles of the Hedges.*

'London Mud' (editor's title). Not published. *Chronicles of the Hedges.*

'London Reflections.' *The Field*, Sept. 27, Oct. 4, 1947.) *Chronicles of the Hedges.* (This is Jefferies' over-all title for many untitled fragments later printed in *Chronicles of the Hedges.*)

'London Scents and Colours' (editor's title). Not published. *Chronicles of the Hedges.*

'London Selfishness' (editor's title). Not published. *Chronicles of the Hedges.*

'London Trout, A.' *Standard*(?). *Nature Near London.*

'Lonely Common, The' (editor's title). Not published. *Field and Farm.*

'Machiavelli: A Study.' *Nineteenth Century and After*, Sept. 1948. Uncollected.

'Magic of the Night.' Not published. *Chronicles of the Hedges.*

'Magpie Fields.' *Standard*(?). *Nature Near London.*

'Makers of Summer, The.' *Chambers' Journal*, May 28, 1887. *Field and Hedgerow.*

'Man of the Future, The.' *Swindon Advertiser*, June 19, 1871. Uncollected.

'Manufacture of Milk, The.' *Live Stock Journal*, Sept. 21, 1877. Uncollected.

'March Notes.' *St. James's Gazette*, March 6, 1883. *Chronicles of the Hedges.*

'Market Gardening.' *St. James's Gazette*, Oct. 20, 1880. Uncollected.

'Marlborough Forest.' *Graphic*, Oct. 23, 1875. *The Hills and the Vale.*

'Masked' (short story). *North Wilts Herald*, Oct. 13, 20, 27, 1866. *The Early Fiction of Richard Jefferies.*

'Meadow Gateway, The.' *See* 'Chronicles of the Hedges.'

'Meadow Thoughts.' *Graphic*, April 5, 1884. *The Life of the Fields.*

'Midsummer 1879.' *Pall Mall Gazette*, July 12, 1879. *Chronicles of the Hedges.*

'Midsummer Hum, The.' *Graphic*, July 15, 1876. *Chronicles of the Hedges.*

'Midsummer Pests.' *Live Stock Journal*, June 22, 1877. *Chronicles of the Hedges.*

'Mind Under Water; or, Fishes as They Really Are.' *Graphic*, May 19, 1883. *The Life of the Fields.*

'Minor Sources of Income.' *Live Stock Journal*, March 16, 1877. Uncollected.

'Minute Cultivation—A Silver Mine.' *Live Stock Journal*, July 26, 1878. *Chronicles of the Hedges.*

'Mixed Days of May and December.' *Pall Mall Gazette*, May 13, 1887. *Field and Hedgerow.*

'Modern Sporting Guns.' *Pall Mall Gazette*, Nov. 17, 1879. *Chronicles of the Hedges.*

'Modern Thames, The.' *Pall Mall Gazette*, Sept. 6, 1884. *The Open Air.* (The first part of the essay only was published in the *Pall Mall Gazette.* This was then entitled: 'Our River: 1. Its Natural Denizens.' Other writers contributed articles under the over-all title.)

'Monkebourne Mystery, The' (short story). *New Monthly Magazine*, Jan. 1876. Uncollected.

'More About Butter.' *Live Stock Journal*, Jan. 11, 1878. Uncollected.

'Mowers and Reapers: Recent Improvements.' *Live Stock Journal*, April 26 and May 10, 1878. Uncollected.

'Mr. Mechi's Budget.' *Live Stock Journal*, April 27, 1877. Uncollected.

'Mulberry Tree, The' (poem). *See* 'The Tree of Life.'

'My Chaffinch' (poem). *Pall Mall Gazette*, March 18, 1887. *Field and Hedgerow.*

'My Old Village.' *Longman's Magazine*, Oct. 1887. *Field and Hedgerow.*

'Mystery of Offal, The.' *Live Stock Journal*, April 12, 1878. Uncollected.

'Natural History of Beautiful Women, The.' Not published. *Field and Farm* (appendix).

'Natural System of National Defence, A' *Swindon Advertiser*, June 26; July 3, 10, 1871. Uncollected.

'Nature and Books.' *Fortnightly Review*, May 1887. *Field and Hedgerow.*

'Nature and Eternity.' *Longman's Magazine*, May 1895. *The Hills and the Vale.*

'Nature and the Gamekeeper.' *St. James's Gazette*, March 13, 1883. *The Life of the Fields.*

'Nature in the Louvre.' *Magazine of Art*, Sept. 1887. *Field and Hedgerow.*

'Nature Near Brighton.' *Standard*, Aug. 28, 1883. *The Life of the Fields.*

'Nature on the Roof.' *Chambers' Journal*, June 21, 1884. *The Open Air.*

'Neglected Pig, The.' *Live Stock Journal*, Feb. 22, 1878. *Field and Farm.*

'New Facts in Landscape.' *See* 'Notes on Landscape Painting.'

'Nightingale Road.' *Standard*, Nov. 26, 1880. *Nature Near London.*

'Nightingales.' *St. James's Gazette*, April 10, 1886. *Chronicles of the Hedges.*

'Noontide in the Meadow' (poem). Not published separately. *Greene Ferne Farm.* (Later printed separately as a poem by Samuel J. Looker in his notes to the Collector's ed. of *Field and Hedgerow*, 1948.)

'Notes A-Field.' *St. James's Gazette,* July 28, 1885. Uncollected.
'Notes on Landscape Painting.' *Magazine of Art,* March and November 1882. *The Life of the Fields.* (This essay was published under two titles in the Magazine of Art: 'The Beauty of the Fields' and 'New Facts in Landscape.')
'Novelty in Literature.' Not published. Uncollected. (*See* Samuel J. Looker, 'Jefferies Unpublished Manuscripts.')
'November Days.' *Standard,* Nov. 14, 1878. Later incorporated into *Hodge and His Masters.*
'Nude in London, The.' *World,* June 12, 1878. Uncollected.
'Nutty Autumn.' *Standard,* Sept. 30, 1881. *Nature Near London.*
'Oak Bark.' *See* 'Thoughts in the Fields.'
'October.' *The Bryanston Miscellany.* Samuel J. Looker, 'Jefferies Unpublished Manuscripts.' Uncollected. (Extract from an early draft of *Bevis.*)
'Old House at Coate, The.' Not published. *The Old House at Coate.*
'Old Keeper, The.' Not published. *Field and Farm.*
'Old Mill, The.' *Graphic,* Feb. 9, 1878. *Landscape and Labour.*
'On Allotment Gardens.' *New Quarterly,* April 1875. Uncollected.
'One of the New Voters.' *Manchester Guardian,* Jan. 24 and 31, 1885. *The Open Air.*
'On the Downs.' *Standard,* March 23, 1883. *The Hills and the Vale.*
'On the London Road.' *Pall Mall Gazette,* April 2, 1885. *The Open Air.* (The title in the *Pall Mall Gazette* was 'Scenes on the London Road.')
'Orchis Mascula.' *Longman's Magazine,* June 1891. *The Toilers of the Field.* (In *Longman's Magazine* this fragment was included in Andrew Lang's miscellany 'At the Sign of the Ship.')
'Otter in Somerset, The.' *Manchester Guardian,* Aug. 27, 1883. *The Life of the Fields.* (In *The Life of the Fields* this essay is incorporated into 'By the Exe.')
'Our River: 1. Its Natural Denizens.' *See* 'The Modern Thames.'
'Our Winter Food.' *Live Stock Journal,* Sept. 14, 1877. Uncollected.
'Out of Doors in February.' *Good Words,* Feb. 1882, May 1883. *The Open Air.* (The last four paragraphs appeared separately as 'The Green Corn' on the later date. *See also* 'Vignettes from Nature.')
'Out of the Season' (short story). *London Society,* Sept. 1876. *Society Novelettes II.*
'Outside London.' *Chambers' Journal,* Jan 17, Feb. 21, 1885, *The Open Air.*
'Pageant of Summer, The.' *Longman's Magazine,* June 1883. *The Life of the Fields.*
'Paradox: Slow Progress of Science, The' (editor's title). *The Field,* July 19, 1947. *Beauty is Immortal.* (Published in *The Field* under the title 'Slow Progress of Science.')
'Parliamentary Measures Affecting the Grazier.' *Live Stock Journal,* Feb. 23, 1877. Uncollected.
'Partridge Hatching Season.' *St. James's Gazette,* June 27, 1883. Uncollected.
'Partridges in 1880.' *St. James's Gazette,* June 29, 1880. Uncollected.
'Pasture and Population.' *Pall Mall Gazette,* Oct. 25, 1877. Uncollected.
'Pasture and Stock.' *Live Stock Journal,* March 23, 1877. Uncollected.
' "Patent" Butter.' *Live Stock Journal,* Feb. 8, 1878. Uncollected.
'Persecution of St. Partridge, The.' *Live Stock Journal,* June 8, 1877. *Field and Farm.*
'Pheasant Breeding.' *St. James's Gazette,* Oct. 3, 1882. Uncollected.

'Philosophy of Mayflies, The.' *The Field,* May 24, 1947. *Field and Farm.*
'Piccadilly.' Not published. *Chronicles of the Hedges.*
'Picture of April', (poem). *Pall Mall Gazette,* April 30, 1885. *Chronicles of th.*
    Hedges. (The title in the *Pall Mall Gazette* was 'April.')
'Picture of Men and Women Living Upon the Land.' Not published. Un-
    collected. (An early synopsis of *Hodge and His Masters. See* Samuel J. Looker,
    'Jefferies Unpublished Manuscripts.')
'Pictures in the National Gallery' (editor's title). Not published. *Chronicles of the*
    Hedges.
'Pigeons at the British Museum, The.' *Pall Mall Gazette,* Jan. 11, 1884. *The Life*
    of the Fields.
'Pine Wood, The.' *Standard,* Sept. 3, 1885. *The Open Air.*
'Place of Ambush, The' (editor's title). *The Field,* April 26, 1947. *Field and Farm.*
'Plainest City in Europe, The' (Paris). *Pall Mall Gazette,* Oct. 20, 1883. *The Life*
    of the Fields.
'Plea for Pheasant Shooting, A.' *Live Stock Journal,* Sept. 28, 1877. Uncollected.
'Poaching as a Profession.' *Pall Mall Gazette,* Dec. 12, 14, 1877. Later in-
    corporated into *The Gamekeeper at Home.*
'Poetry of the Bible, The.' *Broad Churchman,* early 1873. Uncollected.
'Position of the Grazier, The.' *Live Stock Journal,* Feb. 2, 1877. Uncollected.
'Power of the Farmers, The.' *Fortnightly Review,* June 1874. Uncollected.
'Preservation of Game in England, The.' *St. James's Gazette,* Oct. 25, 1881. Un-
    collected.
'Primrose Gold in Our Village.' *Pall Mall Gazette,* June 8, 1887. *Field and Farm.*
'Producers and Consumers.' *Live Stock Journal,* June 21, 1878. Uncollected.
'Professional Bird-Catcher, The.' *St. James's Gazette,* Aug. 4, 1885. *Chronicles of*
    the Hedges.
'Profit from Rabbits.' *Live Stock Journal,* Sept. 13, 1878. Uncollected.
'Prospects of the First, The.' *St. James's Gazette,* Sept. 1, 1882. Uncollected.
'Protection of Hunting, The.' *Live Stock Journal,* May 25, 1877. Uncollected.
'Protection of Nature, The' (editor's title). Not published. *Field and Farm.*
'Queen's New Subjects, The.' *Cassell's Family Magazine,* Aug. 1877. Un-
    collected.
'Rabbits and Hares.' *Pall Mall Gazette,* Aug. 18, 1880. Uncollected.
'Rabbits as Food.' *Live Stock Journal,* Dec. 29, 1877. Uncollected.
'Rabbit Shooting.' *St. James's Gazette,* Feb. 3, 1882. Uncollected.
'Rabbit Warrens and their Returns.' *Live Stock Journal,* Jan. 4, 1878. *Field and*
    Farm.
'Railway Accidents Bill, A.' *Fraser's Magazine,* May 1874. Uncollected.
'Rats, Mice and Game Preserves.' *Live Stock Journal,* Sept. 27, 1878. Un-
    collected.
'Recapitulation' (poem, editor's title). Not published. *Chronicles of the Hedges.*
'Red Roofs of London.' *St. James's Gazette,* Aug. 2, 1884. *The Open Air.* (In the
    St. James's Gazette this was published under the title 'The Roofs of London.')
'Reorganizing the Meat Supply.' *Live Stock Journal,* Jan. 26, 1877. *Field and*
    Farm.
'River, The.' *Standard,* Sept. 10, 1880. *Nature Near London.*
'Roman Brook, A.' *See* 'Bits of Oak Bark.'
'Rook Shooting.' *St. James's Gazette,* May 9, 1882. Uncollected.

'Rooks, The' (editor's title). Not published. *Chronicles of the Hedges. (See* 'A Winter Scene.')

'Round a London Copse.' *Standard,* Dec. 26, 1882. *Nature Near London.* (This essay contains passages which also occur in 'The Spring of the Year' [q.v.].)

'Rural Dynamite.' *See* 'The Field Play.'

'Rural London.' An over-all title for most of the essays published later as *Nature Near London.* They are here listed under their separate titles.

'Sacrifice to Trout, The.' *St. James's Gazette,* March 17, 1883. *The Life of the Fields.*

'Saint Guido.' *English Illustrated Magazine,* Dec. 1884. *The Open Air.*

'Scarcity of Bacon Pigs, The.' *Live Stock Journal,* July 19, 1878. Uncollected.

'Scenes on the London Road.' *See* 'On the London Road.'

'Scientific Culture of Grasses and Clover.' *Live Stock Journal,* Nov. 16, 1877. Uncollected.

'Seasons in Surrey: Tree and Bird Life in the Copse, The.' Not published. *The Old House at Coate.*

'Sea, Sky, and Down.' *Standard,* Jan. 3, 1884. *The Life of the Fields.*

'Seed Inquisition, The.' *Live Stock Journal,* Dec. 21, 1877. Uncollected.

'Selling by Rule of Thumb.' *Live Stock Journal,* May 10, 1878. Uncollected. Sermon on *Luke* xii, 52. Not published. Uncollected. (Listed in Hodgson's Auction Catalogue for April 24, 1959.)

'Shipton Accident, The.' *Fraser's Magazine,* Feb. 1875. Uncollected.

'Shooting.' Not published. Uncollected. (*See* Samuel J. Looker, 'Jefferies Unpublished Manuscripts.')

'Shooting a Rabbit.' *Pall Mall Gazette,* June 25, 1880. *Chronicles of the Hedges.*

'Shooting Poachers.' *Pall Mall Gazette,* Dec. 13, 1884. *Chronicles of the Hedges.*

'Shortest Day Scene, A.' *St. James's Gazette,* Dec. 22, 1884. *Chronicles of the Hedges.*

'Shorthorn in France, The.' *Live Stock Journal,* June 7, 1878. Uncollected.

'Shorthorns on Arable Land.' *Live Stock Journal,* April 13, 1877. Uncollected.

'Shrinking of the Scene in Winter.' Not published. *Chronicles of the Hedges. (See* 'A Winter Scene.')

'Sin and a Shame, A' (short story). *New Monthly Magazine,* Nov. 1875. Uncollected.

'Single Barrel Gun, The.' *St. James's Gazette,* Dec. 19, 1884. *The Open Air.*

'Sipping the Season.' *World,* June 7, 1876. Uncollected.

'Size of Farms, The.' *New Quarterly,* Oct. 1874. *Landscape and Labour.*

'Skating.' Not published. *The Hills and the Vale.*

'Sleight-of-Hand Poaching.' *Pall Mall Gazette,* Dec. 29, 1877. Later incorporated into *The Gamekeeper at Home.*

'Slow Progress of Science.' *See* 'The Paradox: Slow Progress of Science.'

'Small Birds.' *Pall Mall Gazette,* Dec. 30, 1878. *Chronicles of the Hedges.*

'Snipes and Moonlit Sport.' *Pall Mall Gazette,* Nov. 16, 1877. Later incorporated in *The Amateur Poacher.*

'Sold by Auction.' *St. James's Gazette,* Feb. 24, 1885. *Field and Farm.* (In the *St. James's Gazette* the title was 'To be Sold by Auction.')

'Some April Insects.' *Pall Mall Gazette,* April 27, 1887. *Field and Hedgerow.*

'Some Triumphs of Poor Men.' *Cassell's Family Magazine,* April 1877. *Beauty is Immortal.*

'Some Uncultivated Country: Downs.' *See* 'Downs.'
'Some Uncultivated Country: Forest.' *See* 'Forest.'
'Southdown Shepherd, The.' *Standard*, Aug. 31, 1881. *Nature Near London*.
'Specialite Cheese.' *Globe*, Oct. 15, 1877. Uncollected.
'Spirit of Modern Agriculture, The.' *New Quarterly*, July 1876. Uncollected.
'Sport and Science.' *National Review*, Aug. 1883. *The Life of the Fields*. (*The Life of the Fields* includes only part of the original essay whose full title was 'A Defence of Sport' [q.v.].)
'Spring Notes.' *Pall Mall Gazette*, April 23, 1880. *Chronicles of the Hedges*.
'Spring of the Year, The.' *Longman's Magazine*, June 1894. *The Hills and the Vale*. (This essay contains passages which had already appeared in 'Round a London Copse' [q.v.].)
'Spring Prospects and Farm Work.' *Live Stock Journal*, March 22, 1878. *Chronicles of the Hedges*.
'Squire and the Land, The' (editor's title). Not published. *The Old House at Coate*.
'Squire at Home, The.' Not published. Uncollected. (*See* Samuel J. Looker, 'Jefferies Unpublished Manuscripts.')
'Squire's Preserves, The' (editor's title). Not published. *Field and Farm*. (An unused section of *The Amateur Poacher*.)
'Stars Above the Elms, The' (editor's title). Not published. *Chronicles of the Hedges*.
'State of Farming, The.' *St. James's Gazette*, Aug. 3, 5, 13, 1881. *Field and Farm*.
'Steam on Country Roads.' *Standard*, Sept. 13, 1881. *Field and Hedgerow*. (Published in the *Standard* under the title 'Steam on Common Roads.' The essay was revised before book-publication.)
'Story of Furniture, The.' *Cassell's Family Magazine*, June 1877. *Beauty is Immortal*.
'Story of Swindon, The.' *Fraser's Magazine*, May 1875. *The Hills and the Vale*.
'Strand, The.' Not published. *Chronicles of the Hedges*.
'Strange Story, A' (short story). *North Wilts Herald*, June 30, 1866. *The Early Fiction of Richard Jefferies*.
'Straw and Stock.' *Live Stock Journal*, Oct. 12, 1877. Uncollected.
'Strength of the English' (editor's title). Not published. *The Old House at Coate*.
'Study of Stock, The.' *Live Stock Journal*, May 11, 1877. *Chronicles of the Hedges*.
'Summer Day in Savernake Forest, A.' *Globe*, July 27, 1876. *Landscape and Labour*.
'Summer Evening, A.' *Pall Mall Gazette*, July 28, 1881. *Chronicles of the Hedges*.
'Summer in Somerset.' *English Illustrated Magazine*, Oct. 1887. *Field and Hedgerow*.
'Summer Meat Supply.' *Live Stock Journal*, May 17, 1878. Uncollected.
'Summer Notes.' *Pall Mall Gazette*, July 6, 1880. *Chronicles of the Hedges*.
'Sun and the Brook, The.' *Knowledge*, Oct. 13, 1882. *The Hills and the Vale*.
'Sunlight in a London Square.' *Pall Mall Gazette*, Sept. 7, 1883. *The Life of the Fields*.
'Sunny Brighton.' *Longman's Magazine*, July 1884. *The Open Air*.
'Swallow Time.' *Standard*, Aug. 3, 1886. *Field and Hedgerow*.
'Swindon: Its History and Antiquities.' *Wilts Archaeological and Natural History Magazine*, March 1874. Uncollected. (This was a paper read before The Wilt-

shire Archaeological and Natural History Society on Sept. 16, 1873.)

'Tangle of Autumn, A.' Not published. *Field and Farm.* (This essay had previously been printed in the 1941 edition of the *Notebooks*.)

'Thoughts in the Fields' (editor's title). *The Field,* Sept. 13, 1947. *Chronicles of the Hedges.* (This title was used in *The Field* for fragments printed in *Chronicles of the Hedges* separately as 'The Benediction of the Light,' 'The Lesser Birds,' 'Oak Bark,' 'Trees and Birds of the Wood,' and 'Wild Thyme of the Hills.')

'Thoughts on Cattle Feeding.' *Live Stock Journal,* May 24, 1878. Uncollected.

'Thoughts on the Labour Question.' *Pall Mall Gazette,* Nov. 10, 1891. *Field and Farm.* (Only a part of this essay appeared in *Field and Farm.*)

'Three Centuries at Home.' Not published. *The Old House at Coate.*

'Time of Year, The.' *Pall Mall Gazette,* April 9, 1887. *Field and Hedgerow.*

'Tits and the Trees' (editor's title). Not published. *Chronicles of the Hedges.* (*See* 'A Winter Scene.')

'To a Fashionable Bonnet' (poem). *North Wilts Herald,* June 30, 1866. *The Early Fiction of Richard Jefferies* (Preface).

'To be Sold by Auction.' *See* 'Sold by Auction.'

'To Brighton.' *Standard,* Sept. 15, 1880. *Nature Near London.*

'Too Much "Margin".' *Live Stock Journal,* Jan. 25, 1878. Uncollected.

'Training Schools for Servants.' *Cassell's Family Magazine,* March 1878. Uncollected.

'Traits of the Olden Times.' *North Wilts Herald,* March 2, 1866. *The Early Fiction of Richard Jefferies.*

'Travelling Labour.' *Live Stock Journal,* July 6, 1877. *Chronicles of the Hedges.*

'Tree of Life, The' (poem). *Scots' Observer,* Nov. 8, 1890. Reprinted by Samuel J. Looker in the 1941 edition of the Notebooks and in the notes to the Collector's edition of Field and Hedgerow, 1948. (Also known as 'The Mulberry Tree.')

'Trees About Town.' *Standard,* Sept. 28, 1881. *Nature Near London.*

'Trees and Birds of the Wood' (editor's title). *See* 'Thoughts of the Fields.'

'Trees in and Around London' (editor's title). Not published. *The Old House at Coate.*

'Trespass.' *Live Stock Journal,* Aug. 24, 1877. *Chronicles of the Hedges.*

'True Approach to Nature, The' (editor's title). Not published. *Chronicles of the Hedges.*

'True Tale of a Wiltshire Labourer, A.' Not published. *The Toilers of the Field.*

'T.T.T.' (short story). *North Wilts Herald,* Feb. 2, 1867. Printed separately in 1896. Otherwise uncollected.

'Typical Prize Farm, A.' *Live Stock Journal,* Aug. 23, 1878. Uncollected.

'Under the Acorns.' *Chambers' Journal,* Oct. 18, 1884. *The Open Air.*

'Under the Snow.' *Pall Mall Gazette,* Jan. 20, 1879. *Chronicles of the Hedges.*

'Under Tropical Rains.' *Live Stock Journal,* Jan. 19, 1877. Uncollected.

'Unequal Agriculture.' *Fraser's Magazine,* May 1877. *The Hills and the Vale.*

'Untutored Love.' (*The Bryanston Miscellany.* Samuel J. Looker, 'Jefferies Unpublished Manuscripts.') Uncollected.

'Uptill-a-Thorn.' *See* 'The Field Play.'

'Utility of Birds.' *Live Stock Journal,* Aug. 3, 1877. *Chronicles of the Hedges.*

'Value of Grass, The.' *Live Stock Journal,* March 9, 1877. Uncollected.

'Value of Small Things, The.' *Live Stock Journal,* Jan. 18, 1878. *Field and Farm.*

'Varied Sounds' (editor's title). Not published. *Chronicles of the Hedges.*

'Venice in the East End.' *Pall Mall Gazette*, Nov. 5, 1883. *The Life of the Fields.*

'Vignettes from Nature.' *Longman's Magazine*, July 1895. *The Hills and the Vale.* (The first part of this essay had already been printed as the second part of 'Haunts of the Lapwing'; the second part consists of the essay 'The Green Corn' which had already been assimilated into 'Out of Doors in February.')

'Village Churches.' *Graphic*, Dec. 4, 1875. *The Hills and the Vale.*

'Village Hunting.' *Globe*, Aug. 22, 1877. *Landscape and Labour.*

'Village Miners.' *Gentleman's Magazine*, June 1883. *The Life of the Fields.*

'Village Organization.' *New Quarterly*, Oct. 1875. *The Hills and the Vale.*

'Walks in the Wheat-Fields.' *English Illustrated Magazine*, July and August 1887. *Field and Hedgerow.*

'War, The.' *Live Stock Journal*, May 18, 1877. Uncollected.

'Wasp-Flies or Hoverers' (editor's title). Not published. *Chronicles of the Hedges.*

'Water.' *Live Stock Journal*, April 6, 1877. *Field and Farm.*

'Water-Colley, The.' *Manchester Guardian*, Aug. 31, 1883. *The Life of the Fields.*

'Weather and Wages in the Country.' *Pall Mall Gazette*, July 26, 1879. *Landscape and Labour.*

'Weeds and Waste.' *Live Stock Journal*, Sept. 6, 1878. *Chronicles of the Hedges.*

'Wet Night in London, A.' *Pall Mall Gazette*, Dec. 31, 1884. *The Open Air.*

'Wheatfields.' *Standard*, Aug. 17, 1880. *Nature Near London.*

'Which is the Way?' *Cassell's Family Magazine*, Dec. 1876. Uncollected.

'Who Will Win? or, American Adventure.' *North Wilts Herald*, Aug. 25; Sept. 1, 8, 15, 22, 29, 1866. *The Early Fiction of Richard Jefferies.*

'Wild Flowers.' *Longman's Magazine*, July 1885. *The Open Air.*

'Wild Flowers and Wheat.' *Pall Mall Gazette*, July 20, 1881. *Chronicles of the Hedges.*

'Wild Fowl and Small Birds.' *Pall Mall Gazette*, April 18, 1877. *Chronicles of the Hedges.*

'Wild Fowling.' *St. James's Gazette*, Dec. 4, 1885. Uncollected.

'Wild Thyme of the Hills, The' (editor's title). *See* 'Thoughts in the Fields.'

'Willow-Tide.' *Standard*, April 15, 1879. Later incorporated into *Hodge and His Masters.*

'Wiltshire Downs, The.' *Graphic*, June 30, 1877. *Landscape and Labour.*

'Wiltshire Labourer, The.' *Longman's Magazine*, Nov. 1883. *The Hills and the Vale.*

'Wiltshire Labourers.' Letters to *The Times*, Nov. 12, 23, 27, 1872. *The Toilers of the Field.*

'Window-Seat in the Gun-Room, The.' *The Bryanston Miscellany*. Samuel J. Looker, 'Jefferies Unpublished Manuscripts.' Uncollected. (Part of this fragment was used for 'An English Deerpark.')

'Winds of Heaven.' *Chambers' Journal*, Aug. 7, 1886. *Field and Hedgerow.*

'Winter Scene, A' (editor's title). Not published. *Field and Farm.* (This is a composite essay constructed out of various Jefferies fragments. It contains the notes, previously printed separately in *Chronicles of the Hedges*, of 'The Rooks,' 'Shrinking of the Scene in Winter' and 'Tits and the Trees.')

'Women in the Field.' *Graphic*, Sept. 11, 1875. *Landscape and Labour.*

'Woodlands.' *Standard*, Aug. 25, 1880. *Nature Near London.*

BIOGRAPHY AND CRITICISM

I do not intend to provide a lengthy list of secondary sources, preferring rather that the reader should consult Jefferies' own writings. However, two works deserve mention as pre-eminent in their fields: Edward Thomas's *Richard Jefferies: His Life and Work.* (London: Hutchinson, 1909), is the best biography on the author and is likely to remain so. It has recently been reissued (London: Faber and Faber, 1978). Professor W. J. Keith's *Richard Jefferies: A Critical Study*, is far and away the most perceptive critical approach to Jefferies work to date.